Celia Daileader explores the paradoxes of eroticism on stage in early modern England, where women and their bodies (represented by boy actors) were materially absent and yet symbolically central. Her starting point is the theoretical and theatrical problem of sexual acts that take place offstage, which is a paradigm for the limits of the visible in Renaissance theater. The space that lies offstage becomes an imaginary realm, encompassing both spiritual and erotic transcendence. In accounting for its power, Daileader looks to the suppression of religious drama in England and the resulting secularization of the stage. Focusing on the link between absence and desire, and discussing a wide range of drama from Corpus Christi plays to Shakespeare, her argument draws together questions about sexuality and the sacred, in the bodies – of Christ and of woman – that are banished from the early modern English stage.

Cambridge Studies in Renaissance Literature and Culture 30

Eroticism on the Renaissance stage

Cambridge Studies in Renaissance Literature and Culture

General editor
STEPHEN ORGEL
Jackson Eli Reynolds Professor of Humanities, Stanford University

Editorial board
Anne Barton, *University of Cambridge*
Jonathan Dollimore, *University of Sussex*
Marjorie Garber, *Harvard University*
Jonathan Goldberg, *Duke University*
Nancy Vickers, *Bryn Mawr College*

Since the 1970s there has been a broad and vital reinterpretation of the nature of literary texts, a move away from formalism to a sense of literature as an aspect of social, economic, political, and cultural history. While the earliest New Historicist work was criticized for a narrow and anecdotal view of history, it also served as an important stimulus for post-structuralist, feminist, Marxist, and psychoanalytical work, which in turn has increasingly informed and redirected it. Recent writing on the nature of representation, the historical construction of gender and of the concept of identity itself, on theater as a political and economic phenomenon, and on the ideologies of art generally reveals the breadth of the field. Cambridge Studies in Renaissance Literature and Culture is designed to offer historically oriented studies of Renaissance literature and theater which make use of the insights afforded by theoretical perspectives. The view of history envisioned is above all a view of our own history, a reading of the Renaissance for and from our own time.

Recent titles include

25. *Foreign Bodies and the Body Politic: Discourses of Social Pathology in Early Modern England*
    JONATHAN GIL HARRIS

26. *Writing, Gender and State in Early Modern England: Identity Formation and the Female Subject*
    MEGAN MATCHINSKE

27. *The Romance of the New World: Gender and the Literary Formations of English Colonialism*
    JOAN PONG LINTON

28. *Gender and Literacy on Stage in Early Modern England*
    EVE RACHELE SANDERS

29. *The Limits of Eroticism in Post-Petrarchan Narrative: Conditional Pleasure from Spenser to Marvell*
    DOROTHY STEPHENS

A complete list of books in the series is given at the end of the volume

Eroticism on the Renaissance stage

Transcendence, desire, and the limits of the visible

Celia R. Daileader
University of Alabama

CAMBRIDGE
UNIVERSITY PRESS

PUBLISHED BY THE PRESS SYNDICATE OF THE UNIVERSITY OF CAMBRIDGE
The Pitt Building, Trumpington Street, Cambridge CB2 1RP, United Kingdom

CAMBRIDGE UNIVERSITY PRESS
The Edinburgh Building, Cambridge CB2 2RU, United Kingdom
40 West 20th Street, New York, NY 10011–4211, USA
10 Stamford Road, Oakleigh, Melbourne 3166, Australia

First published 1998

Printed in the United Kingdom at the University Press, Cambridge

Typeset in Times 10/12 pt. [CE]

A catalogue record for this book is available from the British Library

Library of Congress cataloging in publication data

Daileader, Celia R.

Eroticism on the Renaissance stage: transcendence, desire, and the limits of the visible / Celia R. Daileader
     p.   cm. – (Cambridge Studies in Renaissance Literature and Culture; 30)
Includes index.
ISBN 0 521 62379 0 (hardback).
1. English drama – Early modern and Elizabethan, 1500–1600 – History and criticism. 2. Women and literature – England – History – 16th century.
3. Women and literature – England – History – 17th century. 4. Erotic literature, – English – History and criticism. 5. English drama – 17th century. – History and criticism. 6. Shakespeare, William, 1564–1616 – Characters – Women.
7. Middleton, Thomas, d. 1627 – Characters – Women. 8. Transcendence (Philosophy) in literature. 9. Body, human, in literature. 10. Desire in literature.
11. Renaissance – England. 12. Sex in literature.
I. Title. II. Series.
PR658.W6D35   1998
822′.3093538 – dc21   97–47555   CIP

ISBN 0 521 62379 0 hardback

PR
658
·W6
D35
1998

Dedicated to the memory of
Dorothy Louise Caputi
1936–1985

Contents

Illustrations

Acknowledgments

I owe thanks to the Research Grants Committee at the University of Alabama for their generous funding toward this project, and to Stan Jones and Hank Lazer for crucial "emergency" funding which helped me complete my work. In addition, I thank the British Library, the Folger Library, and the Library of Congress for contributing illustrations to this book. My research assistants, Tim VandeBrake, John Barret, and Brigid Reardon, were indispensable in helping me to meet deadlines and to cover all the material collected here; their cheerful diligence and dependability will not be forgotten.

For invaluable advice and comments from the book's inception to its completion, I thank Tom King, Coppélia Kahn, and Stephen Orgel. In addition, there are a number of women in the field of Renaissance studies whose more general support of my work and my feminism has made an astonishing difference, in particular, Valerie Wayne, Linda E. Boose, and Linda Woodbridge. Outside the field (and in one case, the profession), Peter Logan, Philip Daileader, and Karen Quinn have cheered me on (and, when necessary, up) in ways that made it all possible; Sharon O'Dair deserves special thanks for her exhaustive (and rigorous!) comments on one draft and for generally "being there." Salli Davis has contributed nothing less than a nurturing working environment, and Elizabeth Meese, my feminist theorist mentor, has helped, inspired, and encouraged me in more ways than I can number.

The deepest gratitude is always the most inarticulate but is also the least content with silence. Without Gary Taylor, this book would have been unimaginable and certainly unwritable; the dream it grew out of, undreamt and unrealized. For every word in this book, I owe a word – a world – of thanks.

1   Entrances: sex, women, God

At the corners of the maps, there are pictures of animals or monsters, or of the four winds.   Marie-Louise von Franz, *Creation Myths*[1]

The trouble began when I noticed a hole in a text. It was that simple. About halfway through reading Thomas Middleton's *Women Beware Women* (1621), I paused suddenly, frowned, flipped back a page, and scanned, again, the stage directions, growing more and more perplexed. The passage disturbed me for reasons personal as much as editorial, for in it a lustful male and a resistant female meet onstage, grapple a moment, exit from stage, and return some three minutes and one ejaculation later, leaving unspoken either the word "rape" or the word "seduction," letting the audience, or at least the reader, guess. This moment provoked me to look, by way of contrast, at other, less ambiguous episodes of offstage sexual activity in early modern English plays, and to think about the fact that this male/female "eroticism" (as it is often called) was performed without recourse to "real" female bodies onstage, and this led me to begin asking questions I thought could not be answered.

Because no sooner had I discovered this hole in the text than I ran up against the difficulty of finding a language in which to discuss that hole, given the fact that our dominant theoretical discourse does not uphold the notion of a "reality" beyond the text, beyond discourse, and therefore would not regard this as a hole at all – or at least, it would not expect me to find anything *in there*, certainly not "sex" and certainly not "women."[2] One might as well be looking for God in that hole. And my conception of something NOT onstage, not in view, not palpably present in a single discursive moment (especially given the fact that this "something" was a sexual something), posed a danger any Foucauldian scholar could see coming a mile away, that of the "repressive hypothesis" debunked so thoroughly in a cornerstone text of contemporary theory on the body.[3] My interest in offstage sex could easily be interpreted as a complaint about the prudishness of the early modern English theater, rather than an exploration of the sexual imagination in all its material and rhetorical splendor. And my focus upon the fictional bodies of women as opposed to the material onstage bodies of boys might appear a naive or heterosexist rejection of post-structuralist theory, rather than an effort to plumb the paradoxes inherent in male/female erotic representations – indeed, an effort to define what this eroticism *is*.

Nonetheless, with these risks in mind, I set out to explore what looked to me like a hole in the text, hoping to return, like a proper constructionist, with lots of clever formulations about the text surrounding this hole, and about the texts surrounding this text, and about patriarchal discourse in general and its construction of "woman" as lack, and so on – but I never expected to find anything in that hole other than, well, a hole.

Then I began having problems. Because instead of focusing on the print surrounding the hole, I continually wondered why it was there in the first place. And that led me to imagine the text without a hole in it, which led me to imagine the "space" it represented, which led me to imagine what "happened" in that space – which got me into trouble.

Because the space of the offstage, I found, was inhabited by all the bodies barred from the stage. Of the surviving dramatic works performed in London's commercial theaters during the years encompassed by this book – that is, between 1595 (*Romeo and Juliet*)[4] and 1621 (*Women Beware Women*) – some 95 percent feature at least one scene foregrounding what we would now call "heterosexual" erotic activity,[5] despite the obvious complication posed by the absence of female performers. And if one scene does not seem sufficient proof of a play's overall sexual focus, there are other means of charting this territory. In fact, a survey of titles alone highlights the prominent role played by women and sex in these womanless playing spaces. Scanning Harbage's *Annals of English Drama* for the same 26-year period,[6] I found 28 titles referring to love, lovers, or lust;[7] 32 titles containing some form of the word "woman"; 36 titular maids, virgins, ladies, wives, mothers, widows, shepherdesses; 11 titular whores, courtesans, vipers, witches, cuckolds; and 1 *Insatiate Countess*. In addition, I noted 8 titles referring to wooing or wedding, and 6 naming Cupid and/or Hymen (a sum which would have doubled had I counted masques). And finally, I should mention – despite my feminist chagrin – 2 appearances of that ever-popular rape-victim, Lucrece, no doubt a sexualized figure to at least some play-goers. All together, this amounts to 124 dramatic works (none counted twice) whose titles suggest a preoccupation with women, sex, and marriage. And considering the number of dramatic works whose titles do not advertise their obsession with heterosexual couples and coupling (to name just a few from the same period: *A Midsummer Night's Dream; As You Like It; Much Ado About Nothing; A Mad World, My Masters; Ram Alley*), this figure of 124 works in 26 years, or (rounding up) 5 works per year out of an average of 26,[8] can only be viewed as the tip of the iceberg.

Results of the content survey and the title survey, viewed in tandem, thus present a high and low estimate for the emphasis placed upon sex in these plays; at least 1 text in 5 and possibly as many as 19 in 20 highlight an act that will not be performed – not even "faked," as it is in contemporary theater, often mimed from beneath bedding or through a translucent screen (methods which do not, by the way, require a female performer). And boy actors aside, the considerable female presence in the *Annals'* cast of starring characters strikes me as curious in itself, given the generally low status of women in the culture which produced these texts. I might add that, in addition to the generic references to women in these titles, there are a large number of plays about prominent (or notorious) individual women, for instance, *The Duchess of Malfi; Medea; Zenobia; The Queen of Corinth*; and, astonishingly enough, *If You Know Not Me You Know Nobody, or The Troubles of Queen Elizabeth*. Not that these plays are necessarily the sexiest of the genre (in my survey of titles I passed over *Patient Grissil, Pope Joan*, and *The She Saint*), but this litany of female names invokes a host of bodies *not* on stage; these are voices from offstage, that space of prohibition.

On the other hand, not all prohibitions are created equal. And, amongst all these erotic bodies, the offstage harbors some surprising presences.

Let us pause for a moment on the case of *If You Know Not Me*. The play was performed on the public stage in 1604, one year after the Queen's death (a sequel followed in 1605); the Queen's death, in fact, may have made the performance possible, as any such representation of the royal person would have been (to put it mildly) frowned upon during her lifetime.[9] The prior censorship presents a delectable irony: thanks to an accident of the British succession, a woman winds up on the winning side of taboo; for a change, she is the silencer, not the one silenced, and thus is spared the insult Shakespeare's Cleopatra so dreads, that of witnessing "some squeaking" actor "boy [her] greatness" (5.2.216). The two taboos – the one, barring female acting, the other, barring the acting of a particular female role – are curiously counter-poised. Though not a direct critique of the all-male stage (indeed, the Queen worked hard to control all other avenues in which her image might circulate[10]), nonetheless, the royal distaste for impersonation casts a positive light on non-representation. While she lived, the Queen was protected from profaning mimicry, unlike her female subjects, who were "boyed" on stage endlessly.

But then again, the injunction against female thespianism was also justified by the imperative to shield the weaker sex from a morally dangerous visibility.[11] When does regulation privilege the viewers, and when does it privilege the (potentially) viewed? Susan Frye relates censorship of the royal image to "the hot debate among Protestants about images of God."[12] And speaking of God. One other work in the same pages of the *Annals* also managed to circumvent censorship, although the text does not survive: a play called *Christ's Passion*. In the wake of the Reformation, the English government had been cracking down on religious drama; this particular play was performed in a private aristocratic residence, and thereby escaped control. Harbage categorizes the work as a "neo-miracle" – one of only two in this period – and the title stands out amongst the lovers and heroes surrounding it, the last breath of a dying breed of plays.

From the perspective of our culture, which in general censors sex rather than piety, the early modern attack on the passion plays may appear downright absurd – especially given the outrageously sexual nature of the plays which survived in the wake of this censorship. All those lovers in Renaissance plays had to step offstage for satisfaction, but dramatists found this convention no stumbling-block: in Middleton's *A Mad World, My Masters*, for instance, an amorous couple can be heard panting and grunting offstage. In the same year as this perform-ance, 1606, Parliament outlawed the speaking of God's name on stage. By 1609 the bleeding body of Christ had been virtually swept from the English stage, but in Beaumont and Fletcher's *Philaster, Or Love Lies a-Bleeding*, the title-page displayed a prone, bare-breasted, bleeding heroine.

Our leap down the rabbit-hole of offstage sex has landed us in alien territory – a murky space in literary history in which sacred and sexual shift shape and intershade. The year 1609 provides a kind of snapshot for the forces shaping taboo and theater. This year witnessed, in addition to the performance of *Philaster* (a play in which a prince is caught – if not literally "caught in the act" – with a courtesan), one of the very last performances of the Corpus Christi plays, in the remote county of Chester. Like *Philaster*, this performance is forced to make use of the offstage, although for very different purposes: the actor playing God must now remain invisible as he speaks his lines.[13] Sarah Beckwith, discussing Christ's body in late medieval texts, views this development as evidence of "the separation of voice and body" which went hand-in-hand with "reformation sensibility."[14] There is, however, more than one separation at work here – not only body and voice, but body and stage, body and audience, body and bodies. I view this pivotal moment in theater history – when God exits, his voice remaining, like an echo – as emblematic of the withdrawal of the sacred from the English stage, a withdrawal which is more gradual, more painful, and more problematized than many scholars have acknowledged, a withdrawal whose repercussions persist even today.

I also cannot help but imagine the *allure* of the offstage voice in the Chester plays. I wonder where the actor stood as he delivered his lines – behind the stage, above the stage, to the right or left? Despite the material differences in the playing space which was Shakespeare's medium, I am tempted to position this veiled figure alongside the ghost in *Hamlet* – or, even more daringly, alongside the lovers in at least two Middleton plays, voicing the pleasure and pain of a sexual or literal "death" from an unseen corner of the theater. And whereas it may seem far-fetched to describe the Chester "God" as a sexual figure, it seems quite fitting to call him an *erotic* figure; indeed, his very distance from the stage defines him as such, creating, for the audience, that dialectic of exclusion and desire which theorists such as Roland Barthes have shown to constitute eroticism. The erotic, as distinct from the sexual, beckons even while it recedes.

And it may be that this distinction in terms is the crucial issue here. If we take eroticism to mean consummation of desire imagined or signified, then offstage sex is eroticism *par excellence*. And it may in fact prove that sex only enters into this discussion by virtue of its material absence in theater; in other words, sexual intercourse only concerns this study insofar as it constitutes – through its absence – the erotic effect.

In this book, we embark on a pilgrimage – toward the sexual signified.

Before setting out in search of this theoretical space, it is necessary to ponder the historical questions framing it.[15] What drove God to seek the company of women? What happened between the composition of the Corpus Christi plays and God's exile from their performance? What transformation of English culture created this particular kind of textual hole?

A time-line may be a good starting-point. The earliest manuscript of the Chester Corpus Christi play was probably composed sometime between 1475 and 1500. Between 1492 and 1504, Columbus conducted his voyages to North America. In 1517 Luther sparked the Protestant Reformation. In 1533 the English Church broke with Rome. The year 1538 produced Gerhardus Mercator's cordiform map of the world, and 1543 witnessed the publication of two crucial – and oddly related – scientific treatises: Copernicus' *De revolutionibus orbium coelestium*, and Andreas Vesalius' ground-breaking anatomy text, *De humani corporis fabrica*. In 1548 the feast of Corpus Christi was rejected by the English Church, while efforts to put down the major cycles continued, peaking between 1569 and 1580. In the interim, Abraham Ortelius put together the first atlas, entitled, interestingly enough, *Theatrum orbis terrarum*, or "Theater of the World." Speaking of which – the first English public theater was built in 1576; one year later, in 1577, Drake began his voyage around the world. The Queen's Men were founded in 1583, the Rose Theatre built probably in 1587, the Swan about 1595, the Globe in 1599. In 1606 the charter for Virginia coincided with the Act of Abuses banning the naming of God on the public stage. In 1609 God was exiled from the Chester stage, while the Virginia commissioners were shipwrecked in Bermuda, and Galileo invented the telescope. By the year 1612 the Corpus Christi plays in England were extinct; that same year, a courtesan took center stage in Webster's *The White Devil*.

This time-line is as selective as any other. But the proximity of developments theatrical, cartographical, epistemological, and theological draws attention to an early modern phenomenon I will call *boundary confusion*. The voice offstage or outside the spectacle is marked in the text as *"within,"* and the spatial paradox of this signature embodies a vertigo peculiar to early modern English culture – a culture perplexed by the shifting frontiers of knowledge, by changing cosmographies, geographies, anatomies. Let us return, briefly, to that doubly significant date in science, the year 1543. Jonathan Sawday calls the Copernicus/Vesalius conjunction "a remarkable coincidence in the discovery of both macrocosm and microcosm."[16] And somewhere between the macro and the micro lies that third realm of "discovery": the Americas.[17] But such drastic shifts in perception can produce disorientation. The drama of the age opens a window into this boundary confusion, and does so – perhaps not accidentally – by way of an architectural structure more or less defined by its circular frame, by its boundaries. At this time, in fact, these structures were becoming more tightly enclosed, and more firmly controlled, as open-air amateur performances in innyards and fair-grounds were replaced – thanks to government action – by walled-in commercial theaters like Shakespeare's Globe.[18] It's as if the walls themselves provided the sense of security necessary for the culture to confront its demons. Within the safe confines of what Shakespeare called the "wooden O," a culture purged its fears and dreams of liminal collapse.[19]

This kind of spatial anxiety is evident already in a play just pre-dating my period of focus, Marlowe's *Doctor Faustus* (*c.* 1590), wherein the conjuror's circle yields a seductive, but dizzying, power over an expanding world map. In scene 1, Faustus anticipates the fruits of his forbidden studies in a way that links necromancy and colonialism.

> Shall I make spirits fetch me what I please,
> Resolve me of all ambiguities,
> Perform what desperate enterprise I will?
> I'll have them fly to India for gold,
> Ransack the ocean for orient pearl,
> And search all corners of the new-found world
> For pleasant fruits and princely delicates . . . .   (1.78–84)[20]

Faustus goes on to ponder walling "Germany with brass" and making the "Rhine circle fair Wittenberg" (87–88), intoxicated by the prospect of manipulating geographical boundaries, creating circular enclosures, little worlds of his own. And the play continues to re-define space, not only through necromancy, but often through theology. Mephostophilis offers a description of hell which departs from the model of the Dantean cosmos. He locates hell somewhere "Under the heavens" (5.118), but can be no more specific than

> Within the bowels of these elements,
> Where we are tortur'd and remain for ever.
> Hell hath no limits nor is circumscrib'd
> In one self place, but where we are is hell,
> And where hell is, there must we ever be . . .   (120–24)

The definition of hell as exclusion from God's presence is not unique to Marlowe, but in this text preoccupied with the conjuror's circle, this refusal to *circumscribe* strikes me as curious. Moreover, the speaker's first replies to the question "Where is hell?" set up false expectations: in the medieval cosmos of concentric spheres, hell is "under" heaven and "within the bowels" of earth, but Mephostophilis, after suggesting this model, suddenly uproots it, replacing the solid, unambiguous globe with the more fluid, more abstract "elements," and finally, discarding the map altogether, defining hell as a non-space.

So much for the macrocosm; what does this play have to say about the microcosm, the human body? There are virtually no women in *Faustus*, and, aside from one bawdy joke about the conjuring circle, there is really no sex either; in this respect, the play calls attention to its marginal periodicity, looking backward toward the fading values of the medieval morality play rather than anticipating the secularization – and the sexualization – of the late Elizabethan and Jacobean stage. Faustus' quest for total knowledge does not necessitate a quest for carnal knowledge (although Helen would be a bonus); but in many later plays the urge to "know," to "see," the desire for "ocular proof" targets female sexuality exclusively. Webster's *Duchess of Malfi* (1612–14), for instance, turns the new tools of science upon the body of a woman who strives to evade patriarchal surveillance.

> We had need go borrow that fantastic glass
> Invented by Galileo the Florentine,
> To view another spacious world i'th'moon,
> And look to find a constant woman there.   (2.4.16–19)[21]

This is one of several references to glass as an optical aid, revealing new worlds, great and small, and hence associated with the hidden world of female desire. The material properties of glass also play a role in discussions of women: "A man might strive to make glass malleable, / Ere he should make [women] fixed" (2.4.14–15). But glass *can* be made malleable, when heated, and this attribute is also used to malign women. Bosola, hired to spy on the pregnant Duchess, detains her midwife with a joke about the "glass-house" and the "strange instrument" that can "swell up a glass to the fashion of a woman's belly" (2.2.6–10). As I will argue in depth later in the book, the image of the glass womb reveals, in Bosola, a fantasy of visual penetration which is no less violent than Ferdinand's killing jealousy.

The specular preoccupations of the supposedly sane males are parodied, later in the play, in the babble of the madmen: "Hell is a mere glass-house, where the devils are continually blowing up women's souls on hollow irons" (4.2.79–80); "If I had my glass here, I would show a sight would make all the women here call me mad doctor" (99–100). And perhaps most telling of all is the Mad Astrologer's desire for a "perspective," or telescope, which may draw "Doomsday . . . closer," and a magnifying glass, which may "set the world on fire" (74–76). Glass, in the hands of men, is a profoundly ambivalent symbol: as a metaphor for the womb, it betrays a killing curiosity; as a specular tool, it can destroy the known world.

The universe of Webster's play – like that of *Faustus* – has been hollowed out by the tools of knowledge. But the primary victim of this dissecting world-view is the human – particularly, the female – body. Here are Bosola's words of "comfort" to the doomed Duchess:

Thou art a box of worm seed, at best, but a salvatory of green mummy: what's this flesh? a little crudded milk, fantastical puff-paste: our bodies are weaker than those paper prisons boys use to keep flies in: more contemptible; since ours is to preserve earth-worms: didst thou ever see a lark in a cage? such is the soul in the body: this world is like her little turf of grass, and the heaven o'er our heads, like her looking-glass, only gives us a miserable knowledge of the small compass of our prison. (4.2.123–31)

At first glance, this seems no more than your standard *contemptus mundi* moralizing – but the looking-glass metaphor adds an unexpected twist, and also introduces (as in the above references to glass) an unsettling ambiguity. Comparing heaven to a mirror seems vaguely blasphemous: mirrors are flat, impenetrable, associated with narcissism and deception; they epitomize *worldliness*. A mirror set beside a bird cage will trick the bird into singing to its illusory "mate"; the mirror, in effect, mitigates the bird's incarceration but offers no final means of escape. What does this metaphor say about our relationship to heaven? It's one thing to view the body as a "temple," as a vessel for the soul, quite another to view it as "a salvatory of . . . mummy" – as a vessel for an extract drawn from a dead, eviscerated body, or (to read the line literally), as a vessel for a vessel made of mummified flesh. Not that Bosola cites a single, stable model for the contents of the human body: the caged lark/soul keeps company with flies and worms in his sequence of metaphors. One can gloss "miserable knowledge" as poor knowledge (the mirror creates the illusion of a larger "prison"), or as knowledge which makes us miserable (the mirror reflects back to us the earth/flesh we want to escape), and the point is the same: we are trapped, in our bodies, in our (mis)perceptions.

Bosola's lecture – like Renaissance anatomy – eviscerates the body, leaves it "mummy"-like. His dark brand of piety also resembles that of the early anatomist, who sought to uncover, in his dissection, the divine truth embedded in the human microcosm. David L. Hodges notes the futility of the anatomist's moral project: "These totalities . . . remain elusive because the anatomist's fragmenting method defers and distances the absolute order he hopes to bring to light. For the anatomist, there is always more cutting to be done." Sawday, likewise, observes anatomy's ability to deflate piety: "For all their continual assertions that the body mirrored the harmonious orchestration of the universe, what they confronted in reality was something else: a structure of such bewildering complexity . . . that the outcome of every such interior voyage hovered on the edge of disaster." Therefore, Sawday argues, "The inwardly directed gaze . . . transformed the body into the locus of all doubt."[22] This inward gaze, along with its attendant disillusionment, produces Bosola's vision of a twice-trapped human soul, peering from the cage of its body into the false depths of a reflecting sky.

The idea of a mirror into the soul is not Bosola's own invention: Prince Hamlet, berating his mother in her bedchamber, imagines a "glass" which will show Gertrude her "inmost part" (3.4.19–20).[23] As in *The Duchess of Malfi*, though, the issue here is a woman's sexual secrets, and the rhetoric is incisive to a degree which complicates its Christian intent. Hamlet's words are likened to "daggers" by himself as well as his victim. Gertrude begs him to stop, crying, "Thou turn'st my eyes into my very soul" (78–79). But Hamlet perceives his cruelty as surgery. He warns her, "Lay not that flattering unction to your soul," for "It will but skin and film the ulcerous place, / Whiles rank corruption, mining all within, / Infects unseen." (136–40). Hamlet's obsession – here, as elsewhere in the play – is with the interior of the human subject, with the spiritual contents of this bodily vessel (as in Sonnet 146, "Poor soul, the centre of my sinful earth"). Or is it? For Hamlet problematizes the traditional paradigm by troping this interiority in medical/anatomical language, by speaking of ulcers, of infection. Sawday sees Hamlet as "a prototype of the new scientist" embodying "the struggle of the imagination when confronted with new orders of spatial organization."[24] As revealed in his conversation with Yorick's skull, Hamlet – like Renaissance anatomy – clings to the medieval belief in the soul, meanwhile fascinated by the body's literal "insides."

In Hamlet's language we detect the collision of two paradigms for inwardness; it is no accident, I hold, that these paradigms collide over a woman's – and, in particular, a *mother's* – body. Lear does the same thing to another erring woman: "Let them anatomize Regan; see what breeds about her heart" (3.6.34–35). According to Hodges, this moment illustrates the tension between empirical and moral approaches to the body, a contrast which becomes even more striking in relation to Lear's earlier, more "traditional" curse directed at Goneril's womb.[25] But Hodges neglects to factor in fully the centrality of the womb in both episodes: in the proposed "anatomy" of Regan, the word "breeds" precedes "heart," suggesting a (dis)location of the spiritual/emotional center somewhere around the reproductive organs. Once again, the eye is directed toward an ambiguously located "inmost part."

What characters like Bosola and Hamlet convey through their dissecting rhetoric is a distinctly *early modern* horror of the physical, inseparable from their attitudes toward what we call the metaphysical. There is a direct relation between Bosola's hollowing of the flesh and his perception of heaven as a mere mirror-trick. (One might also draw a connection between this view of the flesh and his ability to *kill*.) Inventions like the telescope and the magnifying glass, current in Webster's day, when considered alongside the discovery of the North American continent, add up to an explosion of the boundaries of the visible world, both outward, into the heavens, and inward, into the human anatomy. The seeming availability of total knowledge both opened horizons and made the visible world suddenly hollow. The medieval cosmos, with its fixed spatial boundaries, had offered an escape from our bodily cages through proximity to the holy; the early modern cosmos, by virtue of its fluid boundaries, sent heaven flying: hence, as Mephostophilis says, hell is everywhere.

The neuroses of Bosola and Hamlet reflect those of their culture, but it is tempting to describe these symptoms in psychoanalytic terms. Hamlet's response to physicality resembles what Julia Kristeva terms "abjection": "Apprehensive, desire turns aside; sickened, it rejects . . . But simultaneously, just the same, that impetus, that spasm, that leap is drawn toward an elsewhere as tempting as it is condemned. Unflaggingly, like an inescapable boomerang, a vortex of summons and repulsion places the one haunted . . . beside himself."[26] In such cases of existential nausea, the scapegoats are bound to be women. As Mark Breitenberg maintains, "masculine anxiety toward women's sexuality is both prior to and considerably in excess of any 'referent' . . ."[27]

The cover of Vesalius' *Fabrica* portrays a woman's body displayed in the theater of anatomy – the focal point, her opened womb (Figure 1). And, as numerous scholars have pointed out, the appellation is no analogy: it was a stage designer, Inigo Jones, who was commissioned to design such a structure in London.[28] Webster's *The Duchess of Malfi* was not alone in its obsession with the hidden female sexual interior; Shakespeare's *Othello*, and to some degree, *Hamlet*, in addition to a host of other plays, make it their mission to anatomize female sexuality. "The womb or uterus was an object sought after with an almost ferocious intensity in Renaissance anatomy theatres" – and, I would add, in the anatomical imaginary of the theater itself.[29]

The glass-house invoked by Bosola and his mad counterpart was located, interestingly, near the Blackfriars Theatre. And, despite the glass women fantasized by Webster's misogynists, the theater was a more effective factory for male fantasies, and a more active arena for male voyeurism. With the explosion of the margins of all maps – cosmographical, geographical, biological – the female body, or rather female subjectivity (with its most perplexing manifestation, sexual appetite), became the last frontier in the quest for total knowledge.[30] The stage became the primary locus for the playing out of these cultural obsessions, being perfectly designed to serve this function: its very boundedness and visibility made it the most effective medium for exploring questions of specularity and boundary confusion. And the fact that the boundary conditions of the stage debarred women from its compass only intensified the fascination with "woman" as the last great mystery.

Faustus is not the principal conjuror in Renaissance drama.

We must be cautious, on the other hand, not to over-stress the differences between early modern and medieval maps, since, in some respects, all maps are alike. And what most concerns this project, anyway, is not so much the map, but its *margins*, the offstage/edge-of-page space of representation which provides the transhistorical basis for an erotic theoretics. History is only relevant to this investigation insofar as it

Figure 1   Title page of Andreas Vesalius' *De humani corporis fabrica* (1543).

created the preconditions for a specific kind of text, and textual hole; ultimately, though, these holes open into our own universe.

According to John Gillies, the frame of a map has a "perennial poetic function," that of defining "identity in relation to otherness."[31] Renaissance maps, like their classical models, function as mirrors of cultural identity: their margins provide a space for fantasies of the exotic and the monstrous against which this cultural identity can be formed – something I would call a cosmographical abject. Observing a correspondence between map ornamentation and plays like *The Tempest*, Gillies argues that the early modern theater – epitomized by Shakespeare's Globe – was conceived in quasi-cartographical terms: "All the world's a stage."[32]

If the stage is a world, then what world awaits us offstage? Gillies' case for the sexualization of the map's frame further likens it to the theoretical space we are seeking.

Like the Indian caste system, the imagined edges of the ancient map would represent a case of "external boundaries" recapitulating the "internal lines" of prohibitions governing the body and its orifices . . . The link between monstrosity, margins and sexual "promiscuity" is far from casual. Mythological edge monsters such as centaurs and harpies are hybrids, or the offspring of literally "promiscuous" unions between creatures of different kinds.[33]

On the other hand, if the purpose of the frame is, as Gillies says, to define identity against otherness, it is just as easy to deify as to sexualize (which is to say, to demonize) the occupants of these margins. Hence the medieval *mappemundi* situates Christ and his angels outside the globe; the "Psalter Map" presents an interesting variation, in which two serpentine monsters occupy the lower part of the frame, as if cowering from the image of Christ which dominates the top (Figure 2). The margin is not only a wondrous place, but also wondrously ambivalent.[34]

Is there no essential difference, then, between the geographic imagination of the so-called Age of Discovery, and that which preceded it? Gillies questions the distinction between the "old geography of emplacement and the new geography of extension," in light of the fact that the latter self-consciously defined itself against the former while yet clinging "to the imagery of the past."[35] Yet one cannot deny that in Shakespeare's day the edges of the known world (and consequently, of the map) were beginning to be reinscribed in such a way as to render the old monsters obsolete – or, more accurately, to replace them with new monsters based on tales of European contact with native non-Europeans (Figure 3). The new maps offered a different, less reified, less forbidding edge – but an edge nonetheless. The ornamental sea-serpent remained a fixture in maps of increasing sophistication, attesting to a habit of mythologizing the boundary which no amount of new data could quite abolish (Figure 4).[36]

Figure 2   "The Psalter Map."

Figure 3   Petrus Plancius, *Orbis terrarum typus* (1594).

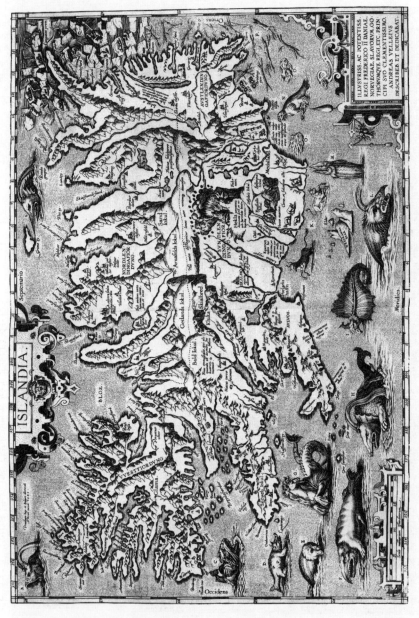

Figure 4   Abraham Ortelius, " Islandia," from *Theatrum orbis terrarum* (1590).

Still, it is necessary to ask what it meant to early modern scholars to realize that the old maps were, empirically speaking, wrong. It is noteworthy, for instance, that Shakespeare's answer to *Faustus, The Tempest*, draws upon sources on the Bermudas, but situates Prospero's island in the Mediterranean (which was, as its name indicates, the middle of the classical world).[37] Shakespeare's geographical conservatism – though not universal in Renaissance literature – suggests a nostalgia for the old *mappemundi* with its safe, landlocked sea and its cosy Christian boundaries. And the old maps were only part of a vast body of revered texts which became subject to critique. Anthony Grafton presents a case for the radical re-thinking of classical texts in response to the discovery of the New World and the birth of "modern science": "The world was no longer accessible only through learned books in Latin; it could be known directly."[38] The desire for this direct knowledge or contact launched the expedition of Columbus – who, of course, did not initially think that the old maps were wrong, but only unwittingly proved them so. Intending to sail from one edge of the map to the other, the explorer plunged into a hole in the map. A hole the size of a continent.

In the case of Columbus, we might safely say that he found *something outside the text*. What was done with this experience of difference fully supports what constructionism teaches: the New World was not so much discovered as "put into discourse" – and often by defining the "new" in terms of the old xenophobic paradigms. This process, however, was by no means instantaneous and by no means simple, and the impact of the initial experience on the European imagination was partially produced by a sense of this experience as a semiotic crisis, as a confrontation with *an unnamed thing*.

In other words, at the boundaries of the world the explorers faced the boundaries of their discourse, the limits of all systems of meaning available to them. Kathleen M. Kirby analyzes the interconnectedness of language and space in post-structuralist theory, but she traces the development of a post-modern spatial sensibility as far back as the narratives of Cabeza de Vaca and Samuel Champlain.[39] Kirby's discussion of the "vertigo" of post-structuralism suggests a prototype in what I have diagnosed as early modern boundary confusion. The *hors-texte* deflected by Derridean theory is prefigured in the horizon of Columbian exploration. Leaving aside the philosophical question of whether such a limit can ever be crossed, I nonetheless hope that this paradigm of semiotic struggle can aid in the exploration at hand, as we prod the boundaries of our own theoretical discourse in the hope of finding a place for that hole in the dramatic text.

But perhaps we are not talking about a hole after all, but rather an opening, an entrance. Offstage sex transpires when two people exit from stage, but the difference between an exit and an entrance is entirely a matter of perspective. In fact, we can only find our way to the realm offstage by exploring the space of the stage itself, along with those onstage spaces occupied by bodies in costume. It is this *material* stage which, turned inside-out, gives rise to my theoretical model:

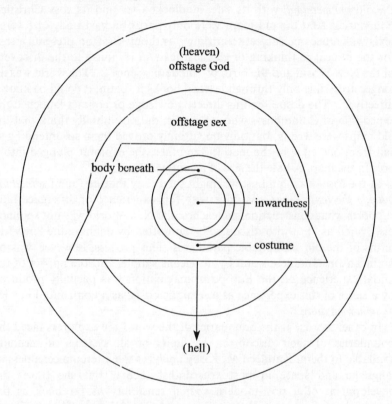

The resemblance to the old geocentric cosmos is not accidental; the concentric hermeneutic spheres radiating from the center of the stage's "little world" are the products of a new kind of theology – a theology of theater – which sprang up quickly in the debris of the medieval stage. Catherine Belsey notes the correspondence between the medieval cosmography and the circular staging of *The Castle of Perseverance* (Mankind, and the audience, placed in the center, God and Belial beyond an encircling moat) and elaborates on the changing "map" of the stage through the Renaissance and Restoration. By the time *Faustus* was written, "the abstractions" had "become relatively peripheral" – and soon would vanish entirely from the visual field.[40] It is this fading periphery which we seek in the offstage, with its spectral, and now sexual, goddesses and demons.

I do not, however, present this model as a definitive, totalizing chart of the early modern "theatrical mind"; my eclectic array of methodologies (French feminism and deconstruction tempered by the more practical tools of performance criticism, historicism, and editorial theory) does not lend itself to sweeping ontological claims. And anyway, we know that maps are conceptual by definition. Most importantly, then, this map serves as a map of the book, whose trajectory is closer to spiral than to linear, its approach essayistic more than argumentative, more concerned with play than with proof. "Offstage sex and female desire" encircles the stage, applying theater semiotics, Derridean theory, and my own feminist critique of modern editorial practice, to four episodes of offstage sex – culled from Middleton's *Women Beware Women* and *A Mad World, My Masters*, and from Shakespeare's *Othello* and *Romeo and Juliet* – in order to unlock the signifying secrets of a body whose "absence" the naked stage or page declares. A crucial factor in the magnetism and magic of such moments, we discover, is the voyeuristic response of the reader/audience, which varies in intensity depending upon the way the textual "gap" is framed by the dramatist, by the editor, and/or by the director. Offstage sex, I argue, encapsulates the paradoxical nature of male/female erotic representation on an all-male stage, and in a male-authored and (largely) male-edited genre,[41] where female "desire" or subjectivity is the central, nagging question.

Ultimately barred entrance, however, to the sexual otherwhere offstage, we turn, in "Body beneath / body beyond," to the onstage microcosm: the fantasy of a female body inside the costume of the transvestite boy actor. In order to penetrate the enigma of the "body beneath," the chapter must unravel the paradox by which a woman's clothes come to embody her body; this only becomes possible if we consider the theatrical body as a spatial construct – a set of contours built of fabric and flesh (two components not always distinguishable) – to which language adds the illusion of depth. And this dissection of body-space has peculiar relevance to the female body, considering the phallocentric figuration of woman/vessel/womb – a model which easily lends itself to architectural tropes. Hence, these pages explore not only the rhetorical treatment of the female interior, but also the ways in which the stage itself projects this interior; to this end, John Fletcher's *The Tamer Tamed*,[42] and Ben Jonson's *Bartholomew Fair*, prove useful sources, for each play focuses on an architectural space – Maria's bedroom, and Ursula's booth, respectively – which figures the body of its female proprietor. Thus, we arrive at the conclusion that the seemingly womanless Renaissance stage is not only – paradoxically – woman-focused, but in fact is woman-like; that is, the stage is a "female" space, both hollow and boundlessly fertile.

Finding the erotic "core" of the stage, however, as elusive as its offstage correlative, "(Off)Staging the sacred" proceeds to the farthest exit, death, observing two female sexual martyrs – the heroines of, respectively, Middleton's *Lady's Tragedy* and Webster's *The Duchess of Malfi* – and detecting in their sacrifices the fingerprints of an exiled Christ. Stepping this far from the Renaissance stage, accordingly, requires a step back in theater history; this chapter, hence, investigates the transition between the two earliest "periods" of English drama – a transition marked by the secularization of the stage and the proliferation of the bawdy – along with its implications regarding modern (and even post-modern) definitions of the sacred and the sexual. Building upon Caroline Walker Bynum's thesis concerning a "feminized" medieval Christ, I argue that the suppression of the Corpus Christi plays – which featured an eroticized sacrifice – created the demand for depictions of sensational, sexualized murders of women. This nexus explains the strange sisterhood in censorship – God/woman – which first led me to conceive of a "theology" of theatrical sex.

"Obscene and unseen" follows the path of God's body back(wards) to the stage (and forward in history) by way of His traces in early modern profanity, traces which dwindled in the wake of the censorship laws of 1606, but which nonetheless lead us to an important juncture in stage and cultural history: the point at which body parts became bawdy parts and the "profane" became prurient. Supported by Foucault's thesis about the rise of *scientia sexualis*, this study claims that, at some point during the seventeenth century, *sex replaced God as the supreme signified*: hence the sacralization of sex and the sexualization of profanity, and hence the ambivalence of the offstage, that locus of fascination and disgust. But the final stage in our journey, I hope, will not leave us stranded in history. As intimated above, this is not, strictly speaking, a historicist work, but rather a theoretical essay, a foray. This chapter returns us to the same four plays with which we began, aiming to locate, in their ribald, oath-strewn pages, a different sort of textual hole: a corporeal kernel within language that can translate to our own discursive field.

The spatial metaphors I have been using (e.g., "discursive field"), together with the spatial paradigm I have etched above, require a certain self-reflexivity on my part. In discussing the vogue in post-structuralist theory for this kind of language, Kirby astutely notes,

Theorists themselves often seem uncertain about whether they are speaking of *real space*, and practices taking place within it, or of a realm purely discursive . . . And sometimes, as . . . [in] the work of Freud, a space that begins as a mere descriptive convenience may turn into a space with referential autonomy: in describing the space of the psyche, language gathers a material weight and body. It tends to become real – and may be the only reality we have.[43]

The skepticism of the last clause is typical of the scholarship I will be engaging; if literary theorists cannot distinguish between real and conceptual space (never mind determining the ontological status of the gendered body) then it would follow that so many intellectuals doubt the existence of heaven, or God. My borrowing from the language of theology in exploring eroticism in drama may provoke questions about the philosophical grounding for my claims: is my sex/woman/God triad "merely" a system of analogies? I might dodge the question by citing Foucault, who claims that the Renaissance *episteme* configured all knowledge as analogy.[44] But it might be more honest to say, "I don't know." This much I can say, though: this book's realm of enquiry is purely conceptual; the "offstage" does not exist. Nonetheless, the objects I will take up throughout my analysis did and do exist: theaters, costumes, wigs, puppets, props, play texts – and the embodied players themselves. Renaissance dramatists themselves were fascinated, not just by the mysterious space of the womb, but by metaphorical spaces more generally: the language spoken onstage is cluttered with circles and spheres. The conjuror's circle – a popular vehicle for bawdy, and a *topos* to be broached in the Conclusion – is only one such figure. But the "magic" of theatrical practice was (and is) its impact upon real bodies; understanding this impact, this force, this "weight," is my ultimate goal in this book.

The danger of eroticism in theater, according to Puritan polemicist Stephen Gosson, is that it ravishes the spectator; it "flatters the sight" and pierces "the privy entries of the eare."[45] Post-structuralist theory says the opposite is true: theatrical "sex" is part of the larger semiotic web encompassing all human experience; it does not enter US, we enter IT. In the following study I intend to skirt the boundaries of dramatic texts and the discursive boundaries of the early modern English stage in search of entrances toward (or perhaps into) what I will call the erotic body – a body defined as female by the very dynamic of exclusion/desire (manifested in but not limited to the taboo against female performance) which renders this search necessary. And if this quest for "the body" might be faulted as essentialist in its conception, I would immediately qualify it as *strategically essentialist*. For I engage in this search knowing full well that any discursive exit I might find, in the space of these pages, can only amount to a Derridean "exit from closure."[46] And one might finally say that the thing I call eroticism is an effect of this very engagement with or teasing of verbal boundaries, is perhaps achieved by way of the illusion that one has touched the edge of the intelligible, the describable, the discursive. Eroticism entails the illusion (if it is one) that it is possible to touch the body directly.

2   Offstage sex and female desire

Rape is defined by the absence of consent, but it cannot be prosecuted where there is an absence of proof. The prosecutor thus faces a paradoxical task: to supply palpable evidence of absence. What often arises from this difficulty is a search for signs that the victim struggled – torn garments and bruises, for instance. That rape can happen without leaving these marks on the victim, and that, furthermore, the absence of consent need not coincide with the will or the power to struggle, are common feminist objections to this legal method.[1] Nonetheless, the method, and thus the paradox, remain.

Proving rape in literature is no easier than proving it in life. And sexual intercourse in early modern drama presents itself largely through verbal testimony – designed, in some cases, to titillate more than narrate, and, in some cases, narrating little at all. This problem creates the disturbing potential of act 2, scene 2, of Middleton's *Women Beware Women*, the so-called "seduction" of Bianca while her mother-in-law plays chess. The text incites questions about what we see onstage, but also, more subtly, about *what we do not see* onstage, and since modern productions of the play are few and far between, the reader is basically on her own. That intercourse occurs offstage is taken for granted; that it occurs *at all* is taken for granted. But of course the question is not "what really happened," because technically nothing "happens" offstage: theatrically speaking, the actors await their cues; textually speaking, narrative is interrupted – both resulting in the illusion that a vital part of the play eludes the gaze. In theorizing this gap and the way the "mind's eye" fills it in, one must ask not only WHAT but HOW this absence comes to signify, and what role is played by editors and directors in this semiotic process.

Because not all such absences are created equal. Middleton's *A Mad World, My Masters* draws our attention to a contrasting episode of offstage sex, this one explicitly and jubilantly consensual; the juxtaposition defines female erotic desire as a "problem" for critics, editors, theorists, and play-goers in the same way it is a problem for the male characters onstage, and it locates that interpretive problem in a textual *aporia*. *Othello* is only one of a number of early modern plays whose plot hinges upon a *reported* sexual incident and the question of its truth or falsity – a question which, in a specular male economy, inevitably boils down to the furtive nature of female desire.[2] And though I begin this chapter with a point about rape, the one "on trial" in these plays is more likely to be female; the subject of interrogation, her sexual secrets – housed in a dark world offstage.

In this way narrative "holes" become stories in themselves – supplying interpretive nodes for both the onstage (male) "jury" and the feminist critic, not to mention the offstage (and generally male) editor/director who mediates (or so we hope) between the first two parties. And what better place to look for a female signified – in a male-authored and male-edited genre – than between the lines? What better place than out there or *"within,"* in the space between *"exeunt"* and *"enter,"* birthed by the voyeuristic imagination? And yes, we, as critics, as readers, are spectators, and hence potential voyeurs. Webster's dictionary defines a voyeur as "One who derives sexual gratification from observing the sex organs or sexual acts of others, esp. from a secret vantage point." Offstage sex appeals to the voyeur in each of us ("Look what they're doing!") in a double gesture which ultimately preserves our sense of decency ("Don't look now!"). One could even go so far as to say that theater offers the voyeur that "secret" or protected vantage point by way of the audience/stage divide. Of course, it is also arguable, and has been convincingly argued by feminist film theorists, that this vantage point is structurally "male";[3] but this is not to say that women don't, can't or shouldn't occupy the voyeur's position. On the contrary: the project at hand requires it. And in any case, early modern theatrical practice never demands full-blown voyeurism; the sexual spectacle always retreats, at the last moment, into its own "secret" place – beyond the tiring-house wall and nowhere at all.

Gillian Rose's feminist geography seeks out "a paradoxical space which straddles the spaces of representation and unrepresentability" because "feminisms imagine an elsewhere beyond the . . . master subject while also trapped within the limits of his desires and fears."[4] Is the offstage a feminist "elsewhere" or another site of misogynist abjection? I believe it may be either or both. The promise lies in the versatility of absence itself as conceived by Derridean theory – not as an ontological quality of "things," or an ontological thing in itself (say: void, vacancy), but as an effect of signification, cradling its own infinitely diverse signifying powers. In order to demonstrate this, I intend, in this chapter, to compare four episodes of offstage sex in four plays by Shakespeare

and Middleton, discussing both textual "clues" and editorial and performative "solutions" to the erotic riddle at hand. By studying not only the
play-text, but also what theater semioticians call the "text" of performance, and by noting the bridge between the editorial para-text (stage
directions, original or interpolated,[5] commentary notes, etc.) and the
offstage space in performance, we may arrive at a better understanding
of the *mise-en-scène* and its relation to the edited text.[6] Ultimately, I aim
to measure the seeming *proximity* of each offstage encounter – a quality
which both constitutes and reflects the pitch of our voyeuristic engagement – in the process noting the editor's or director's power to alter that
engagement.[7] And though I will begin with the simple question of "what
happened," I hope to end by raising some larger questions about *where*
and *how* "it" happened. How does "sex" happen in a theater where
absent bodies play the starring role?

I   **Middleton: silence and sound**

Feminist critics confronting act 2, scene 2, in *Women Beware Women* will
find the text mute in certain daunting ways: no stage directions signal
pursuit, flight, or struggle. Nonetheless, consent is neither stated nor
implied, and Bianca's exclamations, paired with the Duke's pleas of
"tremble not" and "strive not," seem a clear indication of physical
resistance. Modern readers who expect the text to be more explicit, who
look, for instance, for piercing screams and violent strife, may be misled
on two counts, one editorial and one historical. First of all, early modern
drama is notorious for its sparse stage directions, and modern editors –
as we shall see – have done little to clarify the problem of consent, or
highlight the degree of potential struggle. More importantly, though,
even if Bianca chooses to keep quiet, she may have excellent reasons for
doing so, considering the social superiority of her assailant: Suzanne
Gossett argues that early modern rape victims had scanty recourse,
above all when the alleged rapist was a social superior.[8] The sixteen-ish
Bianca (a potential statutory rape victim by our legal standards)[9] may
indeed yield simply because she knows resistance is useless. As the Duke
pointedly reminds her, "I can command: / Think upon that" (364–65).[10]

Yet to me the most rape-like aspect of the offstage encounter is its
duration. Bianca is lured from her mother-in-law (who is distracted at
chess) by the prospect of a tour of the ducal palace and its artifacts
(2.2.295); Bianca is led into a locked gallery and shown "naked pictures,"
intended to whet her otherwise "queasy" sexual appetite (313); her guide
(ironically named Guardiano) slips out as the Duke approaches, unseen,
from behind her (319); the Duke seizes her (322; more on this move

below); she protests; he threatens and cajoles; they leave the stage (389). Meanwhile the chess-game continues between the mother and the Duke's procuress, Livia, whose *double entendres* throughout the game keep the audience alert to the unseen act. The game ends quickly, and Bianca returns alone, ashamed and furious (421). The offstage coupling has occupied the space of thirty-one lines of dialogue, or, in my estimation, no more than three minutes of performance time.[11] My estimate may even be generous: Andrew Gurr notes that in Elizabethan theater "The words were rattled off at speeds markedly higher than we are used to now, if contemporary references to the duration of performances are any guide."[12]

And clearly Middleton meant to emphasize the obscene brevity of the act, as the mother-in-law remarks to Bianca, "Are you so soon returned?" and doubts whether she could have "seen all" on so brief a tour (450–52). As a woman reader sympathetic to Bianca's reluctance beforehand and shame afterward, I find this the most troubling aspect of the sequence. Even setting aside the issue of power disparity and what we would now consider Bianca's minority status, I find it hard to believe that intercourse between strangers which takes the woman by surprise and lasts less than three minutes could amount to anything short of violation. Even if the woman consents, there is little likelihood of her pleasure.[13] Nor has this particular male shown concern for his partner's pleasure – as Livia remarks of her king during the chess game, he "makes all the haste he can" (392).

And if brevity alone does not constitute violation, Middleton uses other clues – not always elucidated in the commentary notes and critical introductions of modern editions. Two devices represent the unseen act: the chess-game, with its plethora of sexual puns – comparing, for instance, Bianca to a pawn, the Duke to a "duke," meaning a rook, who takes the pawn[14] – and the erotic artwork Bianca is shown early in the scene. The dual metaphors embody different aspects of sex: the political and the aesthetic, respectively.[15] Both aspects pertain to Bianca's position as a woman coveted by her social superior for her body's aesthetic value. Neither metaphor suggests mutuality in sex; in chess there is, at the player-level, a winner and a loser,[16] and at the board-level, pieces that take and pieces that are taken; in art there is a buyer and a commodity, a viewer and an object. Of course, a chess-player can enjoy a losing game; a pawn (let's imagine) can enjoy being captured; a prostitute can enjoy the sex she (or he) sells; anyone may enjoy being viewed, by a lover or a stranger. But when the admiring viewer mentions his power to mar the artifice, his appreciation hardly seems generous: in the midst of praising the resistant Bianca's "delicate" beauty, the Duke obliquely threatens,

"Take warning . . . / . . . I should be sorry, the least force should lay / An unkind touch upon thee" (341–47).

These violent undertones have been ignored if not completely effaced by editors from Day One. A. H. Bullen's introduction to the 1886 edition blithely summarizes the sequence as follows: "After no severe struggle she capitulates"[17] – although the Duke himself remarks on the physical "strength" she wastes in resisting him (330). And yet Bullen's cavalier approach at least acknowledges the *potential* for struggle, implying some awareness of the necessary physical contact on stage; this sensitivity is lost in the much later, more "authoritative" Revels edition, the introduction of which, ascribes to "exaggerated nervousness" Bianca's initial cry, " 'Oh treachery to honour!' (II.ii.320), *before the Duke says anything to affront her.*"[18] The editor, astonishingly, has overlooked the Duke's *physical* affront, made obvious by his immediate demand, "Prithee tremble not, / I feel thy breast shake" (320–21). The oversight is somewhat emended in a subsequent edition by David L. Frost, who inserts, as a cue for Bianca's cry, the stage direction *"Embraces her"*[19] – an interpolation which still, to me, begs quite a few questions. Does a rapist "embrace" his victim? Does the victim perceive it so?

Staging could, of course, clarify the question of consent; at the very least, it would *have to* resolve the problem of physical contact. Bianca could make a few half-hearted attempts to rebuff the Duke and finally begin to return his caresses; or she could struggle in earnest and deliver her lines in a near shriek. Or the director might exploit the scene's most brutal potential: the Duke could stifle Bianca's protestations and – at his imperative "We'll walk together" (388) – he could "walk," or rather drag her offstage. Director Terry Hands, in a 1969 Royal Shakespeare Company production, opted for an effect more in keeping with what I believe was Middleton's grittier vision: Bianca was "Grabbed by [the Duke] from behind, both stared out towards the audience . . . [the] Duke calm, firm and matter-of-fact, Bianca stunned and appalled. As he hustled her off after his last long speech . . . there was no hint of compliance in her behavior . . ."[20] Hands' interpretation can hardly be called radical: the Duke's approach from behind is necessitated by the dialogue, and the grabbing and shuffling (as opposed to embracing and leading) is a matter of nuance.

I have argued quite adamantly on behalf of a particular reading of Middleton's famous chess sequence not only because I feel that an entire critical and editorial tradition needs "correction" on feminist grounds, but more importantly because I wish to demonstrate the power of the textual / dramaturgical "frame" in determining a reader's / viewer's response to an offstage event. So perhaps it is worthwhile asking why modern editors (all of whom, by the way, happen to be male) of *Women Beware Women* have chosen to frame this episode as though it were *not a rape*. Does this have something to do with the voyeuristic response, or rather, in particular, with *their* responses as (male) readers and voyeurs? It is tempting to speculate. Perhaps calling it "rape" would spoil the fun; after all, rape, to the class of modern males who have edited Renaissance plays, is not supposed to be sexy. To find rape sexy you must (as a male) call it "seduction."

Of course it helps that we never "see" a woman getting raped; the act itself is materially absent from both written text and "text" of performance. Or is "absence" the proper term? Michael Issacharoff distinguishes between two forms of dramatic space, "mimetic" and "diegetic," or, respectively, that which is shown, and that which is "described" or "referred to by the characters."[21] In light of this model, offstage sex may be said to transpire at the farthest end of diegetic space; never fully described, but only referred to (often obliquely) by dialogue, gestures, and movement on stage. Although I hesitate over the seeming unity of the category, considering the diverse impressions that can cluster about the same diegetic space, the concept nonetheless allows the performative text to embrace, at least in theory, the absence we seek. And the written text? From a Derridean point of view, we cannot work with or work in writing, without making absence our element.

> To grasp the operation of creative imagination . . . one must turn oneself toward the invisible interior of poetic freedom. One must be separated from oneself in order to be reunited with the blind origin of the work in its darkness . . . Only *pure absence* – not the absence of this or that, but the absence of everything in which all presence is announced – can *inspire* . . . [22]

Only one of countless haunting passages in which Derrida maps the non-spaces which make meaning, this may provide, in conjunction with Issacharoff's model, a means to ground our study of performative or textual absences.

I take this turn to theory and away from my critique of editorial practice in its relation to an authorial intention, not because of some anti-positivistic reflex instilled by my post-structuralist training (on the contrary: in this case, I'm quite certain I'm right), but rather because the instances of misreading I have diagnosed here in fact may prove theoretically fruitful. Why have so many readers of this play perceived the gap in act 2, scene 2, as erotic rather than violent? Perhaps because there is something naggingly erotic about any such gap. "Is not the most erotic portion of a body *where the garment gapes*?" asks Roland Barthes; when it comes to "textual pleasure," he claims, "it is intermittence . . .

which is erotic."[23] In a later work, Barthes applies this definition of eroticism to a visual medium, providing an even better analogy: "The erotic photograph . . . does not make the sexual organs into a central object; it may very well not show them at all; it takes the spectator outside its frame . . . as if the image launched desire beyond what it permits us to see"[24] Barthes calls this effect the *punctum* (a typically phallocentric trope): I call it the offstage.

If, as Derrida holds, writing or signification in general arises from "pure absence," erotic writing does so all the more. Yet Barthes' *punctum* allows one to turn this statement inside out, and say that eroticism, paradoxically, makes absence palpable, which is to say, it un-makes it, or rather, unmasks it, in all its semiotic glory. *Eroticism gives absence the lie.* Derrida underscores the erotics of absence in his discussion of "that dangerous supplement" of writing. Of particular interest to this chapter is a passage he quotes from Rousseau's *Confessions*, depicting the youthful narrator's response to the absence of his mother: "How often have I kissed my bed, since she had slept in it; my curtains, all the furniture of my room since they belonged to her; even the floor, on which I prostrated myself, since she had walked on it!"[25] Here the absence of the beloved stimulates the narrator's imagination, with the result that peripheral objects become central, are endowed with signification based on their past contact with the desired body. Physics mandates that a vacuum be filled: the mind's eye imprints the blank text; frame and center, ground and figure switch places. Barthes praises "the intermittence of skin flashing between two articles of clothing," for "it is this flash itself which seduces." He goes on to define eroticism in theatrical terms: "the staging of an appearance-as-disappearance."[26] One wonders whether Rousseau's speaker would embrace "Mamma" herself in quite the state of rapture with which he kisses the bed, the curtains, etc. But there is a striking creativity in his actions, as he circles and recircles the material traces of this presence; objects, like braille, take on meaning when touched, or rather, like clay, take the shape of his desire. Rousseau describes the process of re-presentation, the attempt to make present which underlies all art.

Representation, hence, is an act of lust; sometimes it becomes an object of lust. Orchestrating the Duke's ambush of Bianca, Guardiano tries to "prepare her stomach . . . / To Cupid's feast" (403–4) by showing her erotic artwork. The art gestures toward the "embrace" (in one editor's terms) of the Duke awaiting her, just as the entire scene gestures toward the moment of offstage coupling. But there is much evidence in the text to suggest that Bianca finds the representations more appealing than the thing itself; at the artwork she exclaims, "Mine eye nev'r met with fairer ornaments" (2.2.314), but she has no such praise for the Duke or his overtures. Human beings often pursue the sexual signifier more ardently than the sexual body: the aesthetics of sex, the trappings of sex, the words that entice become the end itself. As Derrida points out, "The sign, the image, the representation, which come to supplement the absent presence are the illusions that sidetrack us."[27]

Yet Bianca herself – or rather, her body – becomes a sexual signifier also. Long before she is shown the "naked pictures" in this scene, she has been likened to an erotic artifact: she is "the most unvalued'st purchase" (1.1.12), a "treasure" (14), a "masterpiece" (41), "a most matchless jewel" (162). Indeed, her beauty is so powerful that her husband feels he must hide her from the eyes of the world, lest she – "the best piece of theft / That ever was committed" (43–44) – should be stolen by another. "'Tis best policy," Leantio ruminates, "To keep choice treasures in obscurest places." Therefore, this "jewel is cas'd up from all men's eyes" (1.1.166–70).

For men's eyes are not to be trusted. One mere glimpse through a window ignites the Duke's fatal lust. And in fact the theme of vision – of the viewing of objects – plays a prominent role throughout the rape sequence: Bianca is *shown* not only the artwork, but the Duke as well: Guardiano introduces him as "a better piece / Yet than all these" (2.2.317–18). The Duke takes hold of Bianca and reminds her, "You have seen me; here's a heart / Can witness I have seen thee" (327–28). He tells her that her face reminds him "Of figures that are drawn for goddesses / And makes Art proud to look upon her work" (341–45). And as the Duke removes Bianca from view, her mother-in-law, oblivious to her ward's plight, loses the chess-game on the lower stage and points out, "My eyes begin to fail" (395). Finally, re-entering the stage, Bianca describes her shame in these words: "I saw that now / Fearful for any woman's eye to look on" (422–43).

The eroticism of the Duke's world rises from the play of vision against obscurity; Bianca herself notes the "infectious mists and mildews" clouding his eyes (424).[28] One wonders whether he would have wanted Bianca had he met her on the street in broad daylight, rather than spying her through the *frame* of a window in Leantio's domestic fortress. Bianca's tour through the Duke's pornographic gallery initiates her into an erotic universe even more tightly sealed than the one she has left behind. In order to show her the "rooms and pictures," her guide needs a key, and the progression from lower stage to upper stage (a place to be discussed later in the chapter) and finally to offstage creates the sense of movement through concentric secret enclosures.

And what about the pictures in this gallery: does the audience see

them? My guess is that they don't. And, given what we know about
seventeenth-century erotica, most likely no one in the audience ever had
seen these particular pictures, or ever would. We can infer that the
"pictures" Middleton had in mind were those referred to elsewhere in his
work as "Aretine's pictures" – a much talked-about but little-seen
collection of graphic erotic engravings published in 1524 and immediately
suppressed by order of the pope.[29] The reference is noteworthy because it
highlights the fundamental paradox behind the eroticism of the play: that
what is least visible is most desirable.

And this is the appeal of offstage sex: it excites voyeuristic desires even
as it appears to frustrate these desires. For voyeurism requires a barrier,
a sense of exclusion *within* proximity (however much the voyeur – from
his "secret vantage point" – purports to escape his self-imposed exclusion). This gulf produced by the *mise-en-scène*, this intermittence, also
translates into theatrical terms the isolation of the Derridean "literary
act." In the distance which makes a "spectacle" of sex we may metony-
mize all those gaps which create meaning: that between reader and text,
between text and commentary; between audience and stage, between
onstage and offstage; between signifier and signified. Representation,
says Derrida, does not simply procure "an absent presence through its
image; . . . it holds it at a distance and masters it. For this presence is at
the same time desired and feared."[30]

One question remains: are all such gaps created equal? Gary Taylor
critiques Derrida's vision of an intertextual cosmos because it mandates
"equiproximity" between signifiers, between texts: a spatial as well as
hermeneutic impossibility. Addressing yet another philological gulf, that
between editor and author, Taylor explains that "the most that an editor
can hope to achieve is not presence, but proximity."[31] In the previous
pages I have faulted various editors for not *approximating* the offstage
sex in *Women Beware Women* in the way the absent author, I believe,
conceived it. And yet in doing so I am behaving, I realize, like a
frustrated voyeur, jostling my way closer to the stage. How close, I
wonder, will Middleton allow his audience?

Voyeurism plays a prominent role in act 3, scene 2, of *A Mad World, My
Masters*, where an adulterous tryst arranged by a third party apparently
takes place before the very eyes of that third party – though not before the
eyes of the audience. As in *Women Beware Women*, the plot centers upon a
wife who is kept locked away by a jealously watchful husband. The would-
be adulterer, Penitent Brothel, employs a courtesan to inspire his beloved,
Mistress Harebrain, to adultery. The courtesan passes herself off as a
religious tutor and thus insinuates herself into the Harebrain household,

where she secretly tutors the wife in infidelity. The longed-for tryst occurs when the courtesan feigns illness, calling for Penitent, disguised as a doctor, and requesting that the mistress pay her last respects. The adulterous union, which takes place in the sick-room as the husband lurks outside the door, may constitute the most ingenious and the most hilarious depiction of sex on (or rather, off) the early modern stage.

The offstage sex in *Mad World* occupies fifty-six lines of dialogue, as opposed to the thirty-one lines in *Women Beware Women*. Even if the episodes were of equal duration, their respective narrative frames create contrasting dramatic effects. In *Mad World*, consent is explicit; the lovers not only exit together, but return together and happily. Both parties have anticipated their union, and the text clearly states the eagerness of their coming together:

> PENITENT. The fulness of my wish!
> MISTRESS HAREBRAIN. Of my desire!
> PENITENT. Beyond this sphere I never will aspire!   (3.2.192–93)

The woman's "desire" – itself providing her lover an earthly "sphere" in which to dwell – presents itself in its "fulness" just before the absent scene of consummation. (And here we should recall that her husband's first name is "Shortrod," indicating a prior, sexual lack which incites this hunger for "fulness."[32]) If the intercourse which follows these lines takes no more than five minutes (my minimum estimate), there are far better reasons for speed here, as opposed to the estimated three-minute episode discussed earlier: in addition to the lovers' heightened feelings for one another, the nearby presence of the husband *necessitates* speed in love-making and quite possibly adds to its excitement. In contrast, in *Women Beware Women*, Bianca and the Duke have every reason to take their time: Bianca is (to put it mildly) a reluctant lover; her husband is miles away, and her mother-in-law is detained at chess, a game notorious for its ability to consume hours.

Middleton emphasizes the brevity of the offstage sex in *Women Beware Women*; contrastingly, in *Mad World*, the wily cover-up speech of the conspiring courtesan is notable for its duration, pointed up by the verbal filler she spins out so that the lovers may enjoy themselves. The scene has scandalous, as well as uproarious potential, for Middleton's text clearly allows – in a way modern editors have been shy to point out – that the lovers *be heard*, if not seen, onstage. Witness the courtesan's clever masking of the sounds of frantic sex:

> COURTESAN. Still, still weeping? Huff, huff, huff. Why, how now, woman? Hey, hy, hy, for shame, leave! Suh, suh, she cannot answer me for sobbing.

> HAREBRAIN. All this does her good, beshrew my heart, and I pity her.
> Let her shed tears till morning, I'll stay for her. She shall have
> enough on't by my good will, I'll not be her hindrance.
> COURTESAN. Oh no, lay your hand here, Mistress Harebrain. Aye there,
> oh there, there lies my pain, good gentlewoman. Sore? Oh aye, I
> can scarce endure your hand upon't.
> HAREBRAIN. Poor soul, how she's tormented.   (3.2.218–29)

The "sobbing" and the "pain" are real enough to the lovers; the
courtesan's monologue serves as a kind of parodic commentary which
may fool Harebrain, but will *not* fool the audience. Even more hilarity is
surely evoked by her wordy farewell with its inventive stream of quasi-
obscenities: "Pray, commend me to the good gentleman your husband
. . . And to my Uncle Winchcomb, and to my Aunt Lipsalve, and to my
Cousin Falsetop, and to my Cousin Lickit, and to my Cousin Horseman,
and to all my good cousins in Clerkenwell and St. John's" (243–49).
Again, I can imagine an ideal performance. Let the courtesan fumble
between each name, glancing offstage in the direction of the lovers; let
her seem to stretch her powers of improvisation, run out of ideas,
stammer, cough loudly, and continue with renewed bravado. The
audience could begin to sense the lovers' unwillingness to break off their
embrace, could begin to get edgy; or, in a more bold production, the
audience could hear the love-making crescendo – cued by Harebrain's
unwittingly crude (but accurate), "Fall back, she's coming" (215).[33] In
any case, the contrast between *Women Beware Women* and *Mad World*
should be clear: the former entails a swift violent act, the latter a simple
"quickie."
  Once again, though (and by now we should be used to this), most
editors don't "get it." The initial "Huff, huff, huff" has been the main
source of confusion; most editions follow Standish Henning in inserting
the stage direction "*Sobs*" in the first of these passages, suggesting that
the courtesan ventriloquizes, by way of these inarticulate sounds, the
mistress' so-called "weeping." But "huff" more closely resembles a
cough than a sob, as do the other nonsense words, including an earlier
handful of "huh"-sounds, before the Mistress is anywhere near
(3.2.34).[34] And let us not forget the Mistress' own worry that her
husband might overhear her and her lover ("Jealousy is prick-eared, and
will hear the wagging of a hair" [169–70][35]). Obviously, then, what's
going on here is a virtuoso sickness act, punctuated by wheezing, sighing,
sputtering, whatever it takes to drown out and/or gloss over the offstage
"oohs" and "ahs." And talk of glossing over. Henning's editing –
wittingly or not – adds another layer of white noise to the scene's loudly
erotic potential.

This tradition of mis-reading places the editor in much the same position as old Harebrain, who hears everything – even his wife "coming" – but misinterprets it, perhaps willingly; the result of this, however, is to twice-remove the reader from the *mise-en-scène*. And the scene has stunning voyeuristic potential – especially when compared to the famous "seduction" in *Women Beware Women*. Even if a depiction of rape has the power to fascinate, any number of psychological responses ranging from fear to guilt may taint viewing pleasure, above all, I believe, for women. Also, the prolongation of the consensual encounter allows for greater imaginative involvement – especially if the production includes audible offstage love-making. Overall, this offstage act is more foregrounded than that in *Women Beware Women*, or, in my terms, it seems not as *far* offstage, bringing the lovers within earshot and therefore almost within view. And even if the viewer or reader resists voyeuristic involvement, she may vicariously enjoy the courtesan's "insider's" point of view. However ambiguous we find the stage directions, we may assume that the lovers *"exeunt"* only as far as some corner of the sick-room; the husband, after all, lurks "prick-eared" outside the door (the pun highlighting the potency of one organ at the expense, perhaps, of another), and the very necessity for the ruse indicates the unavailability of a private niche elsewhere. It is worth noting here that, in Middleton's society, privacy was generally harder to come by than in our own; the people in the audience may in fact have been accustomed to hearing offstage sex (so to speak) in their everyday lives.[36]

The main question, then, is to what extent the supposed patient *watches* the illicit act. Does she throw an occasional glance toward the edge of the stage, while more or less concentrating on duping the eavesdropping husband? Or does she glue her eyes brazenly on the adulterous couple, thereby creating the illusion of their visibility? The onstage voyeur could noticeably gloat in the fruits of her craft, watching with lip-smacking appreciation; her fixed stare would render the act more immediate, and far more titillating to the audience.

But let us not forget the second voyeur in the scene: the jealous husband listening at the door. However foolish the scene makes him out, his physical position renders the success of the ploy uncomfortably tenuous, especially in light of his relentless suspicion throughout the play. In fact, it is not inconceivable that his very closeness to "catching" the lovers is a necessary component in their arousal, transforming an otherwise routine adulterous quickie into a delectable outrage: pseudo-voyeurism meets pseudo-exhibitionism. And, as Michael Neill argues in relation to *Othello* (a work I will discuss more fully below), "Jealousy is itself an extreme and corrupted . . . form of sexual excitement"[37] – with its manifestation in the kind of lurid scrutiny that belies its own moralistic rationale. Like Leantio in *Women Beware Women*, Harebrain plays the role of jail-keeper and warden of his wife: alongside numerous references to keys and locks, the word "watch" recurs as a description of his jealousy, and the main plot with its *literal* robbery of an unguarded home endorses Harebrain's watchfulness.

In fact, Penitent himself, the sexual "thief" in the Harebrain household, also validates the husband's jealousy, which he describes as "a fantastic but *deserved* suspect" (1.1.108; my emphasis). And how can this suspicion be both fantastic – that is, born of fantasy, fabricated – and deserved? What is the relation of fantasy to jealousy, of jealousy to voyeurism, of voyeurism to "ocular proof"? Katharine Eisaman Maus, remarking on the frequency, in early modern drama, of episodes in which "the cuckold is entranced by the scene of his own betrayal," explains that in such cases "sexual jealousy provides a complex analogy to theatrical performance and response."[38] In lieu of a performance, though, the same analogy applies to the reader's response. Voyeurism, like sexual jealousy, involves fantasy, involves story-telling: re-creation in lieu of pro-creation. Any wonder, then, that editors, those powerful re-creators, jealously guard access to the text? (As Taylor himself notes, "Editoriality is territoriality."[39]) We may laugh at the cuckold with his ear to the door, but without editors and directors we are no closer to the "true story" than he. Courtesan, husband, audience, and readers form a voyeuristic spiral with its center in the offstage act.

II   Shakespeare: balconies and beds

Voyeurism leads to laughter in *Mad World*, but in Shakespeare's *Othello* it leads to murder. If there is one quality that distinguishes Iago's cunning, it is his ability to manipulate the voyeuristic imagination toward his own destructive ends. This is apparent from the very first scene of the play, when Iago shouts beneath Brabanzio's window, "Even now, now, very now, an old black ram / Is tupping your white ewe. Arise, arise!" (1.1.88–89).[40] Offstage sex is instantly and urgently evoked, and it is not until later that we, the audience, realize we have been "fooled" as easily as Brabanzio: in fact, Desdemona and Othello do not consummate their marriage until well into act 2.[41]

The entire play thus revolves around two kinds of offstage sex: the "real" sex fabricated by the dramatist, and the "false" sex fabricated by his villain; in Issacharoff's terminology, we are offered two conflicting forms of diegetic space. The "real," legitimate sex between Desdemona and Othello is explicitly marked in the text – taking place between

2.3.8–9 (*Othello*. "Come, my dear love, / The purchase made, the fruits are to ensue") and 2.3.157, when the brawling soldiers wake Othello first and then his bride ("Look if my gentle love be not raised up" [2.3.243]). Yet the dialogue of Iago throughout this scene, and throughout the play, creates a narrative frame that destabilizes and distorts the image of the offstage nuptials created by Othello's own "gentle" remarks to his wife. Iago's machinations not only result in physical chaos surrounding the bridal chamber, but they in fact falsify an alternative offstage event – Desdemona's infidelity with Cassio – capable of violating, symbolically, that same bed-chamber. Iago's own description of the brawl highlights this tension:

> Friends all but now, even now,
> In quarter and in terms like bride and groom
> Devesting them for bed; and then but now –
> As if some planet had unwitted men –
> Swords out, and tilting one at others' breasts
> In opposition bloody.
>
> (2.3.172–77)

The juxtaposition foreshadows the violence that will take place *within* the bed-chamber at the play's end.

We also note how Iago's phrasing echoes his earlier warning to Brabanzio about the Moor "tupping" his daughter – "Even now, now." The connection not only reveals Iago's habit of associating sex with violence, but also points up a persistent tactic of his: the arousing of a sense of urgency, even panic, in his listeners. This "now" also re-introduces the temporal constituents of offstage sex. Though I emphasized the contrasting temporal frames of the two Middleton episodes, it is important to note that both cultivate a sense of offstage simultaneity – an effect which translates to *proximity within time*, if not to real proximity in the small spatial framework of the narrative. Indeed, perhaps what makes offstage sex "work" is this very element of now-ness, which (especially when coupled with here-ness) results in the illusion that our participation is possible. Move quickly and you might just catch them at it.

This urgency on the part of Iago's onstage male audience also signals a need to protect or contain the female body. In the opening scene Iago warns Brabanzio, "Look to your house, your daughter, and your bags. / Thieves, thieves!" (1.1.80–81) and asks "Are your doors locked?" (85). The danger is that of violated boundaries: houses, daughters, and bags are vessels that can be broached. Brabanzio, upon discovering his daughter's absence, cries, "How got she out?" (171), alternating between rage at her escape and fear that, in her innocence, she has been bewitched. Of course, the cross-racial nature of this union is a crucial factor in Brabanzio's panic, but the main goal of Iago's alarum is to create the impression of *sex out of bounds*. As Neill observes, "Iago lets horrible things loose and delights in watching them run."[42] The fictive love-making of the Moor and Desdemona is most menacing in the fact that it *is* offstage, that it is uncontained, that it has escaped surveillance; like the images Iago evokes – of animals, thieves, devils – this transgressive union seems to loom in the dark. Thus Brabanzio calls out for torches and weapons: "Light, I say, light!" is his desperate refrain.

Despite its protective, paternalistic overtones, this urgency cannot be separated from its sexual components. Iago's summons – "Arise, arise!" – suggests male sexual excitement as well as military readiness. And the torches (a recurrent prop in the play) are as vital as the weapons in this quasi-voyeuristic call to arms. *Othello* shares with *Women Beware Women* a thematic focus on the visual, on the struggle of vision against darkness or obscurity and the prying open of sexual secrets.[43] The threat – and fascination – of unseen, unbridled sex brings forth the men of Brabanzio's house; swords and torches are raised in an effort to capture, shed light on, control, contain.

And containment – or the urge to contain – is a key factor in offstage erotics; it is the axis which mediates between desire and fear, titillation and horror; it may even draw the line between gendered responses, onstage and in the audience. The near hysteria of *Othello*'s first scene is even more striking in contrast to *Mad World*, in which the sex is morally transgressive but physically contained, and made safe through farce. The imagined enclosure of the sick-room brings the event closer to the stage – brings it down to scale, so to speak – and the only urgency evoked is that of simple sexual excitement. On the other hand, containment has its hazards for women, as demonstrated by the rape in *Women Beware Women* – a textually contained depiction involving a physically constrained body. In relation to the ominous but fictive offstage sex Iago evokes, the rape of Bianca is more proximate, due to the initial presence of both parties on stage, the dramatic timing, and the subsequent firsthand account of the victim. In Bianca's case, we do not need an Iago to tell us that lust is dangerous.

And it is impossible to account for differences in such episodes without speaking of the person who tells the story, without speaking of the narrative which creates (or re-creates) the missed moment. Iago's role in *Othello* invites comparison to the role of the courtesan in *Mad World*, and to some extent the role of Livia in *Women Beware Women*: all are voyeuristic commentators upon sexual events removed from view. What makes Iago most dangerous is not so much that his commentary is

deceptive, but that it is both seductive and sadistic. Middleton's courtesan might be similar in her cunning, but ultimately her voyeurism is
playful, not venomous. In fact, the two voyeurs fulfill inverse roles: the
courtesan delights in verbally masking the love-making others cannot
see, and Iago delights in *exposing* sex that is not even "really there." And
in doing so, he literally creates a monster, a "beast with two backs."

And this particular image gives pause for thought. Indeed, Iago's
mental menagerie has a weird charm, and perhaps the key to his verbal
seductiveness lies in its dark whimsy, in its mere inventiveness. We are
reminded of Harebrain's "fantastic" suspicion, of the phantasmagorical
nature of jealousy in general. Iago is a story-teller, a dealer in fantasy;
there is a kind of exoticism to his fictions of adultery. Patricia Parker
relates Iago's story-telling to the story that brings together a Venetian
lady and a Moor. "The links between Othello's exotic 'travellours
historie' – its verbal pictures bringing offstage events vicariously before
the eye – and Iago's manipulation of *evidentia* . . . when attention turns
to the domestic secrets of a Venetian woman, become part of this play's
own extraordinary emphasis on bringing to 'light,' on the hunger to
'know' as the desire to 'see.' "[44] Thus the question is whether we, the
audience, will be blinded by Iago's fantasies as readily as Othello has
been. That we are not allows us to appreciate Iago's fabrications for their
aesthetic value. Our position in relation to Othello is similar to our
position in relation to Harebrain: we watch someone "taken in" by a
good story, done in by a smooth talker.

Of course, let us not overlook the fact that Iago is a *male* talker – as is,
interestingly, every speaker in the wedding-night sequence, excepting
Desdemona. Even if we are to take Othello's remarks to his bride as the
"true" referent to the offstage union they frame, we are still looking at a
male narration, a male truth. Othello is, as Parker highlights, a story-
teller himself; he responds to Iago's stories in much the same way that
Desdemona has responded to *his*. That Iago denigrates these as "fantastical lies" (2.1.224) underscores, ironically, a certain brotherhood
between himself and the Moor. Despite Othello's apology for his "rude
. . . speech" (1.3.81), he and Iago both have much to say. Desdemona,
on the other hand, says little; she speaks only one line in the wedding-
night scene, not upon entering, but upon leaving the bed-chamber:
"What is the matter, dear?" (2.3.245). In the clamor of male voices and
the ringing of swords, her silence deserves note.

And it is a lengthy silence. Of the three offstage episodes considered so
far, the union of Desdemona and the Moor occupies the largest textual
space – 147 lines of dialogue, almost triple the duration of the offstage
sex in *Mad World*. The relative looseness of the textual frame works

further to remove the "real" offstage sex from the audience, giving primacy to Iago's cynical and deceptive commentary: the background becomes the focus. That the audience is aware of Iago as, in novelistic terms, an "unreliable narrator" complicates the voyeuristic response but does not lessen the impact of his manipulations. And the question of performance time is further problematized by the fact that the scene ends up encompassing an entire evening – a performative illogicality that often eludes the audience.[45] At the end of the scene Iago remarks, "By the mass, 'tis morning. / Pleasure and action make the hours seem short" (2.3.368–69). Iago's use of the word "action" – a common euphemism for sex[46] – once again underscores, in retrospect, his preoccupation with the "pleasure" happening offstage; correspondingly, the comment reveals the masturbatory nature of his onstage machinations. The chaos of the scene, it turns out, has been fueled by Iago's fascination with the simultaneous, though unseen, "action" within the bed-chamber.

And of course Iago's verbal power hinges upon his understanding of this fascination in other males, particularly in Othello. In response to Othello's repeated demand for "ocular proof" of Desdemona's infidelity, the villain replies:

> Would you, the supervisor, grossly gape on?
> Behold her topp'd? . . .
> It were a tedious difficulty, I think,
> To bring them to that prospect. Damn them then
> If ever mortal eyes do see them bolster
> More than their own! What then, how then?
> . . .
> It is impossible you should see this,
> Were they as prime as goats, as hot as monkeys,
> As salt as wolves in pride, and fools as gross
> As ignorance made drunk. But yet I say,
> If imputation and strong circumstances
> Which lead directly to the door of truth
> Will give you satisfaction, you might ha't.   (3.3.400–13)

Iago here ingeniously incites the voyeuristic impulse while simultaneously provoking a moral discomfort with this impulse. The passage, in fact, crystallizes the dynamic of offstage sex: it is a verbal tease, which asserts at once the desirability and unattainability of voyeuristic "satisfaction."[47] Like the husband in *Mad World*, Othello can only approach the "door" of his wife's secret, sexual "truth."

And what about us, the readers/viewers? Since Shakespeare, as opposed to Middleton, has been (so far) better-edited and more frequently performed, our options are more or less open. Oliver Parker's film makes some surprising, but quite justified, interpolations: the film-maker offers a peek not only into the conjugal bedroom, but also, later, into Othello's jealous fantasies (set in the very same bedroom) where Desdemona and Cassio are glimpsed having what seems to be *better* (or rather, dirtier) sex. Thus, Parker represents on screen the two conflicting erotic narratives, collapsing them into the same diegetic space, thereby demonstrating Iago's pornographic magic.[48]

We began this analysis with the question of whether or not a woman was raped – that is, whether she "got what she wanted." We then turned to another woman who does get what she wants, and we asked how she gets away with it. Now we turn to *Othello* and see our voyeuristic musings mimicked within the text, as the male characters strive (with dubious motives) to delineate Desdemona's sexual desire, its legitimacy, its causes, its ability to be contained. The play's legalistic rhetoric has been connected to contemporary witchcraft trials: Maus, for instance, points out that "Iago encourages Othello" to redefine adultery as akin to "such essentially invisible crimes as treason and witchcraft."[49] And though it is in Iago's best interest to mystify the "crime" itself, the heart of the question is (again) not "what happened," but the dark place inside a woman where such acts are conceived.[50] As Othello laments, "O curse of marriage, / That we can call these delicate creatures ours / And not their appetites!" (3.3.272–74). We must remember that Desdemona's desire is a "problem" from the beginning of the play, as her father prods her for signs that her choice of a transgressive, cross-racial union is not the result of a spell cast upon her. Thus, the subject of our inquiry becomes not so much whether female desire is present or absent, or even how textual absence represents female desire – after all, Desdemona has made her desire for the Moor, and her lack of desire for Cassio, explicit. Rather, the question is how male narratives (and this includes editions and productions) *deploy* textual absence in representing – or misrepresenting – female desire.

In early modern drama, the balcony tends to further voyeuristic purposes. Balcony scenes create the sense of a visual boundary breached; they create an opening into the private world of the characters; they create, in effect, a stage-within-the-stage, whereon we can glimpse an even "truer" narrative. Iago's shouting into Brabanzio's window sets him up as a voyeur, as a person who delights in the breaching of privacies: his words in this first scene constitute a deliberate and malicious intrusion not just into a rich father's peace of mind, but into his daughter's sexual world. In *Romeo and Juliet*, the young hero commits a similar transgression, albeit in the name of love. He learns of Juliet's desire by eavesdropping – which is, as the heroine points out, the only way he *could* have learned of her desire. Once again, female desire is only glimpsed, furtively.

But we, the audience, cannot condemn this nosiness because we are equally guilty. We too position ourselves beneath the balcony and peer into Juliet's chamber. We witness her confessing her love, then anticipating her lover, and, finally, bidding good-bye after a night in his arms. As in *Women Beware Women*, where the use of the upper stage allows us to witness Bianca's progress into the Duke's well-guarded erotic universe, in *Romeo and Juliet* the balcony operates as metonymy for a forbidden world.

Theater companies, we know, had beds at their disposal, and many scenes in plays of the period revolved around this important prop. But by erecting a visual barrier beyond which a bed is implied, one creates a stronger sense of transgression. A peeping Tom loves the wall as much as the hole in it. In fact, of the four sexual episodes discussed in this chapter, only one includes an onstage bed, and even then sex does not happen there. One might even argue that the bed in *Mad World* is particularly conspicuous because sex does *not* occur there – that it is only *witnessed* there – and that this quirk of staging creates the particular humor and sexiness of the moment. Mistress Harebrain and her lover, one might say, are not interested in beds: they are interested in screwing. Right now, right here. Beds are for people with time to lie down. Beds are for dying in.

And that, in fact, is what happens in most Shakespearean beds. We do not see Desdemona's bed until she is murdered in it. We do not see Romeo and Juliet lie down together alive. Taylor argues that "Shakespeare's great love stories are, almost without exception, premarital, or at least pre-consummational."[51] Of course, the characteristic deferral of voyeuristic consummation can be looked at as one of Shakespeare's most effective poetic tools. Stephen Greenblatt holds that "The unrepresented consummations of unrepresented marriages call attention to the unmooring of desire, the generalizing of the libidinal, that is the special pleasure of Shakespearean fiction."[52] Greenblatt, above, addresses comedy in particular, where Taylor uses the generic label of "love stories." But in those great love stories which are also tragedies there is consummation – generally, once – quickly punished by death.

Does death purify an onstage bed? In tragedy, certainly, it provides a morally palatable onstage "climax" shared by the romantic hero and heroine. Neill, among many other critics, highlights the titillation fostered by many performances of Desdemona's murder: "In the most striking of many effacements, it became the practice for nineteenth-century Othellos to screen the murder from the audience by closing the curtains upon the bed ... But the actual effect of the practice was apparently quite opposite, raising to a sometimes unbearable intensity the audience's scandalized fascination with the now-invisible scene."[53] This particular "effacement," unlike the others explored in this chapter, is a directorial rather than an editorial move (reflecting the difference between nineteenth- and twentieth-century dramaturgical mores), but the attempt backfires, inciting instead of calming the audience's voyeuristic lust. This kind of fascination is also evoked by productions of Juliet's mock death in which the curtains are drawn on her supposed corpse. In fact, a noteworthy motif in Renaissance erotica – including what we know of the engravings called "Aretine's pictures" – was the canopied bed, furnishing the artist an excuse to flaunt his skill at texture and shadow, but more importantly, providing the viewer with the thrill of penetrating a private world (Figure 5). It is only fitting that, when Desdemona's bed finally appears onstage, having been mentioned twenty-five times, it is even then enclosed in draperies, veiled before our "anxious fascination."[54] The curtains, in fact, have to some degree survived as a directorial fetish: in Oliver Parker's *Othello*, the sheer curtains around Desdemona's bed play a role not only in the erotic sequences mentioned above, but also in the murder scene.

Of all the offstage encounters I have examined, I would judge *Romeo and Juliet*'s to be the farthest offstage – indeed, so far offstage that many of my undergraduate students fail to notice it. In act 3, scene 5, the lovers are presented *after* their wedding night, bidding a reluctant farewell. When the scene begins, sex has already taken place – Shakespeare lets us visualize the act only in retrospect, and in these terms:

> JULIET. Wilt thou be gone? It is not yet near day.
> It was the nightingale, and not the lark,
> That pierced the fear-full hollow of thine ear.
> Nightly she sings on yon pom'granate tree.
> Believe me, love, it was the nightingale.
> ROMEO. It was the lark, the herald of the morn,
> No nightingale. Look, love, what envious streaks
> Do lace the severing clouds in yonder east.
> Night's candles are burnt out, and jocund day
> Stands tiptoe on the misty mountain tops.
> I must be gone and live, or stay and die.   (3.5.1–11)

What strikes me about this passage is its failure (if one can apply the word to such exquisite poetry) to address explicitly what has just taken place. On the one hand, there is a conventionality to this natural imagery which allows it to be read as erotic, but on the other hand, we have

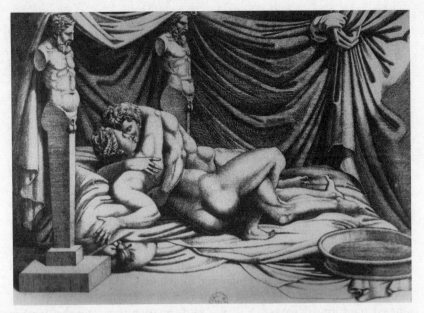

Figure 5   Engraving by Marcantonio Raimondi, one of "Aretine's Pictures" (1524).

already seen that the early modern stage supplies a far raunchier brand of entertainment. In effect, the imagery in this passage weaves a gorgeous and colorful veil for the sexuality of the young lovers. Not only does the consummation of Romeo and Juliet stand outside the play's real performance time, hovering in the nowhere of narrative time, but it also stands essentially outside the play's language. In the fifty-nine lines of this long good-bye, no direct reference is made to the night's connubial joys: the lovers speak, instead, of larks and nightingales, of misty mountain-tops and dawn-lit clouds – all of which, interestingly, *also* dwell in the offstage. With this sleight-of-hand, Shakespeare fills the gap in the sexual narrative with sensual impressions on which imagination can surfeit, rather than (as in *Othello*) with teasing reminders of what cannot be seen. Is this intended to distract the audience from copulative fantasies of these adolescent sweethearts? Sex and sunrise must, due to the limitations of the Elizabethan theater, occur offstage; in *Romeo and Juliet* they become interchangeable.

Or so Shakespeare would have it.

We must also keep in mind, when looking at this passage in the text, that the rhetorical game the lovers play involving the all-too-indisputable sunrise is a game at the expense, one could say, of the audience. Elizabethan performances made do with natural daylight, so audiences had to rely on narrative clues for the telling of time. When Juliet declares (whether in irrational longing, self-mockery, or morning-after delirium) that it is not yet near day, we might, for a moment, believe her, might hope that it is not all over, that we have not missed all the fun; this flash of vain hope renders doubly excruciating Romeo's inevitable departure. It is yet another example of Shakespearean almost-sex, evoking desire in a context that forbids its consummation, aligning sex with the impossible. "Believe me, love," Juliet protests – as if believing could stop time.

And time, as we have discussed, is a crucial factor in determining audience engagement. These lovers have had more than three minutes, more than five minutes, more than the duration of one scene in which to make love; rather, they have enjoyed an entire night together. And yet, the audience has not shared this enjoyment. Jill Colaco links the two "window scenes" of act 2, scene 2, and act 3, scene 5, by way of the respective folkloric "night visit" and "dawn parting" courtly traditions which Shakespeare has ingeniously combined here.[55] Yet the implications of this sequence, in terms of the missing scene of consummation and the tangled question of narrative versus performative time, deserve further consideration. The "night visit" during which Romeo learns of Juliet's love departs from the folk tradition in its deferral of consummation; the "dawn parting" here provides narrative closure without relieving the intervening anticipation. The voyeurs in the audience wonder, "When?" until suddenly realizing, "Missed it" – an effect which drives home all the more strongly the wrenching quality of Romeo's departure. Despite (or perhaps because of) the rhetorical excess of the passage, the audience is left hungry.

Of course hunger can be very effective. And if the goal of the dramatist is to tantalize, a bare stage or a text bare of stage directions can work better than a space crowded with signifiers. Harley Granville-Barker articulates a commonly held preference for the visual simplicity of Shakespeare's medium. "As with costume, so with scene; we shall gain nothing, we shall indeed be the worse for surrendering the freedoms of Shakespeare's stage . . . The place, in fact, is not a place at all, within the modern scenic meaning. If we needs must paint the picture, it will need to be generalized, atmospheric, symbolic . . ."[56] And the sexual imagination – as we learned from Iago – can operate on very little: a handkerchief and some well-chosen words can conjure images of unbounded, animal lust. Guardiano's mere mention of "naked pictures" might cause the audience to shudder. The fact that "Aretine's pictures" were unavailable for viewing may account for their fame in Renaissance literature.

But on the other hand, the departure of Romeo from Juliet's bed-chamber need not be produced as chastely as Shakespeare conceived it. Witness Franco Zeffirelli's 1968 film version. From the ball scene forth, the young lovers are portrayed as shamelessly sexual. Their kisses are violent and prolonged, their hands constantly grasping – not at all what one would expect of bashful adolescents. The film's pictorial lushness only adds to its sensuality. And the dawn scene of act 3, scene 5 scandalously shatters the lovers' mythic innocence: Zeffirelli places his lovers, not "aloft" in their traditional balcony, but naked together in Juliet's bed. The snowy profusion of disordered sheets, the luscious web of shadows and tousled hair, the bare white skin in the dawn light – these elements bespeak sensual and sexual satiation. Before the dialogue begins, Romeo rises languidly and goes to the window, exposing his nude back and ivory buttocks; a few moments later we glimpse Juliet's disturbingly new breasts (the actress, in keeping with the text, was scarcely through puberty during filming). I think it is safe to say this is not a production Shakespeare could have foreseen – especially since the Juliet of *his* stage was not equipped to display any breasts, pubescent or mature.

And yet, however daring one finds Zeffirelli's interpretation, the sexual act itself is not represented onstage (or rather, on screen). And in fact the narrative tells us it may not happen again, onstage or off. This adds even greater poignancy to the moment as Shakespeare imagined it; the film shows us, in a way that the text cannot, what it is that the lovers are threatened with losing. The nudity is in this respect vital, as is the camera's lingering over skin and bedding. And the film's visual lushness until this point – especially with regard to costume – has well prepared the eye for this taste of flesh. One might even say that the entire first half of the film serves as an "appetizer" for the bedroom scene. But by the time we glimpse Romeo's nubile form, he is already turned from us, receding from view.

And this literally hind-sighted view of the nude Romeo is a perfect metonymy for our hind-sighted view of the nuptial embrace. But what is even more curious about this filmic moment is that it gives us, as Peter S. Donaldson points out, *Juliet*'s vantage-point.[57] In the space of textual lack, this male film-maker inserts a woman's desire – or her look of desire – toward an object she is about to lose. Perhaps in Zeffirelli's queer lens, the exposed buttocks promise as much as they withhold, compel as strongly as signal retreat; in any case, no one wants to see him go. And the scene's homoerotic orientation provides (not for the first time in film history) a more comfortable space for the (straight) female viewer, in effect reconstructing Shakespeare's stage to accommodate her point of view. We are no longer outside Juliet's room, like Romeo in act 1, peering into the secret, female world within; we are, instead, inside Juliet's private space, gazing longingly at a body about to disappear into the outside world. This is still voyeurism, but inside-out.

Of course, it is a standard argument that film in general cultivates voyeurism. But the question appears to have personal significance to this particular director. Donaldson cites an anecdote from Zeffirelli's auto-biography which places his interpretation of act 3, scene 5, and in fact this entire analysis, in a new light. Zeffirelli, who was an illegitimate child, shuffled from one care-giver to another, recounts occasions during his childhood when he shared a bed with his mother and his visiting father; the boy would watch " 'fascinated,' as his parents made love."[58] This story underscores the dynamic of intimacy and exclusion inherent in the voyeuristic gaze. Although this need not be true of voyeurism in general, we can surmise that the boy's fascination was charged with the threat of separation which saturated his life. The same dynamic stands out in the nuptial scene in his *Romeo and Juliet* – voyeuristic fascination, darkened by the awareness (both in the characters and the viewers) of imminent separation,[59] and also darkened, more subtly, by our aware-ness of the separation between voyeur and object, audience and perform-ance. Romeo's exile is, in some sense, our own.

In this chapter I have juxtaposed four dramatic episodes to determine the differences in their representations of sexual activity; in order to do so I have taken these episodes more or less out of context, treating the offstage event as the invisible kernel of which the surrounding dialogue forms the shell. Looking at each of the episodes in isolation, we see four very different types of sex: in *Women Beware Women*, sex which is brutal and objectifying; in *Mad World*, sex which is frenzied but light-hearted, merely naughty in the play's moral universe, and, for that reason, comical; in *Othello*, sex which is legitimated by marriage, but socially questionable enough to play into the hands of a villain; in *Romeo and Juliet*, sex which is passionate, sublime, but above all innocent. Absence, it seems, comes in many flavors.

I will return to each of these plays toward the end of the book. For now, we need only determine how these four episodes fit into their respective contexts, how each erotic kernel fits into each play as a whole. *Women Beware Women* ends as darkly as one would expect of a play about a woman's love-affair with her rapist. *Mad World* ends with jollity and forgiving. *Othello* ends in sexualized violence and suicide. *Romeo and Juliet* ends with the majestic and terrible death of the lovers, an ending which inevitably leaves audiences elated, if tearful. In each of these four cases, the ending suits the spirit of the sexual encounter the play

technically omits. In each of these cases, the absence creates: the hole in
the text begins to look like its womb.

We have come a long way from the rape/seduction problem with which
this chapter began. Maus' work on inwardness in English Renaissance
drama makes a good case for the connection between legal discourse and
theater, especially when the subject is a sexual secret.[60] And, as my
mock-trial of the Duke indicates, the jury is still out on a number of sex-
crimes in this body of texts. Or is it, the text-crimes in this body of sex?

Whose body is it, anyway? Maus' chapter on "prosecution and sexual
secrecy" relates the "self-limiting voyeurism" of the Renaissance stage to
the impotence proceedings in the famous Essex divorce case, which
allowed Frances Howard to "prove a long-lost virginity" by way of a
veiled body-double.[61] And it occurs to me that we, too, have been
looking at (or looking for) the wrong body. As Howard's veiled virgin
surrogate reminds us, the voyeuristic "tease" of offstage sex becomes a
double-tease, when considered in light of early modern theatrical practice. Ontological questions of desire or resistance, legalistic proof of
consent or refusal, all our musings over the editorial/dramaturgical/
theoretical issues raised by the sexual *aporiae* of these four plays . . . all
recede into the larger *aporia* of the absent biological female. And as if
this isn't enough of a theoretical maze, we must also consider the early
modern construction of female sexuality as lack, epitomized in the
"single sex" view of anatomy, mapping the female reproductive system
as an inversion of the male.[62]

Sue-Ellen Case offers a reading of this paradox of the early modern
stage which verges on a feminist dismissal of an entire genre: "The
celibacy of the stage was maintained by omitting the presence of the
female body and by representing physical sexuality in the language . . .
The fictional 'woman' . . . simply mediates and enhances the homoerotic
flirtation between two males."[63] The key word here is "simply." I believe
there is nothing simple (or celibate) about the dynamic which Case
addresses. The presence of the boy actor does not negate the heteroerotic
plot any more than the presence of the female character negates the
homoerotic energy produced in the exchange. Despite the normative
female/male paradigm upon which my study focuses, we must realize
that to view early modern eroticism as *either* hetero- or homo- in its
essence is not only to espouse dualistic thinking, but also to overlook the
fact that "homosexual" as a human category did not exist in early
modern culture.[64] Case's argument risks eliding homoeroticism and
misogyny, and equates the discursive representation of "physical sexuality" with erasure or omission of the physically "real."

Case is not alone in blaming misogyny, at least in part, for the prohibition against female acting. Stephen Orgel, though he does qualify the characterization of the public stage as all-male,[65] points out the uncanny correspondence between the demand for the boy actor and the demand that the romantic heroine he plays, time and again, should assume a male disguise. "The dangers of women in erotic situations, whatever they may be, can be disarmed by having the women play men, just as in theatre the dangers of women on the stage (whatever *they* may be) can be disarmed by having men play the women."[66] There can be no doubt that these anxieties played some role in keeping women offstage; I only hesitate in granting the boy himself so much visibility. I will explore further, in the next chapter, the role of the transvestite costume and the enigma of the gendered body beneath it. My main concern here is that we look at the presence/absence question at the heart of these erotic performances in terms of production rather than erasure. For the presence of the boy actor tells us more about the "woman" he signifies than that she is absent. The same is true of the erotic dialogue in which he takes part.

Obviously the prohibition against female actors, working in tandem with social decorum, encouraged the offstage placement of heterosexual intercourse; paradoxically, to make it remotely convincing, it would have to remain unseen. And given this technicality, the erotic postponement Greenblatt presents as Shakespeare's hallmark appears less his personal idiosyncrasy than an exaggeration of patterns built into the genre. Richmond Barbour, for instance, cites Greenblatt in order to contrast the "teleological" eroticism of Shakespearean comedy with the "modes of aroused being" offered by Jonson,[67] but the distinction between a necessarily *thwarted* teleology and a cultivated state of arousal strikes me (at least in crude biological terms) as a fine one. Nonetheless, that this erotic diffusion or deferral is required by the genre does not make it less of an aesthetic triumph. The four scenes we discussed are anything but workmanlike in their erotic "detours," and this suggests that their crafting was inspired by more than prudery and more than pragmatism. Perhaps, in the back of each dramatist's mind lurked a pre-Derridean sense of the frailty of the signifier, a nagging sense that sex simply does not translate. We might even take the notion of offstage sex, along with the very indeterminacy of desire or resistance in a female character, as a kind of emblem for male authorial (and later, editorial) limitation, as a gesture – conscious or not – toward the enigma of female subjectivity. Derrida writes, "It is impossible to dissociate the questions of art, style and truth from the question of the woman . . . And she is certainly not to be found in any of the familiar modes of . . . knowledge. Yet it is impossible to resist looking for her."[68]

If women were excluded from the stage, however, they were not excluded from the audience.[69] The voyeuristic spiral created by act 3, scene 2, of Middleton's *Mad World* includes not only a "woman" character onstage, but also the women in the audience, many of whom (I presume) would have taken more vicarious pleasure in Mistress Harebrain's situation than in Bianca's. Barbour supplies an alternative to Case's view of the transvestite theater: he argues that the indeterminate gender of the boy actor attracted female hetero- as well as male homoerotic interest: "boys helped make room . . . for women's eroticism."[70] And Barbour's idiom strikes me as a fortunate choice, given the lack of "room" onstage for female performers. In a similarly optimistic move, Linda Woodbridge argues that women playgoers of Middleton's time in fact enjoyed some influence over theater companies, an influence which resulted in certain plays which championed women (including one play to be examined in the next chapter, Fletcher's rebuttal of *The Taming of the Shrew*).[71] Freud's question "What do women want?" thus pertains not only to the women represented onstage, but also to the women in the audience who wanted to see the "woman" onstage get what "she" wanted.

And this, come to think of it, is what motivated me to examine these four texts. If I spent enough time peering into the margins, poring over the stage directions, the commentary; if I pried apart the strata of four centuries' worth of male-biased editing, I might just make contact with the real woman in the text – I might just set her free. Of course, the best I could do was to approximate the woman a male author had imagined. I happen to agree with T. S. Eliot, who said that Middleton "understood woman . . . better than all the Elizabethans – save Shakespeare alone."[72] But it irks me to hear this from a male critic. And how perfectly fitting that one obvious innuendo missed by the Middleton editors was old Harebrain's incomprehending declaration, "She's coming!" In a recent study of pornography, Linda Williams highlights the male quest after the elusive "frenzy of the visible" as embodied in the mystery of female sexual pleasure.[73] It seems that Othello's demand for "ocular proof" (3.3.365) is still pertinent. Given the invisibility, the internality of female pleasure as perceived by a male specular economy, it is a necessary paradox that this "fulness" appears as a textual lack, that this inwardness is forced into the margins, or even (depending on the editor) outside the page entirely. Yet, as I have attempted to show, non-representation has advantages too; it may leave room, in readers and viewers of both genders, for imaginative play. The union of Romeo and Juliet does have something in common with the sunrise they speak of in parting: it is too large for the stage. Does the text encircle the sunrise, or does the sunrise encircle the text? Wherever it is, the world offstage looms largest.

3   Body beneath / body beyond

The startling nude scene in Franco Zeffirelli's *Romeo and Juliet* achieves its impact partially by way of the film's preceding (and subsequent) richness of costume; the nudity of the young lovers constitutes the erotic core of the film, enveloped, on both sides, by cinematic ornament. Yet viewers can scarcely overlook the sensual appeal of many preceding scenes, in particular the dance sequence, where Romeo first spies his love-object from behind a gilded mask. The juxtaposition demonstrates two types of eroticism – constituted by fabric and by skin, respectively – which, placed side by side, make up the "flash" Barthes defines as eroticism at its height.[1] And these two types of cinematic eroticism have their rhetorical prototypes, as epitomized by the ornament of Shakespeare's dawn parting and the starkness of Middleton's unseen, silent rape.

This equation points up another way of looking at offstage sex. Where the fabric of the text gives way, where poetry falls silent, we glimpse the offstage, or rather the offstage body. Stage directions could do as much for the *onstage* body, if they were more frequent in dramatic texts of the period: the simple, italicized *"kisses her"* shines like an inch of naked skin through the weave of *textus*. As readers of a play, we are reminded of the bodies onstage; as viewers of a play (seated, we hope, near the stage), we hear the tell-tale smack or the long, wet pause and perhaps think – for a split second – of the actors as real people, perhaps wonder if the woman playing Juliet even *likes* her co-star, or whether he has bad breath.

Again, though, this is to speak of a modern production, in which Juliet is played by a woman. What did early modern audiences think when Romeo and Juliet kissed? Were play-goers conscious of the male body beneath Juliet's gown, or were they lost in the fabric of the erotic fiction, dreaming their way to Juliet's skin? Perhaps viewers had their own Juliets, gendered to their various tastes, and perhaps the awareness of alternative fantasies enhanced the frisson of any one choice.[2] Peter Stallybrass, in his essay, "Transvestism and the 'Body Beneath': Speculating on the Boy Actor," explores those theoretically fraught moments

51

when the boy actor playing the cross-dressed romantic heroine sheds the male disguise, thus revealing his character's essential femininity.[3] But Stallybrass concentrates on audience speculation about a gendered body beneath, leaving open the question of whether, or in what sense, it exists; I take up this question hoping to find clues in our search for missing (female) persons. The previous chapter has sketched a theoretical "space" encircling the stage; this chapter aims to fill in that model by attention to the female bodies that were (or were supposed to be) imagined onstage. For the notion of a "real" offstage bedroom in which lovers consummate their expressed desire presupposes the illusion of a "real" onstage female body, complete with anatomical and perhaps even psychical interiority. The compelling nature of the latter, and its inextricable connection with the former, is the subject of this chapter.

For the body, like the stage, is a *space* in its own right; therefore, bodies onstage operate as mimetic spaces, with a potential for diegetic interiority. And the female body in particular not only occupies space, but, in phallocentric discourse, operates as a metaphor *for* space; its boundaries and contents are continually searched, prodded, and fetishized by the very discourse which delineated this space to begin with. This chapter will focus on two assertive, and assertively physical, female characters – Maria in Fletcher's *The Tamer Tamed*, and Ursula in Jonson's *Bartholomew Fair* – and will examine the manner in which these plays – or at least the men in them – metaphorize and attempt rhetorically to penetrate these women's bodily interiors, at the same time that the women themselves strive for bodily self-determination. In addition, I hope to demonstrate the centrality, in each play, of an architectural space which projects (and, in Maria's case, protects) the female body who inhabits it. Maria's chamber in *The Tamer Tamed* and Ursula's booth in *Bartholomew Fair* function as havens for fleshly indulgence, whether exclusively and rebelliously female or promiscuously trans-sexed; we might call them, in fact, potential matrices for sexual anarchy. Both spaces also harbor a curious creative power, manifested in the material and rhetorical *copia* surrounding them. In short, both spaces are mini-theaters in themselves – as flamboyant, and as fecund, as their mistresses.

This may appear a strange sisterhood: Maria, the well-to-do virgin bride, and Ursula, the corpulent pork-vender and bawd; Maria, a Renaissance proto-feminist, and Ursula, a seeming misogynist grotesquery. But both women are outspoken, are defiantly pleasure-seeking, and both capitalize on male lust – Maria, by staging a sex-strike on her wedding night; Ursula, by selling sex outright. Both women "enlist" other women in the cause of (literally) material gain: "liberty and clothes" for the women in *The Tamer Tamed*, and "the life of a lady" for Ursula's well-dressed whores. Both women overturn gender norms: Maria dons breeches (figuratively, if not literally); Ursula smokes a pipe.

In other words, I have chosen these two figures because of what they DO with their bodies – and they do it despite, or perhaps because of, what phallocentrism does to them. And their "doings" are theatrical doings. Maria mobilizes an army of women and orchestrates a virtual carnival; Ursula draws a crowd to her booth and generates gluttony, drunkenness, hilarity, social chaos. Both women fill the space surrounding them, even literally: both are larger than life.

My hope is that taking a look at these heavyweights will help us understand how the theater builds bodies. And as the above architectural parallels point out, there is something hauntingly "female" about theatrical spaces in general. Perhaps, therefore, the gap in the boy actor's bodice is not the best place to look for the erotic body – at least not at this distance from the early modern stage (and after all, even Zeffirelli's flash of skin filled an entire screen). Speculating on the spectacle might have its own pleasures, and most likely did, for some audience members; but a spectacle, by definition, does not invite scrutiny ("That is not a ghost; this is not a forest"). In a medium as expansive as theater, the fabric of "sex" must be flashier than skin.

I   Women in breeches: *The Tamer Tamed*

Written in reply to Shakespeare's *The Taming of the Shrew*, some twenty years later, Fletcher's *The Tamer Tamed* grants Kate her posthumous revenge; this is one of a handful of plays championing women (including Middleton's *The Roaring Girl*, with its cross-dressing, street-fighting heroine) that Linda Woodbridge cites as evidence of an increasingly vocal female audience.[4] Fletcher's play begins with the wedding of the now-widowed Petruccio to a woman determined not to follow Kate's example. The feisty bride, Maria, begins married life by barricading herself in her chamber, refusing to consummate the marriage until her notorious shrew-tamer husband comes to her "easy as a child / And tame as fear" (1.2.113–14). Nor does this wife protest alone: Maria quickly gathers a troop of female companions-in-arms who stock up her room with food and wine and then swear by their Amazonian foremothers to bring the male sex (through carnal deprivation) to their knees outside.

> MARIA. By the faith I have
> In mine own noble will, that childish woman
> That lives a prisoner to her husband's pleasure
> Has lost her making, and become a beast

       Created for his use, not fellowship.   (1.2.135–39)[5]

Thus, with the war-cry of "let's all wear breeches" (145), the women take possession of the upper stage and the battle ensues. The men gather below, bewildered and chagrined; they urge obedience, and are answered, from above, with mockery. In this twist on the "night visit" motif touched upon in the previous chapter, the upper stage again delineates an off-limits female world – but this time the context is siege warfare, not wooing. And this time, the male sexual objective is not veiled in poetry. We note, by way of contrast with Shakespeare, Fletcher's frankness about the bridal bed, an inaccessible but powerful presence, and, for Maria, the ultimate weapon.

> MARIA. 'Tis bed time.   (1.2.92)
>
> LIVIA. Devest you with obedient hands; to bed.
> MARIA. To bed? No, Livia   (99–100)
>
> PETRONIUS. Will you to bed, son?   (1.3.13)
>
>   Will you to bed, son?   (17)
>
> PETRUCCIO. Is my fair bride a-bed?   (32)
>
> PETRONIUS. Not a-bed yet?   (34)
>
> MARIA. I am gone
>   To bed . . .   (1878–8)
>
>   go to bed and leave me . . .   (207)
>
> PETRUCCIO. I must not to bed with this stomach, and no meat. (223)
>   tender me
>   All the delights due to a marriage bed.   (228–29)
>
> BIANCA. To bed, sir.   (258)
>
> MARIA. To bed, to bed Petruccio.   (261)

As the above lines make clear, this is a battle waged over "pleasure" or the right to pleasure – over sex, food, clothing, entertainment. But, at a deeper level, the play also concerns survival. Before Maria appears on stage, we learn "She must . . . not eat, / Drink, . . . piss" without her husband's permission (1.1.45–46), and that he may "bury her / . . . within these three weeks" (47–48). When Maria decides to protest, she is asked whether she has "a stomach to't" (1.2.63). She does, and she must, for the sake of her stomach, for the sake of self-preservation. Therefore, the food smuggled into Maria's chamber serves as a kind of defense. The men are told,

> They are victualled with pies and puddings,
> (The trappings of good stomachs), noble ale
> The true defendor, sausages, and smoked ones,
> If need be, such as serve for pikes, and pork

(Better the Jews never hated): here and there
A bottle of methaglin, a stout Briton
That will stand to 'em . . .   (2.4.78–84)

The metaphors are phallic but even more so military, highlighting the
fact that in siege warfare food is the most essential "armor."

And in a world which deprives women of stewardship of their own
bodies, feasting and drinking can be revolutionary gestures. So as not to
become "prisoner[s] to . . . [men's] pleasure," Maria and her peers create
a sanctuary for their own pleasure.

Throughout this protest, Petruccio bemoans his sexual starvation, but
also vows to "starve out" his bride, and the men as a group swagger and
threaten a phallic assault. "I'll see all passages stopped," vows the father
of the bride, " . . . We shall have wars indeed"; "Let's in," urges
Petruccio, "and each provide his tackle, / We'll fire 'em out, or make 'em
take their pardons, / . . . on their bare knees" (1.3.282–90). With all the
talk of stopped passages and starving out, the barricaded bridal chamber
becomes a metaphor for the virginal body within. And as the conjugal
antagonism intensifies (and with it, apparently, Petruccio's sexual frustration), the men threaten to fight back in even more visceral terms:

> PETRONIUS. Give her a crab-tree cudgel.
> PETRUCCIO.   So I will;
> And after it a flock-bed for her bones,
> And hard eggs, till they brace her like a drum.
> She shall be pampered with –
> She shall not know a stool in ten months, Gentlemen.   (2.4.28–32)

Petruccio would suit the punishment to the crime. His wife seals her
body against one form of penetration, so he threatens to seal her up
entirely: what he imagines is a kind of indirect and gradual anal rape.
And these male threats escalate.[6] One of Petruccio's cohorts urges the
men,

> Arm, arm, out with your weapons,
> For all the women in the kingdom's on ye;
> They swarm like wasps, and nothing can destroy 'em
> But stopping of their hive, and smothering of 'em.   (2.4.33–36)

Maria's protest provokes sexualized aggression (at least on the verbal
level) because it is perceived as a sexual act; correspondingly, her upstairs
room inspires voyeuristic fascination. The butler reports to the men after
having "peeped in / At a loose lansket" (2.6.42–43) that the women
upstairs "have got a stick of fiddles, and they firk it / In wondrous ways"
(36–37). The sexualization of the women's entertainment may be the
product of the speaker's fevered imagination, but the suggestion of

fiddles as phallic substitutes (used in "wondrous ways") can hardly ease Petruccio's sexual anxieties. And the news gets worse:

> The two grand capitanos
> . . .
> Dance with their coats tucked up to their bare breeches
> And bid the kingdom kiss 'em . . .   (37–40)

The gesture of disrespect, combined with the auto-erotic fiddling, takes on a distinctly sexual flavor; this is a kind of aggressive exhibitionism, which, in the context of a sexual rebellion, adds insult to injury. The dance both celebrates and holds aloof a vibrant female physicality.

As we see, this is not the usual female bodily protest, epitomized by the hunger strike which killed Lady Arbella Stuart.[7] But as in a hunger strike, the cell becomes a stage for the enactment of bodily resistance. Therefore, Maria's greatest test comes when her husband agrees to her conditions and crosses the threshold, expecting an immediate sexual reward. And now it becomes clear that the men's military metaphors were just that, metaphors; Petruccio wrestles with her but stops short of rape, bewildered by her resistance. His self-pity afterward echoes Othello: "I might take her body prisoner, / But for her mind or appetite" (3.3.14–15). The irony is that Maria has been fighting in the name of "appetite" or "pleasure" all along. And this is the catch-22 of phallocentrism: it courts female desire in one channel, while attempting to curtail it in others. But Maria affirms the dignity and integrity of her desiring body. When Petruccio threatens to relieve his lust with her chambermaid, she threatens the same with his own butler (3.3.30).

The morning after the truce, Maria's army departs, beating pans and shaking their fists at Petruccio; in their wake the men of the household swap scandalized stories of female drunkenness and debauchery. But the crude joking about "how they tumbled" belies the larger sense in which the women have triumphed; theirs is the victory of the Rabelaisian feast: "In the act of eating . . . the confines between the body and the world are overstepped by the body; it triumphs over the world, over its enemy . . . grows at the world's expense. This element of victory . . . is inherent in all banquet images. No meal can be sad."[8] And the text itself is a virtual feast, brimming over with lists of food and drink, and with references to hunger, eating, and drinking: my latest count totaled 128, but I am sure I missed a hogshead or a pie. Molly Easo Smith likens events of the play to popular rebellions such as the Essex food riots in 1622 and 1629, also led by a woman.[9] But I will return later to the issue of food in the text: here we need only recognize the banquet as a place where the body oversteps its "confines." Although Maria's protest begins in the confines of her chamber, its effect is to burst the confines Petruccio would enforce on her body; she asserts her right to grow "at the world's expense" – or (even worse) at her husband's.

And grow she does. Maria descends from her chamber the morning after, and proceeds to act on the terms of her contract, ordering fine clothing, silk hangings, "fourteen yards of satin" (3.3.61), horses, hawks, and "twenty acres" of gardens (87), amongst other accessories. Petruccio, still nettled by the night's events, balks at the expenses and half-threatens to "drag" her to her (sexual) "duty," at which point Maria, once again, calls his bluff (126). He winds up alone, bemoaning "this whirlwind, that takes all / Within her compass" (150–51). The battle moves onto new ground.

Maria's main tactic is to seize control of space; therefore, her move from upper stage to main stage marks an expanding sphere of power. One of the servants remarks: "If this house be not turned within this fortnight / With the foundation upward, I'll be carted" (3.1.18–19). And by the end of the third act, Maria has done nearly that. Petruccio has stooped, out of desperation, to the undignified "feminine" ploy used by Middleton's courtesan, that of feigning illness; Maria responds by declaring him a victim of the plague, stripping the house, and leaving him locked inside with an elderly nurse. The moment foregrounds the gendered valences of the outside/inside binary; in response to this new affront to his masculine privilege, her husband hurls threats from off-stage. "Will ye starve me here?" he cries (3.5.42). The last straw comes when she sends a doctor in to bleed him. "*As I am a man*," he howls, "I'll beat the walls down" (69; emphasis added). Petruccio's reaction to the indignity of enclosure within the domestic interior is much the same as his reaction to the indignity of being shut out, and the mere prospect of enduring starvation and bleeding – the same bodily invasions with which the women rebels were threatened – throws him into a rage. He finally breaks open the door and bursts onstage with a loaded gun.

But the stage is empty; Petruccio's "weapon" proves useless. Once again, Maria has deflated and deflected phallic aggression; once again, she makes space her ally. It is this continual short-circuiting of Petruccio's patriarchal power which drives him to abandon it altogether; he finally resorts to the most feminine of all possible devices, a fake death, designed to bring his wife to contrition. This climactic final scene plays out – in an inverted parody – the play's initial prophesy that Petruccio will "bury" his bride; the scene also marks the culmination and triumph of Maria's on-going *battle for space* against the smothering reign of a confirmed phallocrat. In a last, desperate effort to gain possession of her body, her husband shuts his body in a coffin. His "resurrection" coincides with an anguished protest against physical confinement: "Unbutton me," cries the beleaguered bridegroom, " . . . I die indeed else" (5.4.39–40). The line mimics Lear's final enunciation of heartbreak, "Pray you, undo this button" (*King Lear*, 5.3.285) – and though Petruccio's "misery" over his bride's willfulness may indeed cause him a smothering sense of grief, the sexual innuendo of his "rising" at Maria's cue (coupled with the orgasmic "I die") affords a cruder reading of the doleful imperative and invites us to view him as "done in" by his own lust. The combined effects of wounded pride, disappointment, and sexual frustration are more than he can bear: he literally comes apart at the seams.

Petruccio's defeat is so total that Maria's yielding, at this point, sacrifices little of her hard-won dignity, and her offer of "service to" – rather than imprisonment to (an important distinction) – his "pleasure" constitutes an entrance into the sexual partnership celebrated in the Epilogue. Pausing for breath between kisses, the bridegroom turns to his former comrades-in-arms, and exclaims, "O *gentlemen*, I know not where I am"; he is told, "Get ye to bed then; there you'll quickly know, *sir*" (50–51; emphases added). That Petruccio explicitly addresses his male friends is significant; the reply, which turns him from the homosocial to the heterosexual, is even more so. In a world re-shaped to accommodate female will, it is no surprise this hero needs re-orientation. Maria's bed – no longer closed against him – shelters his whole world.

"Devest you with obedient hands; to bed." (1.2.99)

The trouble began with Maria's refusal to do just that. In fact, she was determined to do just the opposite, to accrue rather than to strip, to amass rather than to shed – to amass food, clothing, money, space: a protective circle around her vulnerable flesh. "Liberty and clothes," the first items on her marital contract, ought not to be dismissed as pure bathos; the connection between sartorial freedom and freedom of movement is clear enough in Maria's mind. The jubilation of the "breeches" dance affirms the intimate relationship between cloth and skin, and Petruccio's "Unbutton me" proves that he is made of the same mortal cloth.

On the other hand, the injunction "devest you[rself]," which Maria defies, throws us against the theatrical problem of the "body beneath." And this particular situation onstage – wherein the boy actor is expected to undress – would constitute, for Stallybrass, another "startling moment of indeterminacy" with regard to gender – depending, I suppose, upon how long the audience was held in suspense.[10] In this case, no such suspension seems likely: Maria's refusal to disrobe is immediate and final, and I mention the potential slippage only in order to pose a new way of looking at – or for – her body. I would like to emphasize, in contraposition to much recent theory, the very seamlessness of this portrayal of gender, a seamlessness in part maintained (paradoxically) by Maria's refusal to conform to one particular patriarchal dictate. This is a useful counter-example to that of Desdemona – a main peg of Stally-brass' argument – whose emphatic and prolonged undressing for bed/death allows the dramatist to undo the fiction of her femaleness at the very moment that the fiction has her literally and brutally *undone*. I hesitate to suggest a parallel between the deconstruction done by critic (and, seemingly, by playwright), and the destruction done within the play itself. But the fascination of recent criticism with these rifts in the illusion, these moments of potential breakage in the female/fiction, strangely reiterates the penetrative masculinist economy which strong female characters, by definition, must resist. As Stallybrass himself asserts in a different essay, "Cloth matters so much because it operates on, and undoes, the margins of the self."[11] Therefore, my search for a body beneath will linger a while on the fabric of the fiction, to explore the role of clothes in the affirmation of the "female."

Fletcher's text gives us little indication as to whether or not the exclamation "let's all wear breeches" is meant to be taken literally. It is noteworthy that the pants-dance occurs offstage: the audience hears the account of the male eyewitness and hears the offstage song celebrating "the woman who wears the breeches" – but we are not treated to the sight of the dancers' breeched buttocks. And the notion is clearly meant to titillate. Why is the garment referred to as "*bare* breeches" (emphasis mine)? The seeming oxymoron underscores the fetishization of the cross-gendered garment,[12] but it also highlights the play's more general tendency to conflate the sumptuary and the sensual. Livia, scorning her old, rich suitor, asks, "Can his money kiss me?" but quickly concedes that it can kiss her "Behind, / Laid out upon a petticoat" (1.2.29–30). And Maria insists upon these kinds of kisses, trading her sexual favors for satin and silk. Fletcher's play is keenly aware of the contact between fabric and skin.

Not that the flesh/clothes association was always material for comedy.[13] Christian contempt of the world, epitomized by the *memento mori* tradition in art, condemned bodily adornment as vehemently as any other fleshly pursuit, and never tired of pointing out that your rich attire would only rot in your grave along with your rotting carcass; the "Homilie Against Excesse of Apparell," preached throughout Renaissance England, thunders, "wee are but wormes meat, although we pamper ourselves never so much in gorgeous apparell."[14] And even in theater, where ornament is essence, this ideology finds expression, most notably in the mouths of malcontented male characters such as Hamlet or his Middletonian counterpart, Vindice of *The Revenger's Tragedy* – both of whom introduce a death's head on stage. What is the difference between Fletcher's comedic treatment of the flesh/clothes linkage, and the dark and paradoxical iteration of the same equation in tragedy? And what does the death's head, grim inverse of the carnivalesque, tell us about the fabric(ation) of the female?

I have designated the two heroines to be discussed in this chapter as "heavyweights." And the association between women and flesh (which, if the truth be said, in fact amounts to what we now call "fat") necessitates a look at its antithesis, bone, in its relation to women. Vindice pontificates over the skull of his dead mistress, Gloriana: "Be merry," he tells it, " . . . thou terror to fat folks, / To have their costly three-piled flesh worn off / As bare as this" (1.1.44–47). Death, according to Vindice's metaphor, will undress every body down to bare bones. (That, in fact, is the use to which he eventually puts Gloriana's skull, dressed up in a wig and painted with poison for the grimmest bed-trick in Renaissance drama.) As Hamlet says to Yorick's skull, "Now get you to my lady's chamber, and tell her, let her paint an inch thick, to this favour she must come" (5.1.188–90). One drawing in Holbein's famous series entitled "The Dance of Death" portrays a lovely duchess getting dressed, with Death beside her, adding a necklace of bones (Figure 6).

Hamlet's "I know not seems, madam" – that phrase which has so fascinated critics[15] – is rarely quoted without the appended "madam"; the common distrust of "outward show" seems to require a female target. As Claudius says, gendering his crime as female: "The harlot's cheek . . . / Is not more ugly to the thing that helps it / Than is my deed to my most painted word" (3.1.53–55). Woman, as the more fleshly creature, was more likely to indulge in material excess, to pile, first, flesh upon flesh (gluttony being another typically female vice), and then on top of that, layer upon layer of, for instance, "three-pile" velvet or "paint an inch thick," until inward worth or essence was not simply obscured, but perhaps smothered altogether. It is hence only fitting that the Elizabethan stage represented "woman," as Stallybrass points out, by way of prosthetic additions to the body of the boy actor – primarily wigs. The boy actor playing the cross-dressed "girl" in many plays reveals "her" true feminine self by removing a masculine wig and then letting loose the locks of the "real" woman's hair worn beneath.[16] Do clothes make the man? Well, they certainly make the *woman*.

I call attention to one additional image in circulation at about the same time that *The Tamer Tamed* (1611) and *Bartholomew Fair* (1614)

Figure 6 Etching by Wenceslaus Hollar (1651), based on Hans Holbein's *Death and the Countess*, from his famous series, "The Dance of Death" (1538).

were performed. The illustration for a broadsheet entitled "Mistris Turners Farewell to all women" (1615) juxtaposes the soberly clad, pious, repentant Mistress Turner with an outrageously ornamented "Lady Pride" representing Lady Frances Howard (Figure 7).[17] Yet what is most remarkable about Lady Pride's outfit may not be obvious at first glance: the pearl-encrusted bodice is cut in such a way as to reveal her breasts, which, oddly enough, are barely noticeable amidst the profusion of ornament. The effect is to expose the breast as just another female gaud.

And the subject of breasts brings us back to the puzzle of the boy actor. Lacking material evidence for the use of false breasts in early modern performances, Stallybrass emphasizes the *rhetorical* prominence of the absent breast in scenes such as the suicide of Cleopatra, where Shakespeare deliberately departs from his source in order to highlight that imaginary body-part. Stallybrass also points out that, later, on the gender-inclusive Restoration stage, the revelation of the cross-dressed heroine often required the actress to display her breasts, in addition to the traditional loosing of her hair.[18] Can we extrapolate backwards from this theatrical development a certain consciousness, in audiences of the preceding era, of the *missing* breasts of the body beneath – or of the missing (female) body beneath the breasts? Or, on the contrary, does the material absence of "real" breasts and bodies only demonstrate the power of the fiction?

Recent theorizing of the boy actor renders "the sexualized body" a *"prosthetic"* body;[19] I would go so far as to say that such theorizing renders the female body a hollow body. Exploring the clothing/flesh parallel allows us to unravel the paradox by which clothes come to embody the body – but it also presents the theorizing process as a postmodern analog for the anatomist's craft. Mario Perniola views Renaissance anatomy texts such as Vesalius' *Fabrica* as evidence of an "erotics of dressing" which is more than skin deep: the internal organs in these illustrations are treated as "finer and more praiseworthy fabric" than that of the outward flesh – itself "as external and glorious as a garment" to Baroque artists.[20] Yet, as I noted in the Introduction, dissection also poses a philosophical problem: the inward truth of the soul is put to flight with each new layer exposed by the scalpel. Stallybrass' essay, with its relentless exposure of gender "indeterminacy," undertakes a similar attack on the doctrine of biological essence – but in doing so he (intentionally or not) permits the reader to assume an equally essentialist default position, privileging the "real" body of the actor as the empirical object of gender dissection, as the male skeletal basis supporting the female exterior.[21] And although there can be no denying

Figure 7   "Mistris Turners Farewell to all women" (1615).

the value of either intellectual exercise – that is, deconstruction or dissection – we also must remind ourselves of what is lost in the process: the appreciation and validation of the sumptuous surface.

Laurie A. Finke views Vindice's address to Gloriana's skull as manifesting the male "obsession with woman as a *memento mori* masked by a beautiful facade."[22] But the misogynistic appeal of the death's head lies not in any feminine attributes, but rather in its symbolic *annihilation* of all things feminine; as Vindice puts it, "Here might the scornful and ambitious woman / Look through and through herself" (3.5.95–96). And the rejection of beauty – for Vindice as well as for Hamlet – amounts to the rejection not only of theater, but of life. To risk stating the obvious, there is no surviving what Augustine calls "the contest of . . . the flesh."[23] When Hamlet contemplates Yorick's skull, he faces the *reductio ad absurdum* of his own attack on "outward show." Who would you rather invite to dinner, Holbein's Death or his female victim? The hollow woman of theater seems a cuddlier companion.

We might now draw up a pair of antithetical equations related to the *memento mori* and to the carnivalesque, respectively:

woman = flesh = ornament = "outward show" = theater = death
woman = flesh = ornament = "outward show" = theater = life

Theater, unlike other art forms, uses living bodies as its media; theater literally takes warm flesh as its "material." In other words, theater does to the male actor what the flesh/spirit binarism does to woman: it denies him essence, treats him as pure clay, and whether this is viewed as killing or creating depends upon one's outlook on both process and product. In fact, Laura Levine argues that Renaissance objections to the cross-dressed male actor betrayed an underlying fear that the female costume could literally transform men into women. The role "shapes the man who plays it."[24] Thus, by exploding the notion of inward truth, by positing surface as central,[25] theater demonstrates, time and again, the power of the palpable.

Of course, nothing on stage is *literally* palpable – at least, not to the audience. But the three-dimensionality of theater, the array of textures and forms, in coordination with the contact between bodies on stage, creates the illusion of palpability; like holography, it entices touch. Like the flesh, it compels. Theater is an essentially fleshly, even a fleshy medium: it fills space and engages the senses; it arouses. And this fleshiness can be rendered visually, as well as rhetorically through sumptuous verbal display.[26] As I mentioned above, Fletcher's play – like the offstage bedroom which forms its center, its navel – is filled to bursting with food and drink: it ends, as it begins, in feasting. This list bears witness to the overflow:

pudding eat drunk ripe eat drink wine egg muscatel stomach starved starved fasting fruit eggs buttered parsnips victualled drunk drunk drunk drunk stomach meat feed fast meat pie sauce puddings pastries custards custards pastries appetite eat starved palate eaten beef meat drink cakes meat tripe wine beer fruit cheese eaten fruit eating eggs ale drink drunk pies puddings stomachs ale sausages pork bottle methaglin methaglin ale health drink quaff tipple tipple drunk drunk ale vessels sack sack ale bottles dairy supper tun wine dead-drunk veal capons sack drunk drink ale tippled Toast-and-Butter drunk spoon fasted appetite stomach meat starve stomach broths feed eat onions clove fruiterer eat pudding apples leek-porridge oysters meal meats dish lemon-waters surfeit comfits peas drink starve eggs meat hogsheads butter bread dinner drink drink.[27]

The list is a mouthful – I know because I have read it aloud. But these gathered chunks of text warrant a place in the chapter because they demonstrate, in a way the bare tally of "128 words" cannot, the unwieldiness, the brimming-overness, the aural and oral overabundance of this excessively meaty play. And if the play's "carnivalesque" elements cannot "contain fully the danger of the anarchic behavior" it describes,[28] therein lies the play's spacious potential. In the end, Maria's place is open to all.

II   Breaching Ursula's booth: exteriors, interiors, posteriors

Maria's strategy is to close her door to men; Ursula opens her booth to men and their money. And these more permeable spatial boundaries figure Ursula's more permeable and permeating physical frame. Gail Kern Paster's work has broken new ground in feminist criticism by confronting the stereotypically incontinent woman at all levels; Paster argues persuasively that in city comedies such as *Bartholomew Fair*, where a woman's need for a public chamber-pot leads to her initiation into prostitution, all female orifices are equally suspect and all forms of incontinence are interchangeable. Early modern medical discourse asso-ciated women's bodies with fluids, and "uncertainty in the lower parts bespeaks unreliability . . . in the constructed woman" so that "a woman who leaves her house is a woman who talks is a woman who drinks is a woman who leaks"[29] – is a woman who wants sex.

Paster's analysis foregrounds Ursula, the fat and loquacious vendor of roasted pig and warm women, along with the booth which projects her incontinent body, as the focus of the play's discussion of female appetite. Ursula's booth, like the "pot" contained within it, represents the "leaky vessel" of woman and womb. Here, however, I wish to emphasize what may at first seem a trivial point: that Ursula's booth does not, in fact, house a chamber-pot, but rather "the bottom of an old bottle" (4.4.202–3)[30] which serves the same purpose. The difference highlights, first of all, the fact that booth, body, and "pot" are only three of many vessels cluttering the fairgrounds; but more importantly it reveals the play's concern with a bizarre process of transmogrification (I am tempted to call it a "perversion") of the gustatory to the excretory, of vessels to receptacles. I wish to place Ursula and her booth amidst the text's more general proliferation of vessels – vessels animate and inanimate, biological and gastronomical – and to argue that the abundance and interchangeability of these objects (along with those ambiguous recurrences of the word "hole") highlight the text's confused fetishization of all female orifices and its obsessive concern with their control, or, rather, their uncontrollability. In the end, I hope to demonstrate that there is something magical, something infinitely (if disturbingly) productive about this economy of (w)holes, over which Ursula reigns as unholy *mater* – goddess of the wholly matter.

Bartholomew Fair, like *The Tamer Tamed*, is about women who eat too much, drink too much, spend too much. Jonson's play is also about women who pee too much (or at least, too often). For all of these problems are really the same: excess consumption (physiologically, sexually, or financially) implies excess expenditure and vice versa.[31] The female body, with its porous skin and running holes, operates as both metaphor and metonymy, both symbol and symptom, of excess in general. This excess – or in the terms of Jonson's play, this "enormity" – may be either enacted socially or projected physically (through, for instance, Ursula's layers of fat or Win's much talked-about velvet accessories), but it always, inevitably, comes down to sex. Therefore it is no accident that these two plays which are so preoccupied with female sexual "availability" similarly juxtapose rich female attire with "vulgar" female physicality. Jonson explodes class distinction among female bodies, emphasizing instead common biological functions. The focus upon Win's velvet accouterments renders doubly obvious (and doubly embarrassing) her urinary desperation. I would add, also, that this deflating treatment of female upward mobility persists in contemporary wise-cracks – for instance, "Stick with me, baby, and you'll be farting through silk." The crass humor of the expression has a long history, dating to Rabelais and beyond, and its socially leveling implications in fact echo Christian contempt of the world.

And the Christian background to *Bartholomew Fair* deserves at least a cursory glance, as it helps us to frame Ursula as unholy mother and to view her booth as a kind of profane tabernacle. As Frances Teague points out, the historical fair evolved from the collision between a profitable cloth market and a priory on the same tract of land.[32] And in fact the unique staging of Jonson's play can be traced to medieval morality plays like *The Castle of Perseverance*, which also requires booths and simultaneous staging. There is, however, one important distinction: this medieval play situates its audience at the center of the performance,[33] while Jonson's play centers upon Ursula's booth. The idea that "all the world's a stage" takes on new meaning – especially since Ursula herself is likened to "the World," along with "the Flesh and the Devil," those "three enemies of man" (3.6.33–35).

It is piety which sets the events of the play in motion; piety also provides a target for satire, as appetite propels Jonson's Puritans to the profane pleasures of the fair – and, consequently, into deeper and deeper hypocrisy. Dame Purecraft warns her daughter, Win, not to let "the enemy . . . enter" at the "door" of her mouth by eating the "unclean beast, pig" (I.6.6–7). She explains that the pig, or rather, the temptation it represents, "broacheth flesh and blood" (17), and must be resisted. But by the end of the scene, Dame Purecraft and her pious suitor concede that "we may be religious in the midst of the profane" (72), and the Puritans make their way toward the fair and "the tents of the wicked" (71).

However profane, a certain mystery surrounds Ursula's booth. Like Maria's upstairs chamber, it is the play's inner sanctum; although editors have often allowed act 4, scene 4, to reveal, momentarily, the interior of the booth, there is nothing in the original text which necessitates this staging.[34] Like Maria's chamber, the booth stands at the center of a carnal universe, providing a space for riotously physical activities: feasting, drinking, urination, fornication, the sale of "flesh," both human and animal. We recall Fletcher's final reference to Maria's bed, as encompassing her husband's world: Ursula's booth does the same, and for far more men. Overdo speaks of the tent as "the very womb and bed of enormity, gross as [Ursula] herself" (2.2.102–3), setting out a three-way metaphor by which bodies, wombs, and beds collapse into one great (gross) *ur*-trope of enclosed fecundity.

Womb-images, of course, were very popular among Renaissance authors;[35] what is unique to this text is its magnification and multiplication of such vessels. Even the conflation of "womb and bed" images sets up a dynamic whereby female fertility endlessly multiplies – or conversely, endlessly consumes – its own production: Ursula's tent is a womb which encloses other wombs, brought to bed for sexual and thus, potentially, for *breeding* purposes (the breeding of, perhaps, additional bodies with wombs). And the literal sense of a "womb of enormity" conveys the mind-numbing paradox of a space whose limits contain, even breed, the unlimited – a kind of Renaissance anticipation of the Derridean *mise en abyme*.[36] Add to this picture the notion of Ursula as World and the implications are dizzying. In this abyss of concentric wombs, there is no escape from the flesh – or the female.

Thus Overdo's hesitation before the booth typifies the patriarchal response to the mystery of the womb, the response of abjection. One can only be ambivalent in the face of this vortex of fecundity; for the womb, which creates, is too much like the belly, which devours. Kristeva writes, "devotees of the abject . . . do not cease looking . . . for the desirable and terrifying, nourishing and murderous . . . inside of the maternal body."[37] And in fact, both belly and womb justify the trip to Ursula's in the first place; prompted by her husband, Win uses pregnancy to legitimate her appetite for the fair and its goodies, as she pretends a hormonally induced "longing for pig." That Jonson does not clarify whether Win's pregnancy itself is faked (a question I'll return to) only highlights the ambiguity surrounding the womb's relation to the stomach: Littlewit, for instance, conflates the two organs as he speaks of the "little one . . . that cries for pig so i' the mother's belly" (1.6.99–100).

And it is worth noting here that pork, in the play, is always spoken of as "pig" – as if the animal were eaten alive.[38] This emphasizes the carnivorous nature of the characters, as does the reference to Lubberland, where "the pigs run about, ready-roasted, and cry 'Come eat me!' "[39] And Littlewit's depiction of his baby enhances these carnivorous – even cannibalistic – undertones: by placing the fetus in the "belly" he almost suggests that Win has *eaten* the child, and this in turn equates the child with the "pig" destined to fill the mother's belly.[40] We remember that Ursula, similarly, is named "mother o' the pigs" (2.5.70), which makes her not only an animal, but an animal that eats its own (or feeds them to others). The metaphorical fusion of Win's womb and stomach gives birth to a grotesque image: a live animal crying to eat another live animal from inside the belly of a third (human) animal. In mathematical terms, this is appetite squared. Once again we face a disturbing series of concentric bodily "vessels" – but rather than birthing, each swallows the next.

And Ursula, as the archetypal earth mother, both expels and devours capaciously.[41] Quarlous and Winwife describe her as a "quagmire" or a "bog," and joke that any man who would "venture" to have sex with her "might sink into her and be drowned a week ere any friend he had could find where he were"; Quarlous imagines, " 'Twere like falling into a shire of butter" (2.5.83–91). And the fact that it is butter is no accident, for this "fine oily pig-woman" (Induction 110), as avatar of appetite, is easily likened to that which she sells, is easily troped as mouth, vessel, or nutriment. When she scalds herself, the necessary treatment calls for "cream," "salad oil," "the white of an egg, a little honey, and hog's grease" (2.5.152–74). Her body is equated sometimes with food – meat, in particular – sometimes with the livestock from which we take meat. Her leg, inadvertently cooked, is now "dressed" like a leg of lamb; Knockem even speaks of the limb as a "pastern" as he treats the injury.

But the more common gustatory references in *Bartholomew Fair* focus on liquid – grease, in particular, which is a by-product of meat and therefore a kind of secretion. Once again, liquification is central. Ursula herself contributes to the pile-up of liquefying metaphors, describing herself as "juicy and wholesome" (hole-some?). When we first meet Ursula in front of her booth, she calls attention to her own sweating form: "I am all fire and fat . . . I shall e'en melt away to the first woman, a rib again, I am afraid. I do water the ground in knots as I go, like a great garden-pot; you may follow me by the S's I make." (2.2.48–51). Here Ursula manages to evoke all the components of Eden – woman, garden, and rib, even to the snake-like path her swaying hips trace on the ground. Yet there is something curious about this Eve. We are used to seeing Eve consume; here she melts, fecundating the ground as she does so. I am reminded of Irigaray's feminist theorization of fluids; the following passage could be describing Ursula: "continuous, compressible, dilatable, viscous, conductable, diffusable" or better yet, "unending, potent and impotent owing to its resistance to the countable."[42] It is the potency, not the impotence, which I would emphasize in regard to Ursula. For her self-portrait entails a subtle self-deification: she reverses, re-winds, undoes God's creation of woman, thereby, in effect, claiming the power to shape or re-shape herself. Ursula's fable stresses the nourishing power of the flesh and its secretions, and positions the female as engendering agent: the "great garden-pot" in the sky.

We cannot proceed, however, without confronting the indelicate matter of the other prominent "pot" in this play: the chamber-pot. And indeed, as Paster demonstrates, the female bladder attracts a remarkable amount of attention in the text, even from act 1, when Wasp thus scorns Littlewit's precious box: "Let your little wife stale in it" (1.4.58–59). One thinks of Pandora's box, the classical version of Eve's apple. But then again, it is important to emphasize that, despite Win's urgent search, the chamber-pot, as the more polite receptacle, eludes her in the end. After all, a chamber-pot belongs in the chamber, not on the fairground. Therefore Littlewit can only comfort his wife with the prospect that Ursula might supply her "a dripping pan, or an old kettle, or something" (3.6.122–23); the "something" proves to be a broken bottle.

And, again, the confusion of eating vessels with excretory receptacles deserves note – as do the bizarre associations linking pots, bottles, bottoms, and sex. Faced with poor Win's embarrassed request, Ursula testily informs her that her "vessel is employed"; she will have to wait for the "honest proctor and his wife" who "are at it within" (4.4.202–4).

Noting the secondary sexual sense of "at it," Paster quite aptly names this "chamber-pot," such as it is, "bawd."[43] And the bottle has already made an appearance as something with unusual powers: Overdo calls the tapster a "child of the bottles" (2.4.23), as if a bottle could give birth. On the other hand, the logic which likens a body to a bottle does permit such fantastical transmutations. The question is whether we wind up with a humanized object or an objectified human. Do you picture a Disneyesque dance of kitchen utensils? Or a plastic, pornographic blow-up doll? Here is another example: Ursula orders her tapster to "froth" the beer before serving by jogging the "bottles o' the *buttock*" (2.2.94; my emphasis). I suppose that a woman who sells women and who also sells beer might at times get the two commodities confused – hence the sexualized bottle, the jogging, the froth. But I must confess that my feminist deconstructionist analytic detachment cannot suppress a sense of wonderment here; there seems an odd magic in this bottle.

Perhaps the magic has to do with the sheer abundance produced by bottles and bodies alike. Indeed, the cynical purpose of Ursula's instructions to the tapster – that of cheating customers by filling half their glasses with foam – cannot be separated from its observable effect of *overflow*. Ursula goes on to teach the tapster another trick: bottles and cans should be taken away and replaced "before they be half drunk off" (97–101), thereby creating a bottomless bottle, a bounteous flow of beer (and, in the other direction, of cash). This profane parable of loaves and fishes suits the spirit of Ursula's re-telling of Genesis, and re-duplicates the fructifying power associated with her foaming flesh.

On the other hand, the overflow of Ursula's booth, from her bottles and her smoky cooking-pit, might as easily disgust as tantalize. The Puritans hungrily pursue the scent of roasting meat to its source (3.2.73–82), but Overdo stands outside the tent and expounds upon the dangers of smoke:

> OVERDO. The lungs of the tobacconist are rotted, the liver spotted, the brain smoked like the backside of the pigwoman's booth, here, and the whole body within, black as her pan you saw even now without. (2.6.39–42)

This passage adds three more internal organs to the list of metaphors for Ursula's booth, the "within . . . without" parallelism pointing up the biologism which permeates the play. And in keeping with the anatomical tropes, the booth is given a "backside" which seems to be the part with the worst leakage problem. We also note the gratuitous reminder of Ursula's pan, one of the vessels considered for its potential use as a chamber-pot. Overdo adds to this warning a reference to a disfigurement caused by syphilis (erroneously attributed to tobacco smoking) which creates in effect a "third nostril" through which smoke can be vented (45–50). His disgust with the habit of tobacco clearly arises from the smoke's apparent threat to bodily integrity, its ability to invade, even to erode, the body's delicate surface. Holes can figure illness and decay as well as birth, abundance, and growth.

As the preceding pages have shown, this "hole in the nose" is only one of the many holes inhabiting the text. We remember the hole at the center of Ursula's booth: her cooking-pit. In fact she speaks of the entire place as her "pit" (also, notably, a term for the theater, the "cock-pit"), referring to the guests who "fill" it (3.2.101–2). And considering the heat and smoke of the place, highlighted by Overdo in his anti-smoking lecture, the parallel with hell, itself a common metaphor for the vagina, is only too clear.[44] Also, we have all the "hole" jokes surrounding the stocks – as if the aperture itself, not the instrument overall, were the offending part. It is noteworthy that the stocks compete with Ursula's booth as one of the most prominent props, for these two objects are clearly related in the misogynist rhetoric voiced by Quarlous and Winwife, depicting Ursula's body as a devouring "bog." This ridicule partakes of a long tradition associating the female genitals with entrapment and damnation – the "sulphurous pit" Lear abhors (4.5.121–26).

The metonymizing impulse by which the stocks are reduced to their holes bears comparison to the rhetorical treatment, throughout the play, of Ursula's body. But let us not forget that this body also figures the World. Not a hole, but a whole. And herein lies the "catch" to any circular metaphor, and the power behind the circle as symbol. What do you see inside? A face. Zero. A sun. An eye. Whether Ursula's beer-glass is half-empty or half-full largely depends upon your attitude toward froth – which, like the body, swells, self-generates, and dies. In the Introduction I quoted Webster's *Duchess of Malfi*, where Bosola describes the flesh as "fantastical puff-paste." I would now suggest that the nausea he and Hamlet share is as easily inspired by reproduction as by death and decomposition. Hamlet contemplates the way "the sun breed[s] maggots in a dead dog" (2.2.183–84), and likewise views Ophelia as a potential "breeder of sinners" (3.1.124). His obsession with this, so to speak, "bad breeding" helps explain Overdo's over-reaction to a fat pork-vendor and the smoke of her fire. The multiple womb-images in *Bartholomew Fair* – and the collapsing of these vessels upon one another – amplifies fertility to an almost menacing degree. Ursula's bottle-trick, and the womb-and-bed trope with its endlessly widening hermeneutic spiral, create a sense of infinitude in (re)productivity which projects the "female" everywhere and, consequently, desacralizes the world. The miracle of the loaves and fishes becomes a nightmare when taken out of

Christ's hands. The incarnation makes matter bearable. Ursula, the she-bear, is heavy indeed.

There is one type of hollow object in this play which remains a topic to be broached: toys. This is a play, let's not forget, which includes puppets in its list of "Persons," and these toys might tell us something about the hollow women on stage. Leatherhead, the puppet-master, sells "rattles, drums," and baby dolls (3.6.51) – all hollow by implication, if not by definition. Bartholomew Cokes, delighted and duped by the Fair which bears his name, demonstrates an almost literal appetite for these toys, at one point provoking his servant to groan, "Would the Fair and all the drums and rattles in't were in your belly for me!" (1.5.86–87). Once again, Jonson's text yawns, and we see no bottom to this *abyme* of bellies.

Are the women in the play also puppets, toys? After all, Win is prostituted while her husband watches the puppets perform his play. And he himself has delighted in dressing her up for the Fair, praising the status-symbol of her velvet cap, by which she comes to be identified. Ursula, in fact, speaks of Win as if she were a doll in the making: under-staffed with prostitutes, Ursula determines to "work the velvet woman" (4.5.18–19). And Win's velvet takes on a life of its own as a lure for prospective customers. Punk Alice vents the rage of the regular prosti-tutes toward the "tuft taffeta haunches" of this upper-crust threat to their business: "The poor common whores can ha' no traffic for the privy rich ones; your caps and hoods of velvet call away our customers and lick the fat from us" (67–70). By a curious logic, the second skin of Win's attire *eats away* another woman's flesh. Alice's tirade echoes Ursula's concern about melting down to a rib, but Alice adds a cannibalistic agent, the well-dressed whore feeding off her sister's fat.

Whoredom, like the transvestite theater, equates women with their clothing, offering males the invitation to "enter in at Urs'la's and take part of a silken gown, a velvet petticoat, or a wrought smock" (4.6.18–20). The parallel between Ursula's booth and the enclosure of costume could not be more blatant – each, in its turn, provides entrance. And where *is* the body beneath the gown, the petticoat, and the smock? Word order here deserves note: syntactically, the prospective customer is invited to penetrate, in the proper sequence, each layer of a woman's attire . . . and then . . . ?

Again, the hollow woman of theater gives rise to two antithetical feminist readings which I would label "pessimistic" and "optimistic," respectively. As an isolated statement about the value of real women, the empty petticoat is a grim specter indeed. However, placed in the context of the play's circular economy, the cloth signifies in excess of its surface. I see, in this image, not so much the negation of a body as the mystification of its outer shell. How do these boundaries of cloth accrue such power? I am reminded of a puzzling moment in act 4, when a challenge passes from one man to another by way of a circle drawn on the ground. The drunken games in front of Ursula's booth break into a brawl when one rogue "break[s] circle" (4.4.136) or, to apply a more familiar idiom, "crosses the line" with another. On the one hand, the moment can be seen as exposing the arbitrary nature of social boundaries, including those which cordon off the female body. But on the other hand, the chaos which results from this territorial transgression attests to the *pregnancy* of such delineations.

And let us not forget the circular frame of the theater itself, a symbol so potent it lends itself to comparison with the conjuror's magic circle. The Prologue to Shakespeare's *Henry V* relates the signifying power of theater to the mystical properties of math and necromancy:

> Pardon, gentles all,
> The flat unraisèd spirits that hath dared
> On this unworthy scaffold to bring forth
> So great an object. Can this cock-pit hold
> The vasty fields of France? Or may we cram
> Within this wooden O the very casques
> That did affright the air at Agincourt? (8–14)

The Prologue apologizes for the limits of the "wooden O" of theater, punningly disparaging the players as dull "unraisèd spirits" in contrast to the "great" ones they would conjure, or "bring forth" within the circle. But in the next two lines the diminutive "O" becomes the mighty zero, that "crookèd figure [which] may / Attest in little place a million" (15–16). This is the mathematical translation of that puzzling concept, the "womb of enormity." I will return at the end of this book to the conjuring trope as it pertains specifically to the erotic in theater, but it is crucial that we note here the infinite creativity linked to the "female" space occupied by the stage. The vaginal "pit" or "O" of theater becomes the site of boundless production.

The sequence of concentric enclosures belched forth by Jonson's text is no less hermeneutically pregnant than the delineations of the stage itself, in this age before footlights. In fact, it appears that the problem of the transvestite costume which this chapter has been trying to unravel might best be figured along these circular lines. We might, therefore, take the actor's costume as a vessel itself, analogous to Ursula's tent, that Pandora's "pig-box" of signification. After all, the riddle of the body beneath arises from the indeterminate relationship between surface and interior and the possibility that *there is more than one layer of disguise*. As Stallybrass points out, when the "disguised" romantic heroine sheds "her" masculine wig, we have no way of knowing that the long locks released from beneath are not also a wig[45] – perhaps the same worn, in another production, by Gloriana's skull.

But there is another possibility than that of multiple layers, or of a woman's body or a boy's body beneath any number of layers: what if there is *nothing* underneath the disguise? Levine explores this possibility as it relates to the scene in which Busy, absurdly, lectures to the puppets against cross-dressing. A puppet replies that this "old stale argument against the players . . . will not hold against the puppets" who "have neither male nor female amongst us" – and he lifts up his garment to prove it (5.5.90–99). The "nothing" under the costume of the puppet represents, in Levine's analysis, the worst fears of the antitheatricalists: the empty costume bodies forth (for lack of a better idiom) transvestism's hollowing effect upon gender, its emptying out of referentiality. "In the world the puppet presents to Busy, there is no such relationship between sign and thing because there is no 'thing' under the sign, no genital under the costume . . . [The puppet] forecloses the very possibility of meaning and therefore of knowledge itself."[46]

But what is the relationship of this sexless vessel to the sexual *plenum* of the fictional Ursula's body? Does Ursula, as all-woman, as a figure for pure carnality, merely project outward, in layers of fat, the surface of the hollow puppet? Or does her boundless sexuality "fill in" that troubling void under the garment? Or does it depend, once again, upon one's point of view? Levine views Ursula as an anti-erotic figure, embodying, with her "mountainous fat," the play's "sterile sexuality"; I, however, am suspicious of this judgment, which smacks of a distinctly twentieth-century aversion to a female body-type celebrated by Renaissance artists such as Rubens. And as this entire analysis has shown, the imagery surrounding Ursula, read *in bono* in the garden-pot or *in malo* in the chamber-pot, is anything but "sterile." (Levine even cites the "pot" as evidence of this sterility – a startling moment of illogic in an otherwise brilliant analysis, attesting to the strength of our own cultural biases.[47]) A more empathetic approach is offered by Grace Tiffany, who points up parallels between Jonson's Ursula and Shakespeare's Falstaff, as well as making the case for Jonson's own identification with his chubby champion of appetite:

Ursula's imaginative conversion of fatness to virtue should remind us of the several Jonson poems and epigrams in which the poet defensively celebrates his own inordinate bulk. Jonson consistently employs images of physical weightiness as symbols of goodness, wisdom and creativity . . . The frequency of flesh and food metaphors in Jonson suggests the degree to which "fatness" was crucial to the playwright's self-image.[48]

I am reminded of another fat poet with whom Jonson, like any other educated Englishman, would have been familiar: Geoffrey Chaucer, who never penned a "mean" fat character, whose hallmark is his celebration of "God's plenty,"[49] and who represents himself in the fictional world of *The Canterbury Tales* as "a popet in arm t'enbrace" – as a huggable "poppet," a doll.[50] Today, we'd call him a teddy-bear.

So we are back to toys again – puppets, dolls. According to Scott Cutler Shershow, early modern culture associated the puppet with "threatening social types" including "the effeminate social climber," the player, and "the 'painted' woman"[51] – an attitude evident in the deadly puppet made of Gloriana. But we also should take into account the religious origins of European puppetry: the word "marionette," in fact, means "little Mary," from the early Christmas plays that first used puppets.[52] This curious fact strengthens the parallel between Ursula and the puppet; after all, Mary is the divine answer to Eve – the womb of *God's* enormity. Not hollow, but hallowed (if there is a difference).

But all of these, so to speak, "serious" readings of the puppet run the risk of obscuring one simple and important fact. This is *play*. And I mean that in more than the theatrical sense – as a verb as much as a noun. Hence my somewhat unscholarly delight in the play's biologized bottles, and my insistence that we look at the puppets primarily as toys. And Ursula? She may be the biggest toy of all, the mother of all toys. And this, paradoxically, is what makes her capable of life. In short, she is what you make of her.

At the risk of sounding naive, I would point out that what we are talking about when we discuss theatricality is imagination. In this chapter, I have compared the text's metaphorical mirror-tricks to the *abyme* of deconstructionist critical theory: the comparison likewise helps explain the conflicting responses to Ursula's booth and everything it represents. We may look into the abyss and see either a hell of ungrounded reference or an Elysium of textual abundance – it all depends upon your attitude toward the *play* of signification. The same is true of our attitude toward players and puppets at Jonson's Fair. Levine uses the puppet to demonstrate the way that "again and again, Jonson arouses, only to frustrate, the expectation that he will define an alternative to theatre."[53] I feel there is no need for him to do so, playing, as he does, to (or with) an audience who loves the illusion. Still, one must be cautious not to over-emphasize the "nothing" under the puppet's costume, as Jonson has made the distinction between the "Puppets" and the other "Persons of the Play" quite clear. That the latter *do* have bodies beneath their costumes – bodies that "long," that leak, that lust – has been loudly proclaimed since act 1, and loudest of all in act 5, when Mistress Overdo wakes from her drunken swoon, calls for a basin, and then vomits. Moreover, there is reason to believe that Jonson *himself* may have been the "body beneath" a central character, Ursula. And the play culminates in a series of unmaskings, punctuated by Quarlous' announcing himself "mad but from the gown outward" (5.6.64–65), thereby positing an essence beneath the gown.

I believe Jonson does, in the end, present an alternative to theater: the feast. Quarlous invites everyone to supper at Overdo's house, urging him to "drown the memory of all enormity in your bigg'st bowl at home" (100–1). And the last lines of the play can be read as including the audience in the revelry: "Bring the actors along, we'll ha' the rest of the play at home" (113–14). The "wooden O" encompassing the stage thus expands like a ring of smoke, and the word "play" comes to mean something larger than theater, not a "thing" but an activity, its compass a state of mind.

One Christmas, as a child, I received a hand-painted wooden doll from Russia. Amidst the litter of green and gold paper and the thrill of opening and discovering, my eager fingers soon detected the groove in the doll's belly which allowed me to open it and find another surprise, another doll, inside. Much to my amazement, I learned that even this smaller doll carried another in its belly, and so on, down to a minuscule, featureless pea at the center.

I cite this anecdote because it came to mind while reflecting upon Stallybrass' essay, in particular when he points out the potential layering of wigs, of disguises, upon the body of the boy actor. I think that audience engagement in these theatrical unmaskings (and perhaps, on some level, in theater generally) bears a resemblance to the child's excitement at the prospect of a multiplicity of surprises, one enfolded inside the other. The mystery at the center is less important than the process of discovery. Had I found a pearl at the core of the Russian dolls, rather than a particle of dry matter, I don't think I could have been more delighted by the gift.

On the other hand, though, this doll, like many of its kind, was a "female" – an aproned matron in a babushka. And the logic of the nesting dolls does seem to require a female vessel. It's harder to imagine a male body *doing* this.

Maus demonstrates that male Renaissance poets sometimes analogized their own creative powers in terms of female fertility, comparing "the issue of the brain" and "the issue of the womb," thus troping for themselves a safe enclosure, an interiority within which creation can happen.[54] And, as this chapter highlights, the stage seems a uniquely appropriate place for the playing out of this metaphor. Yet the womb-image is also, so to speak, slippery in all the ways that Ursula is: all-nourishing and all-devouring, containing all and nothing. Divine and monstrous at once, the phallocentric figuration woman/womb holds forth the promise of nurture, of protection, but also the threat of imprisonment; the promise of birth, and the threat of annihilation. Maus explains the double-edged nature of the enclosure trope: "The unread-ability that seems so attractive in oneself seems sinister in others; one man's privacy is another woman's unreliability."[55] It all depends upon who's inside and who's out.

What defines entrance is the space entered; what defines space is its demarcation. Stallybrass deliberately shrugs off the question of essence, of interiority, refusing to define a body – any body – beneath the costume, for what matters in theater is the question itself. "It is as if the eroticism comes not from the body 'beneath,' but rather from the shifting, clothed surfaces."[56] I highlight, here, the critic's placement of the preposition in quotation marks. Similarly, Tennenhouse contends that in early modern theater "meaning . . . resided in surface rather than depth," thus abolishing the notion of a body beneath or beyond the spectacle.[57] Although I agree with these critics in their approach toward clothing as constitutive of identity, I resist the flattening effect of the insistence upon "surface": theater is, after all, a three-dimensional medium. And one of the foremost elements of the vivid cultural moment we call the Renaissance is, let us not forget, the flowering of the visual arts, and in particular, of sculpture. Sawday explains that "for the artists of the period, certainly, the discovery of interior space was as important as the ability to render surfaces into convincing registers of depth. Failure to understand the disposition of the body's interior, they argued, would render all attempts at depicting its exterior futile. Conversely, the surface should suggest an interior."[58] If the viewer of a painting or sculpture was expected to respond to the evocation of depth, it seems likely enough that a play-goer, watching breathing bodies in real space, would do the same. Perhaps, then, there is a place in this discussion for the prepositions attached to theatrical bodies. For the antitheatricalists clearly saw something *in* the transvestite disguise that they didn't like; they saw a male body – or rather, they saw what *should be* a male body, but wasn't *quite*. They saw, in short, their own confusion, embodied.

The problem is that all theatrical bodies are, in a sense, imaginary, are, in a sense, offstage. And on the early modern stage, where nudity was taboo, the "real" flesh of the actor was less visible and therefore less likely to distract viewers from the fantasy. Let us not forget that all of the bodily processes and actions which constitute the carnivalesque in these plays *were performed* – the imbibing and the vomiting, certainly – and that, come to think of it, most of these processes are not particular to women at all (men eat, drink, sweat, leak), despite their gendered associations. Even Win's pregnancy cannot be counted an exception, as this may be, like her symptoms, pure fiction. And it is also significant that the cue to "play the hypocrite" (1.5.148) and stage these supposedly natural female frailties came from her husband, who, as Paster notes, thereby displaces his own appetites onto her, exposing the hypocrisy of all such masculinist stereotypes.[59]

And anyway, the same questions we have posed about the theatrical body beneath, we may ask of the "real," gendered bodies beneath the male and female costumes we wear each day. On the one hand, the puzzle of Win's potential pregnancy can furnish yet another peg in our own games with metatheater; it might even serve as a reminder that the body beneath the costume can *only* play pregnant. But on the other hand, we all know that pregnancies can be quite mysterious to the "real women" who have them, and in the theater of life a woman may find herself pondering a (tiny) body beneath (or not) her own bodily garment. Judith Butler, among other post-structuralist theorists, "considers the very notion of 'the body,' not as a ready surface awaiting signification, but as a set of *boundaries*, individual and social, politically signified and maintained. No longer believable as an interior 'truth' of dispositions and identity, sex will be shown to be a performatively enacted signification (*and hence not 'to be'*)."[60] Although I have some problems with the most extreme application of Butler's theory (I will address these issues later in the book), this understanding of the body can help us out of the theoretical dead-end of an over-emphasis upon "indeterminacy." The body, according to Butler, is – if it "is" anything – its boundaries. Between "beneath" and "beyond." Its essence arises in those exchanges which define its space – socially, sexually, chemically. In other words, the body is what it does, and this is not to offer as essence the "nothing" beneath the puppet's garment, but rather the plenty of the Rabelaisian feast. And I certainly would not be the first to say that the body is only fully realized in moments of contact, verbal or physical, in moments of exchange: eating, pissing, giving birth. So, if the body "is" its boundaries, then the theatrical body is its costume, or costum*ing*. The female body need not be present onstage to be everywhere, to be nowhere. Simply draw a circle and look inside.

4   (Off)Staging the sacred

Our search for an erotic body "beneath" the costume has only deflected us farther offstage, in pursuit of that fleeing signifier, the "beyond" of Ursula's fleshly infinitude. But this expansive corporeality is closely tied to the carnivalesque and the comic. Tragedy offers a different "beyond" for (or through) the erotic body, a beyond which perhaps affords dramatist and playgoer (if not feminist critic) a more clear-cut resolution to the problem of flesh versus spirit: death.

Why take up death in this search for female bodies? Aside from the very basic fact, touched upon in chapter 2's discussion of *Romeo and Juliet*, that death looms as a romantic heroine's alternative "consummation," and aside from the tired tropes linking wombs and tombs, beds and graves, the spatial theology of theater calls attention to death as an *exit*. One of the theatrical and editorial problems posed by death in Renaissance plays is that it requires a literal exit: how do you get the actor's "dead" body offstage? In modern theaters you can close the curtains or dim the lights; on the Renaissance stage, someone must *exit with the body*.[1] And the actor must convincingly portray his own exit *from* the body.

How far is this exit from those entrances which define the erotic body – or the erotic text? Perhaps not far at all, considering the fact that early modern censorship singled out worldly and otherworldly matters alike. References to "tools" and "pisspots," for instance, were censored from *The Tamer Tamed*,[2] and Desdemona's cry of "O Lord, Lord, Lord!" was excised from Shakespeare's murder scene.[3] And the "Lord" called upon may have been in bodily danger Himself: as Shakespeare penned this scene, the Corpus Christi plays were dying a slow and painful death all across England. Nor can we abandon our quest for absent bodies in theater without considering the body of Christ, legally expelled from the stage by the Protestant reformers of the mid sixteenth century.[4] Not that the body of Christ was ever "really" present in the passion plays – as Catholic doctrine proclaims it present in the Eucharist – but the early genre's fascination with this divine body prefigures the later genre's obsession with the elusive female body; in other words, both bodies stand as objects of erotic desire materially thwarted by the ontology of the stage or of the world's stage.

There is no question that the body of Christ was an erotic object to both worshippers in church and spectators at a passion play – and the reformers' systematic suppression of its theatrical representations only testifies to the erotic power this body continued to hold in their day (evident, for instance, in the devotional poems of John Donne and Aemilia Lanyer). And indeed, the theatrical body of Christ may share more with that of woman than the allure of taboo or the fact of existing, in Derridean terms, "under erasure," ~~crossed out~~. Turning from comedy to tragedy, from the carnivalesque to the macabre, this chapter will analyze two female sexual martyrs, that is to say, women who literally "die for love" – Webster's Duchess of Malfi and the heroine of Middleton's *The Lady's Tragedy* – in order to uncover a medieval basis for the powerful, if morbid, eroticism which surrounds these figures.

What does sex have to do with the sacrificial body, and what role do both play in the social body? Historian Christopher Hill notes the centrality of the Bible in "all intellectual as well as moral life in the sixteenth and seventeenth centuries";[5] Debora Kuller Shuger relates this influence to literary texts specifically, stating that "Renaissance biblical narratives . . . need to be read as *cultural* documents in the broadest sense."[6] Shuger argues, furthermore, that the secularization of society following the Protestant Reformation affected attitudes toward both the spiritual and the erotic, and did so by altering a discourse which encompassed them both: the discourse of sacrifice. For sacrifice and sex (as we now call it) both entail *excess*; both require an overflowing of the boundaries of body and self in the direction of an other – an other who is, if not transcendent, then at least transcendentally desirable.[7] Thus, if the female body, recalling Paster's thesis, is figured in terms of excess or overflow, one can argue that any sacrificial body is feminized by definition. Seen in this way, the bleeding body of Christ bears an uncanny resemblance to the "leaky vessel" of woman – indeed, seems a sister to our "fine oily pig-woman" who, like Christ, *feeds* the faithful on the flesh for which she is named.

Caroline Walker Bynum has demonstrated the way medieval culture associated food with flesh and with woman, and the way this episteme allowed for a feminized Christ, complete with metaphorically lactating breasts/wounds.[8] The ensuing pages will explore the possibility that this figure re-emerged in a later, "female" incarnation, on the early modern English stage. In addition, I hope to address a few unresolved questions about the eroticism of both figures. Although Bynum's most influential work notes the erotic component of female mystical "eating" of Christ, a separate essay, published later, cautions scholars against presuming a modern sense of the "erotic or sexual" in their interpretations of the same iconographical and devotional material.[9] The key, again, may be to distinguish the terms themselves, as Bynum does implicitly, Shuger explicitly; one symptom of secularization examined by the latter is the reduction of eros to (genital) sexuality, a point to which we will return.[10]

This chapter, then, aims for more than a cursory backward glance – or even more than the discovery of surprising parallels between two dramatic modes so often treated as antithetical. Rather, this chapter will explore the paradigmatic shift which occurred between medieval and early modern drama as something which gave rise to our distinctly modern notions of the erotic and the profane. We have briefly touched upon the nexus of sacred and profane when we looked at the puppets in *Bartholomew Fair* and paused over their religious origins. *Hollow* becomes *hallowed* with the help of the unseen God. And the invisibility of the offstage removes both sex and the spirit-world from the purview of the spectator. Theater requires a certain faith: it requires, in fact, more "poetic faith" than poetry itself, for the "willing suspension of disbelief," in theater, should happen *un*willingly.[11] As noted of the medieval world map and the medieval stage which reflected it, heaven and hell were reified in the frame, but moved beyond it (offstage) in the Renaissance.

In short, this analysis which began with the departure from stage propelled by male/female sexual desire can only lead to our scrutiny of a woman's ultimate departure from life.[12] That both entrances into the unseen, on the woman's part, are eroticized by the male authorial pen demonstrates the urgency, the centrality of these moments; that both are subject to censorship, that both require an exit from stage or an "X" over the text, points to their shared space in discourse, their common ground in taboo, their overlapping origin. Above all, though, sex and death similarly tax the limits of representation. Therefore, whether we can *follow* these exits remains to be seen.

I   Blood and alabaster: *The Duchess of Malfi*

From a feminist perspective, puppets such as those in *Bartholomew Fair* disturb us not so much for the "nothing" under their garments, but primarily for the almost invisible something – a system of strings – which subjects them to the control of a puppet-master. As Shakespeare's Kate, Maria's "shrewish" predecessor, complains to Petruccio, "Belike you mean to make a puppet of me" (4.3.103). The difference is that, at this point in the play, Kate moves and acts independently of her would-be master, as a puppet cannot, and even at the end of the play there is hope that, if her strings were cut, she could do so once again. In many plays of the period, however, the heroine is not so lucky; when she resists the control of a male authority figure – when she refuses to be "tied down" or "strung along" – male authority severs the thread of her life.[13] In scenes involving a violent female death, the alternative to the boy actor was the dummy, essentially a puppet without strings.

From act 1, the Duchess of Malfi is conscious of the ornamental object that her brothers would make of her: "This is flesh, and blood, sir, / 'Tis not the figure cut in alabaster / Kneels at my husband's tomb" (1.2.369–71).[14] With these words she offers herself to Antonio. But the distinction between flesh and stone is not precisely what concerns us here: the more crucial and more problematic distinction in this tragedy is that between animate and inanimate *flesh*, between bodies capable of motion and bodies permanently at rest – a tricky question in the darkness of Malfi, and an even trickier question from our seats in a darkened modern auditorium. In my Introduction I cited this text as one of many early modern works which emphasize male specular control of female sexuality: here I intend to expand the question of specularity to include, along with the Duchess' pregnancy, the execution which results from her pregnancy. For death, like the womb, is dark; the soul's exit from the body, like its entrance into the womb, compels speculation (and thus, potentially, titillation) in witnesses in the play and in the audience. And either sex or death may compel – even, arguably, *be compelled by* – art. The Duchess' scorn, in the above quote, for the clichéd metaphors of female chastity introduces a pattern of imagery which culminates, ironically, in her resemblance to those very tropes. That she *is* "flesh and blood," or rather, that she *bleeds* – as a mortal, but even more so as a woman (and, soon, a mother) – is reiterated throughout the play in the invasive and violent rhetoric and abuse precipitated by the very state-ment, "This is flesh, and blood"; finally, facing death, she is likened to the "reverend monument" invoked and defied in act 1. Thus, blood and alabaster – the blood of sexuality and of sacrifice; the stone which marks the passage of the soul – prove to be opposite poles on the same axis of imagery, by which we may follow the Duchess' progress first through the torture resulting from her pregnancy (never mind the torture of preg-nancy itself), and then toward, and beyond, the boundary of death. Through this two-step analysis, I hope we will arrive at an understanding of Webster's play as a kind of proto-feminist passion play – haunted by the dream of resurrection for this female sexual rebel.

Finke describes the process by which the Duchess becomes her own *memento mori* as " 'killing' a woman into art,"[15] citing Webster's play as

one example amidst a large body of male texts – Jacobean tragedy in
particular – which inflict this fate upon their heroines: "A male poet of
the Renaissance could and did acknowledge, and even wallow in, his
fears of mortality by emphasizing death's essential contiguity with the
feminine . . . But much more frequently he attempts to deny mortality
and neutralize the threat posed by woman's carnality by transforming
her . . . through art, into an ideal, eternally changeless because essentially
lifeless."[16] Interestingly, though, Webster's play does depict what seems
to be an alternative to this killing art, and that is an art which breathes
life into death, Pygmalion-style. Very early in the play, shortly before the
Duchess renounces her sepulchral likeness, she herself is associated with
the puppeteer's power to animate a lifeless body. Antonio says,

> She throws upon a man so sweet a look,
> That it were able to raise one to a galliard
> That lay in a dead palsy . . .   (1.2.117–19)

The echoes of Lazarus are both endearingly romantic, on Antonio's part,
and subtly ominous in context. Even the bawdy innuendo in the
Duchess' power to "raise" does not quite counteract the morbid ring of
the phrase "dead palsy"; shortly afterwards, the Duchess makes a similar
gratuitous reference to death: "Make not your heart so dead a piece of
flesh / To fear more than to love me" (367–68). And Antonio's fanciful
commendations in act 1 become increasingly ironic as events in the play
unfold, as a jealous brother manipulates the Duchess into a life of greater
and greater immobility, as he drains her of the very life-force she is seen,
by her beloved, to embody. For underlying Ferdinand's lust for total
control of his sister is a dream of the same godlike power which Antonio
imagines in the social superior who will soon become his wife. As Mary
Beth Rose notes, "The Duchess recognizes her brother's grotesque
misogyny and Antonio's rapturous idealization as equally life-
denying."[17] For the real-life translation of the Pygmalion myth is the
power to take rather than give life, to make immobile what moves and
breathes, since the gift of breath remains a mystery.

And this mystery, this thin-as-air difference between death and life, is
most often embodied in the womb – hence the focus of Ferdinand's
sadistic machinations upon the Duchess' pregnancy and maternity.
Misogyny often manifests itself in a jealous fascination with gestation;
the machines of patriarchy are designed to plumb the secrets of the
womb, to harness its power. Finke views the verbal or physical mutila-
tion of women in Jacobean tragedy as evidence of this "masculine
attempt to control life and death, to thwart or coopt the feminine power
of reproduction."[18] The Pygmalion myth (or, alternatively, the God

myth) thus serves as a male compensatory fantasy – but God help the woman who proves the myth a myth.

Ironically, Antonio's praise of the Duchess is the first myth to go. His idealized vision, his "picture" of her "sweet . . . look" and "divine continence" here constitutes a rhetorical counterpart to the alabaster figure she will repudiate in the very same scene. He speculates that:

> Her days are practis'd in such noble virtue,
> That, sure her nights, nay more, her very sleeps,
> Are more in heaven, than other ladies' shrifts.   (1.2.123–25)

And, as his emphatic "sure" almost guarantees, he is shortly proven wrong, when the "flesh and blood" Duchess takes center stage and her reproductive capacity becomes the play's obsessive focus. That he delights in the revelation of her fleshly appetite should not obscure the threat posed by those men who only suspect its existence, who fear being kept, so to speak, in the dark. Ferdinand, less secure in his knowledge of her nights, taunts her, "Your darkest actions: nay, your privat'st thoughts, / Will come to light" (235–26).

So the Duchess must marry in secret, conceive a child in secret, and plan to give birth in secret. Since control, in a male specular economy, is closely linked with the power to see, to uncover, the very interiority of the womb – itself a metonymy for an even more mysterious appetite – dooms a woman to continual surveillance. Hence any visible signs of pregnancy provide a target for the controlling male gaze; by the same token, any reminder of the hiddenness of procreation may taunt the excluded male voyeur to violence. It is above all the Duchess' effort to conceal her already mysterious pregnancy that seals her fate at the hands of a tyrannical misogyny.

And Bosola seems perfectly chosen for the task of scrutinizing the Duchess. He proves an astute observer of pregnancy's symptoms – "she pukes, her stomach seethes . . . / She wanes i'th'cheek and waxes fat i'th'flank" (2.1.67–69) – even in regard to the father: "Methinks 'tis very cold, and yet you sweat" (2.3.19), he tells Antonio. Symptoms, however, do not constitute irrefutable proof. Upon first detecting the symptoms, Bosola blames the Duchess' farthingale and "loose-bodied gown" for obscuring "The young springal *cutting* a caper in her belly" (2.1.153–55; emphasis added) – his choice of idiom betraying the "cutting" impulse driving his inspections. Nonetheless, such a discovery requires more penetrating tools than the naked eye.

Hence Bosola devises a test. His drugged apricots cause the Duchess to sweat, sicken, and produce the "spring yields" of a premature birth. The joke with which he detains the midwife reveals an intense fascination with these results.: "There was a young waiting-woman had a monstrous desire to see the glass-house . . . And it was only to know what strange instrument it was, should swell up a glass to the fashion of a woman's belly" (2.2.5–10). As I mentioned in the Introduction, including this passage among a number of references to glass as a specular tool, the image of the glass womb is the creation of a mind obsessed with penetrating a woman's "inner" or sexual secrets; Bosola's "desire to see" is, in his own words, "monstrous." The image, as voyeuristic fantasy, vividly enacts the Duke's threat to the Duchess that her "darkest actions . . . Will come to light" under his and Bosola's scrutiny. And in fact, Bosola's pregnancy test aims to achieve this very effect. Because he cannot actually penetrate the Duchess' womb – like the anatomist on the cover of the *Fabrica* - he must administer a purge of its contents. Now the evidence, it seems, is incontrovertible.

Evidence, one might ask, of what? Is the child itself the real focus of Ferdinand's, and by extension Bosola's, fascination? Is the child itself such a threat to the order of things in the play? Patrilineage does not seem to be an issue here. Rather, the child is a threat only insofar as it represents, literally embodies, the forbidden act by which it has been engendered. Upon receiving word of the secret birth, Ferdinand responds in a hysteria reminiscent of Othello's: "Talk to me somewhat, quickly," he tells the Cardinal, "Or my imagination will carry me / To see her in the shameful act of sin" (2.5.39–41). However familiar this sort of prurient fascination, its context and severity should give us pause; in his ranting about his sister's "shameful act," Ferdinand virtually ignores her more recent "act" of giving birth – an act many women in the period died performing.[19] Giving no thought to the presumably dangerous, premature labor the Duchess has just survived, his mind instead races backward to reconstruct the obscure moment of insemination. Act 2 closes with his swearing, "Till I know who leaps my sister, I'll not stir" (2.5.78). Thus, even the birth is not evidence enough. Just as Othello demands "ocular proof," the Cardinal, like a doubting Thomas, asks, "Can this be certain?" (2.5.11–12), and Ferdinand vows to break into the Duchess' bedroom and "force confession from her" (3.1.79). And whereas we might accept at face value Ferdinand's stated goal of determining the father, the word "force" betrays here a rapaciousness that has little to do with facts.

The Duke wants to *get inside* his sister. Not satisfied with the purging of her womb, he now speaks of making her bleed. The text, in fact, is filled with references to her blood,[20] and not merely in its abstract sense of lineage or birth. Ferdinand threatens to "make a sponge" of "her bleeding heart" (2.5.16) and "to purge [her] infected blood" (26); he offers his handkerchief (in a moment recalling, again, *Othello*) with which "to make soft lint for" the Duchess' "wounds" after he has "hewed her to pieces" (30–31). He tells the Cardinal, " 'Tis not your whore's milk, that shall quench my wild-fire / But your whore's blood" (48–49). He speaks of "the witchcraft [that] lies in her rank blood" (3.1.78).[21]

This emphasis upon the blood of the Duchess calls to mind the "leaky vessel" discussed earlier; in fact, Paster includes a separate chapter on the bleeding body in her extensive analysis of the humoral body and its manifold, gendered embarrassments. Yet here Paster's argument makes a surprising – and wholly convincing – turn: the act of bleeding, unlike the ambiguous, characteristically female act of "leaking" discussed else-where, could be marked as either vigorously male, or passively female; moreover, blood, according to humoral theory, came in many forms, male blood being (you guessed it) the purer, and female blood (menstrual or otherwise), the more "excrementitious."[22] This is not to say that male bleeding cannot be viewed as effeminately passive or female bleeding as willful and virile (Paster supplies examples of both[23]), but the distinction itself raises the question: do these references to the Duchess' blood invoke the traditional female involuntary leakage or the more active, voluntary bleeding of Christ?

Curiously, though, we witness only *rhetorical* bleeding on the part of the Duchess, and this sharply distinguishes her from the men in the play – especially Antonio, who suffers a highly effeminizing nose-bleed at the very moment his wife gives birth offstage (2.3.42). And Paster's humoral paradigm brings further re-genderings to light. Behind Ferdinand's obsession with his sister's blood lies the conviction that her blood is in fact his: "Damn her! that body of hers, / While that my blood ran pure in't, was more worth / Than that which thou would'st comfort, call'd a soul" (4.1.119–21). It was common in the period to speak of the body as a vessel for the soul, but here even the soul (which only God can claim) is devalued in favor of the brother's patriarchal stake in his sister's blood. According to this anatomy lesson, the Duchess owns only her exterior shell; the "flesh and blood" by which she proudly defines herself is emptied – drained, for the sake of *quenching*, as he himself puts it, the Duke's passion. And this verb is no accident; the Duchess' last words recognize her brothers' bloodthirst: " . . . When I am laid out, / They then may feed in quiet" (4.2.232–33).

Like the references to bleeding, this "feeding" gives rise to not only sexual but, even more so, Eucharistic associations. Ferdinand's fantasy about the "whore's milk" and "whore's blood" calls attention to the nutritive powers of her (maternal) body; medieval and early modern physiology in fact considered breast milk a purified form of menstrual blood.[24] I am reminded of Bynum's work with iconography, in particular those images which counterpoise Christ's wound and the Virgin Mary's breast.[25] And there are Renaissance examples as well: Shuger points out the "particular stress on bodily fluids" which characterizes Calvinist passion narratives.[26] When Ferdinand asks for a "cupping-glass" with which to "purge" her "blood" (2.5.26), I can see him licking his lips, curling his fingers around an invisible "cup." Is the Duchess a female Christ? Certainly, she more closely resembles the sacrificial lamb than the "excellent hyena" (2.5.39) her brother sees in her: not devourer, but devoured. Antonio echoes and inverts the hyena trope when he boasts of his wife's child-bearing skills, declaring her an "excellent / Feeder of pedigrees" (3.1.5–6); this is a more benign caricature, clearly, but it does leave ambiguous the precise manner in which these canine offspring are fed (*on* her, or from her hand?). Ferdinand himself would "Have her meat served up by bawds and ruffians" (4.1.123); likewise, she explains, "many hungry guests have fed upon me" (4.2.198).

Of course, these tropes – part of a larger pattern of bestial imagery not immediately pertinent here – do not in themselves constitute the Duchess' deification, and one might argue that they say more about the predatory nature of the heroine's environment than they say about the Duchess herself. But Webster frames the Duchess' victimization in language that – paradoxically – increases her stature. Ferdinand himself grants the Duchess a certain divine status: "I do think / It is some sin in us, Heaven doth revenge / By her" (2.5.65–7). She makes numerous references to Heaven, to the sacraments, and to prayer. And as her persecution continues and her death draws near, we can hardly ignore the parallels to Christ. "Go," she cries, "howl them this: and say I *long to bleed*" (4.1.108; emphasis mine). Surely, this is a willed sacrifice. In the next scene, when she meets her executioners, she, like Jesus, forgives them.

As was true of Jesus, the Duchess' death approaches slowly, heralded by signs. From the alabaster figure she mentions in act 1, through the wax effigies of her husband and children which she takes to be their corpses, the action of the play progresses against an iconography of death. And although one may find Bosola unpalatable as a mouthpiece for the play's ruling philosophy, nonetheless, it is he who articulates the logic underlying the text's progressively macabre images.

> Though we are eaten up of lice, and worms,
> And though continually we bear about us
> A rotten and dead body, we delight
> To hide it in rich tissue . . .   (2.1.58–61)

Bodies, thus, are dead while still living; that we cover them in "rich tissue," in layers of fabric or of fat, does not fool the likes of Bosola. Indeed, the Duchess can be said to have carried her own dead body through the course of the play – haunted, as she is, by her own tomb effigy, and by other foreshadowings of her death. Moreover, as Bosola speaks these lines in act 2, he already suspects that she bears, in fact, literally *hides* in her womb the child whose birth will condemn her to death.

And at times, especially toward the end of the play, the division between the living and the dead grows thin. When the Duchess receives her parting kiss from Antonio, she remarks, "Your kiss is colder / Than I have seen a holy anchorite / Give to a dead man's skull" (3.5.85–87). An entire two acts before Antonio will die, the Duchess senses in his touch the coldness of death, while her own perhaps sardonic analogy casts her as a death's head – as though she saw in herself the walking *memento mori* that her brothers would make of her. The scene directly anticipates the moment when Ferdinand makes her kiss a dead man's hand, first passing it off as his own living hand, and then as the severed hand of her dead husband, who in truth still possesses his hands and his life. Just before she is strangled she asks Cariola, "Who do I look like now?" and is answered with comparisons to her "picture in the gallery" and to "some reverend monument / Whose ruins are even pitied" (4.2.31–35). Similarly, the Duchess tells Antonio from her grave: "*Thou art a dead thing*" (5.4.38) – already.

Ferdinand's visit to the Duchess is worth a closer look, as it marks the point in the play where death makes its entrance as a palpable, though invisible, presence. Ferdinand visits the Duchess in darkness, having her believe he has vowed not to see her. It is the first time he openly demonstrates ambivalence toward the sight of her, but his insistence on darkness now suggests, retrospectively, that he initially hired Bosola to "observe" his sister because he feared implicating himself in his own voyeuristic fantasies ("Talk to me somewhat, quickly, / Or my imagination will carry me"). Also, the Duchess has been associated with light ever since Antonio's commendations ("She stains the past: lights the time to come" [1.2.131]), and this light must indeed be great, for Ferdinand has spoken of placing her in "eclipse" (2.5.80). There is even a hint of religious awe in Ferdinand's kissing her hand in the dark, as Bosola describes it: "He *dares not* see you" (4.1.28; emphasis added). Upon entering, the Duke remarks that "this darkness suits [her] well" (30) for she had been "too much i'th'light" (42); and though he alludes, here, to the public eye, not his own, we note that he hurries away the moment she does call for lights. What is he afraid to see?

Perhaps what he fears looking in the face is his own incestuous lust. The darkness in which Ferdinand visits his sister allows him to present her the dead hand, which, if read as a sexual symbol,[27] makes the exchange a kind of morbid bed-trick. The Duchess, however, is not completely fooled: "You are very cold," she notes, "I fear you are not well," and, immediately discerning what it is that she holds, she cries, "Ha! Lights: Oh horrible!" (51–53). Interestingly, the lights reveal only the horror, not the hand's lifelessness, which touch alone communicated. And indeed, in this world where living bodies resemble dead ones and where dying bodies revive at the gates of death, vision alone cannot be trusted to detect the threads which connect us to life. In the light that reveals the severed human hand, the Duchess mistakes a wax counterfeit for her husband's corpse; she cries, "bind me to that lifeless trunk, / And let me freeze to death" (68–69).

Once imagined giving life to the dead, the Duchess now longs for a fatal embrace. For good reason, though, she does not trust her remains in the hands of her brother, who seems a strong enough candidate for necrophilia. Thus she makes her last request: "Dispose my breath how please you, but my body / Bestow upon my women, will you?" (4.2.224–25). The Duchess' statement once again posits a division between the material body and the invisible force which animates it: the manner of her death, strangling, not only literalizes her injunction "Dispose my breath," but allows her soul to exit, so to speak, under cover and on tiptoe. Ferdinand leaves his sister in darkness, believing (as the audience believes) her dead by his own order. He then returns to her cell, to view what appears to be her corpse, and, whether in horror, guilt, or superstition, he "dares not" look upon her long; "Cover her face. Mine eyes dazzle," he declares, "she di'd young" (259). A few lines later he changes his mind, asking to "see her face again" (266); he goes on to rail at Bosola, "Get thee into some unknown part o'th'world / That I may never see thee" (320–21); as he slinks off, he speaks of this "deed of darkness" (329). Yet at this point, the deed – or the death – is not quite complete. The Duchess revives before the guilt-stricken Bosola, in a culminating moment of life/death liminality.

> She stirs; here's life.
> Return, fair soul, from darkness, and lead mine
> Out of this sensible hell. She's warm, she breathes:
> Upon thy pale lips I will melt my heart
> To store them with fresh colour.   (4.2.335–39)

Again, the difference between the dead and the living appears as insubstantial as breath, and this momentary revival, like Desdemona's, only fools us into longing for miracles. Bosola, in a moment of uncharacteristic passion, dreams that his kiss has the resuscitating power that Antonio first imagined in the Duchess' look (and that he will later, as he dies, imagine in her name). The "fresh colour" he would apply to her lips also evokes Pygmalion's doting paintbrush. But Bosola's wish, of course, is in vain. With a sigh of "mercy" – either in prayer or in blessing – the Duchess finally dies.

And how is it that, even in death, the Duchess "dazzles"? Her philosophy of death is worth quoting here:

> I know death hath ten thousand several doors
> For men to take their *Exits*: and 'tis found
> They go on such strange geometrical hinges,
> You may open them both ways.   (4.2.215–18)

I do not agree with the standard reading of these lines as referring to suicide;[28] given the play's relentless whittling down of the wall between the living and the dead, the image of the double hinges seems to promise intercession from the afterworld. And the Duchess' revival some hundred lines later in the same scene, not to mention her speaking from her crypt in act 5, only reinforces our sense that she is somehow greater than the death her brothers have inflicted upon her. In at least one recent production, the "dead" Duchess returned to stand onstage through the final act, a spectral presence in a "diaphanous gown," silently meting out justice.[29] This interpretation only literalizes and expands the moment when Antonio, walking by her grave, sees her face in "a clear light" and is inspired to leave his exile and defy her persecutors, "For to live thus, is not indeed to live: / It is a mockery, and abuse of life" (5.3.46–47). In just this spirit, we recall, the Duchess defied the "mockery . . . of life" embodied in an alabaster wife.

Looking back over the play, one cannot help but feel that these images of death – these verbal or material props – have played as much a role on stage as the real actors; and this seems curiously appropriate, considering the fact that living bodies, in the play, "play dead." But if, indeed, "to live" in Malfi "is not . . . to live," nonetheless, to die in theater is not to die. The same is true, as we have noted, of making love, being pregnant, giving birth. The presence of the living actress onstage in act 5, in the recent production mentioned above, may appear to undermine the fiction of death, but no more so than the modern curtain call or the early modern jig – that moment of release and relief we all long for, particularly after a tragedy.

The Duchess herself enjoys a comparable moment of relief, when she learns that she has been deceived by the wax effigies, that her children and husband still live. In fact, we can expand this analogy: the response of the audience viewing the heroine's death resembles her own response to the artificial corpses. The language in which she describes the experience further foregrounds the magic of representation: the sight disturbs her more than her "picture, fashion'd out of wax, / Stuck with a magical needle, and then buried / In some foul dunghill" (4.1.63–65). Outside the witchcraft to which the Duchess alludes, how does a doll – a "poppet," as the witch's wax image was called – acquire the power to cause harm to a living body? May we not apply the question to the women figures presented (often to be abused) on the all-male early modern stage? What does the Duchess' suffering mean to the audience – to the women in the audience?

The Duchess' metaphor might perhaps hint at some awareness, on her part, that the figures she views are "only" wax, but, more importantly, it surprises us (in our more skeptical era) because it compares the spectacle of a real death with a superstitiously prefigured death. Yet the events of the play disprove such skepticism, for, as David M. Bergeron has pointed out, the wax figures in fact prophesy the deaths to which they refer,[30] according to the logic of the witch's wax doll and needle. And after all, a director might opt to use the same dummies for both the "false" and the "real" corpses of the children, shown strangled in the very next scene. An image proves as good as the real thing; some people *still* consider it bad luck to break a mirror.

Or we can reverse the equation. As the Duchess approaches her death, she resembles more and more closely the marble woman defied in act 1: Bosola's desire to paint her lips with "fresh colour" highlights her *waxen* appearance. And in fact we don't know for sure whether wax figures were used in performance: it would be easier (and cheaper) to have the living actors play dead.[31] And as to which is scarier – a "lifelike" dead thing or a corpselike living thing – it hardly seems worth arguing. But there's one even scarier thought: that of *not knowing which* we are seeing. Either way, this is a frightening play for a woman to watch.

What are the threads which connect image to referent? How are these mock-deaths joined to our lives? In medieval theater, the death of Christ communicated salvation through its mere enactment: *imitatio Christi* was, after all, a performance, and I have contended here that the Duchess does in some respects imitate Christ. But despite the religious allusions in Webster's play, despite its supernaturalism and its collapsing of death into life, and aside from the odd production which might interpolate an onstage ghost, there is, for the Duchess, no resurrection, no re-entrance through the double-hinged door. There is no encore. Kent

Cartwright analyzes audience engagement in moments of onstage death: "Playgoers require, at some level, that Juliet die" – but they also long, in vain, to call her back.[32] Bosola's desperate kiss – arguably the most intensely erotic moment of the play (her response of "Antonio!" may mean she mistakes him for her husband[33]) – seems to channel spectatorial anguish toward the lips we imagine breathing their last. But this exit we cannot follow.

II   Sex and the crucifix: *The Lady's Tragedy*

Imitatio Christi was a performance, and the actor who played Christ in the medieval passion plays was expected, even required, to endure real physical pain; at least one player on record nearly lost his life in the act.[34] The stage directions can be startling; for instance, when Christ is *"betyn . . . til he is all blody."* [35] And even aside from the rigors of this particular performance, the performance of any death can test an actor's physical powers, whether that means collapsing believably without hurting oneself in the process, or simply holding still for an unnaturally long period of time; "no performer can create full verisimilitude."[36] And the death of any major character inevitably constitutes a dramatic climax: attention is fixed upon the body of the actor as in no other situation.

Perhaps it is this intensity of the spectatorial gaze that lends any performance of death a potential erotic charge. But this is particularly true, in early modern drama, of the death of the female lead – a death which, more often than not, is connected in some way with her sexuality, either resulting from an offstage sexual encounter (real or rumored), or from her resistance to such an encounter. The Duchess of Malfi, Desdemona, Bianca, Beatrice-Joanna, Juliet, Evadne . . . we can even include the "fake" deaths of Hero and Hermione, designed to redeem their slandered honor – not to mention the farcical last rites of the courtesan in *A Mad World, My Masters*. Despite all the ink spilled over the sex/death linkage in Renaissance poetry, and despite the habitual editorial nod toward the "dying" euphemism for orgasm, the centrality of death in so many female roles, and the spectatorial titillation it tends to foster, have yet to be fully explained.

One is tempted to account for this phenomenon by generalizing about the thanatotic obsession in western art, or more specifically in western drama. Through the tragic/comic distinction, death defines one of the two major categories of dramatic texts – or, arguably, death constitutes both categories either by its presence or its absence. (I've never heard one play-goer warn another, "Be prepared. It's a comedy: everyone *lives* at the end!") The role of death in a play determines its genre, and in titles the term "tragedy" often precedes the name of the main character. In other words, the first thing we know about a tragic heroine or hero is that she or he will die during the course of the play. Thus, even before the Prologue, we anticipate the climax.

The title of *The Lady's Tragedy* has been almost as disputed as its authorship,[37] but word order in this permutation of the standard formula emphasizes the heroine's possession of her tragedy, her possession, in a certain sense, of her death. Yet perhaps the syntax of this title obscures the degree to which *her death possesses her*. The Lady, like the Duchess, is the vehicle of her death. In the words of Webster's Cardinal, "Wisdom begins at the end" (1.2.247), and this motto aptly summarizes the eschatology of the tragic art. Interestingly, though, the Lady's "end" happens in the middle of her story: she dies in act 3 (earlier even than the Duchess, who dies in act 4). At the heart of the play, a heart stops beating; the action of the play surrounds a tomb.

Similarly, Christ's death defines his story – if only insofar as it allows for his resurrection. And his "passion," over the centuries, has defined the word "passion" (a point to which I will return).[38] Anne Lancashire points out that *The Lady's Tragedy* is heavily influenced by medieval Christian sources such as saints' lives and passion plays; she compares, for instance, the visit to the Lady's tomb in act 4 with the biblical visit to the tomb of the resurrected Christ, and compares the Tyrant's four soldiers to the four soldiers of the passion play.[39] Middleton's free use of these materials demonstrates Shuger's theory about the pervasiveness of biblical discourse, but it also demonstrates, more subtly, the longevity of a distinctly *medieval* brand of biblically inspired discourse. We shall soon see how these medieval ghosts came to foil Middleton's seemingly Calvinistic intents.

The Lady, like the Duchess, is a powerful figure. The Lady enters in act 1 as the immovable and immutable center of her world; her first words in the play are, "I am not to be altered" (1.1.123). Her rejection of the Tyrant's love symbolically removes his usurped crown, and her fidelity to the true king compensates for his lost kingdom.

> TYRANT.   There's the kingdom
> Within yon valley fixed, while I stand here
> Kissing false hopes upon a frozen mountain,
> Without the confines. I am he that's banished;
> The king walks yonder, chose by her affection,
> Which is the surer side, for where she goes
> Her eye removes the court.   (1.1.142–48)

As in Antonio's commendations of the Duchess, a woman is associated with powers bordering on supernatural. When she exits, "the day e'en darkens at her absence" (212).

The Lady has the power, it seems, to make or unmake kings: "the king" is whoever is "chose by her affection" – a statement which, considering the doctrine of divine right, nearly deifies her. And the theme of choice presents another parallel to the Duchess. The trials of both heroines begin with a sexual choice. Although Lancashire cites the classical story of Virginia as another possible source for Middleton's play,[40] the Lady dies in order to preserve not her virginity but rather her sexual fidelity to Govianus, and for all we know she is not a virgin when the play begins (certainly, she is never called a virgin or a "maiden" in this text). Less openly sexual, perhaps, than Webster's Duchess, the Lady nonetheless defiantly kisses her love before a disapproving father and otherwise makes no secret of the fact that her love of Govianus is physical. And the extremity of the Tyrant's desire endows her with a kind of sexual aura which her fierceness of heart only amplifies. The Lady is sexual enough that the Tyrant hopes to win her desire; rape is not in his plans.[41] Also, the play's structure encourages the doubling of her role with that of the sub-plot's sensual Wife,[42] thus subliminally enhancing her erotic appeal.

Strangely enough, the play is also rife with bawdy. Perhaps it is the Christian homiletic background of the play which renders the sexual innuendo, at times, uncomfortable for modern readers. Indeed, the Lady's death-scene entails a curious combination of martyrological echoes and phallic punning. Surrounded by the Tyrant's soldiers, the Lady begs her lover to kill her for honor's sake: "My lord, be as sudden as you please, sir. / I am ready to your hand." Govianus holds his faltering blade, and laments, "'Tis the hard'st work that ever man was put to. / I know not which way to begin to come to't" (3.120–23). She encourages him, " . . . Dying thine, / Thou dost enjoy me still" (145–46). He faints in the attempt to kill her, in the second of three false deaths – oddly, all male – in the play. While he lies senseless, the Lady picks up his sword and kills herself. Govianus then wakes and describes his failure to kill her in terms that suggest a sexual failure:

> O, 'tis done,
> And never was beholding to my hand.
> Was I so hard to thee? . . .
>   Why, it was more
> Than I was able to perform myself
> With all the courage that I could take to me.
> It tired me; I was fain to fall, and rest.   (168–74)

The act of falling can connote either sexual (phallic) failure or moral failure. Here it may also allude to Christ's falling under the weight of the cross. Govianus falls, more or less, under the weight of his sword (and on the stage a large weapon with a pronounced hilt could effectively point up the parallel to the cross), which the Lady then succeeds in wielding against herself. We are reminded of the symbolic paradox of the crucifixion, by which Jesus falls in order to rise, and even in the process of falling is raised on the cross, pointed heavenward by the very hands that would put him in the earth.

Following the scene of the Lady's death, the action and imagery of the play moves earthward, into the tomb. At the end of act 3, Govianus laments over his beloved's body:

> The whole world
> Yields not a jewel like her; ransack rocks
> And caves beneath the deep. O thou fair spring
> Of honest and religious desires,
> Fountain of weeping honour, I will kiss thee
> After death's marble lip. Thou'rt cold enough
> To lie entombed now by my father's side.   (3.246–52)

Even before descending to the crypt with the body, Govianus' language evokes the cold, subterranean space – parallel to the Duchess' prison – where events of the play reach their climax. At the same time, though, the metaphors of spring and fountain counter this downward motion with the suggestion of revival or ascension, a motion parodied in the bawdy punning about "taking up" the Lady's body, which we will see in a later scene. This dialectic of vertical forces – gravity versus animation – encapsulates the paradoxical nature of the resurrection story; also, the phrase "by my father's side" (a gratuitous reference to an otherwise absent figure) further adds to the Christian resonances. The water symbolism is also inescapably Christian, and although Lancashire glosses the "weeping honour" as a reference to the Lady's bleeding wound (situated perhaps, like Jesus' wound, in the breast), this image, together with the "marble lip" which prematurely invokes her tomb, also anticipates the imagery of the tomb sequence, where the Tyrant describes the moisture on the Lady's monument as tears.

The monument itself – this "weeping" vessel at the heart of the play – also deserves our attention. The stage directions at the top of 4.3 call for the discovery of a "*tomb . . . richly set forth*," bearing, most likely, a marble effigy like that which haunts Webster's play (Figure 8). The previous chapter has delineated a model of theatrical space based on the metaphor of the Russian doll; here is a similarly humanoid vessel, its

Figure 8   Tomb effigy, Church of St. Margaret, Paston, England.

contents no less indeterminate, as we shall soon see. And the task of "breaching" this space – in the nervously ribald terms of the Tyrant's reluctant soldiers – bears comparison to the attempted penetration of Maria's chamber in *The Tamer Tamed*, not to mention the more benign entry into Juliet's chamber by Romeo. Does this enclosure, then, correspond to an offstage space? Elisabeth Bronfen states that "because death and femininity are excessively tropic, they point to a reality beyond and indeed disruptive of all systems of language."[43] Thus, alongside the offstage nuptial bed we may place the coffin. Even in non-theatrical space, the coffin metonymizes absence – since the important thing is not so much the dead body inside as the live body no longer outside. Like a window bricked-over or an empty eye-socket, its shape contains its own negation: the grim void inside the chalked outline of the victim. Fashioned after the human form, it cradles the antithesis of flesh. In this sense, the coffin is the artifact which mocks artifice by signifying the futility of representation, the inability of the image to capture the life it so lovingly copies. The coffin is the body under erasure.

Therefore, the Tyrant's reaction to the Lady's tomb is doubly curious. He cries, "The monument woos me; I must run and kiss it" (4.3.9); in medieval liturgical drama, the apostles John and Peter engage in a race to Jesus' tomb.[44] The Tyrant continues to personify the tomb; he describes the stone "weeping" and proceeds to address it in the second person. Yet in light of the previous analysis of *The Duchess of Malfi*, this attribution of life to an inanimate object should not be dismissed as mere lunacy; after all, the relatively sane Govianus has recently indulged in a kiss nearly, if not quite, as cold as the Tyrant's. And we recall Bosola's fantasy of a resuscitating kiss to the Duchess. In other words, we are looking at Pygmalionism. The Tyrant's attempt to endow the tomb with life is a precursor to his fantasy involving her corpse. In fact, he calls the tomb a "creature," emphasizing both its created-ness and the animation it lacks.

And the Tyrant's necrophilia is – like, presumably, most necrophilia – an act of self-deification, an attempt to appropriate the powers of a creator god, to bring the dead back to life. And, as Bergeron points out, the text associates this hubris with art.[45] So the Tyrant disinters the Lady's body and proposes to revivify her corpse by means of "the treasure house of art" (121). He likewise calls the body itself a "house," vacated by its "mistress" (112), thus breaching what might have seemed the last of our proliferation of onstage enclosures, the tomb, only to delineate another more mysterious enclosure, the dead body within. As his soldier servants rather queasily remove the Lady's body from the tomb, the Tyrant cites the Talmudic legend of Herod, who "preserved" the body of his beloved "dead in honey" (119). The honey, as a symbol, operates on several levels. On the most immediate level, it underscores the Tyrant's perverse carnal greed, with its cannibalistic undertones: as one of the soldiers remarks of the empty sarcophagus, "The lid's shut close when all the meat's picked out" (133). But let us not forget that the eating trope carries a double meaning here; in addition to sexual eating, there is also the Eucharistic eating of the body of Christ; Bynum's scholarship brings to light numerous references to a honey-flavored Eucharist in Christian mystical writings, along with instances in which a holy woman secreted sweet fluid – oil, milk, honey – rather than blood or sweat.[46]

The reference to honey calls to mind another product of bees which is even more effective in preservation: wax. And whereas the connection to Bosola's wax figures may seem weak, both Middleton's tomb-sequence and Webster's torture-scene manifest a concern with the image and its relation to mortality. Like the sonnets that boast their power to immortalize the youthful beauty of a mistress, gummy substances like wax or tree-sap may preserve the form of a mortal model – either mimetically (the witch's doll), or literally (amber). This is an important distinction, too: one need only compare early modern sepulchral art to the sarcophagi of ancient Egypt. The latter vessel – a coffin with a difference – also mimicked the living shape of its human contents, but its purpose was to protect those contents from physical decay or damage: the body, already armed against putrefaction by the holy art of mummification, wore its sarcophagus like armor; sometimes, as in the celebrated case of the Pharaoh Tutankhamun, it wore *several*, one inside the other like Russian dolls. So if the Herod anecdote appalls our modern sensibilities, I would only point out the almost hysterical fascination with which twentieth-century America greeted the "treasures of Tutankhamun" – or, predating that by far, the mesmerized tones in which archaeologist Howard Carter described "Tut's" gradual bringing-to-light, as the old "boy king" shed, layer by layer, his gilded pajamas.[47]

I take this detour into a distinctly non-western and decidedly anti-Protestant funerary method in order to highlight the cultural gulf between some of Middleton's sources and attitudes toward the body and its images ascendant in his day. The "art" of embalming which the Tyrant proposes runs contrary to the moral of the *memento mori* and contrary to the Lady's own professed distrust of surfaces and "outward show" (Govianus shares this belief; later he speaks of "Sorrows that . . . dwell all inward" [4.4.8]). The Lady's first appearance on stage, dressed in black, invites parallels with Hamlet; the Tyrant rebukes her for her funerary weeds, urges her to go and change her clothes and to return "like an illustrious bride / With her best beams about her" (1.1.119–20). The Lady defies him: "I come not hither / To please the eye of glory, but of goodness" (128–29). And she keeps her black robes for as long as she lives in the play; interestingly, it is only when she reappears on stage as a spirit that she resembles a bride *"all in white, stuck with jewels, and a great crucifix on her breast"* (4.4.42.-01–42.-04). This attire is, of course, meant to contrast – on a symbolic if not a visual level – with the Tyrant's adornment of her corpse, first with *"black velvet . . . a fair chain of pearl . . . and [a] crucifix"* (5.2.13.01–13.03) and finally with a mask of paint.

The Tyrant's "art" with regard to the Lady's corpse is allegorized at length by Lancashire:

The many Protestant attacks on Roman Catholicism in Jacobean England focused on Roman Catholic "worship" of saints and images . . . ; and the "Homelie against perill of idolatrie" presents the true Church of England and the "idolatrous" Roman Catholic Church in allegorical terms easily associated with the [play's] living Lady and her dead, painted . . . body. The "idolatrous" Church is likened to an adorned harlot . . . while "the true Church of GOD, as a chaste matron, espoused . . . to one husband, our Sauiour Jesus Christ . . . " is content with "her naturall Ornaments," since Christ "can well skill of the difference betweene a paynted visage, and true naturall beautie."[48]

Lancashire makes a good point but fails to take into account the complication which arises when the Lady's *spirit* arrives on stage "stuck with jewels" enough to rival the painted puppet the Tyrant makes of her body. In allegorical terms it is easy enough to contrast true or "naturall Ornaments" with a "paynted visage," but in theater *everyone* is painted (the Lady must be painted from the start, in order to be a lady, not a boy), and the dramatist has not made the problem any easier by using the same props (jewelry, a crucifix) to represent glory both *in malo* and *in bono*. Of course all allegory may run up against this problem, but this play in particular risks self-contradiction because the very image-worship it condemns makes up the fabric of its sources: how can a Calvinist dramatist attempt an attack on Roman Catholic "idolatrie" using a medium made possible by an "idolatrous" theater? How can art be wielded against "art"?

An examination of the biblical sources brings further contradictions to light. Christ was stripped before his crucifixion – something highlighted in the passion plays[49] – and the Visitation to his tomb by the three Marys was occasioned by their wish, in fact, to embalm him; in other words, to counteract the stripping and scourging of his body by lavishing it with fragrant layers which would "prevent / The blessed flesh from putrifying."[50] The parallel between this Visitation and the tomb sequence in *The Lady's Tragedy* has been well noted but not carried through to its implications regarding the role of the Tyrant. Like the three women who loved Jesus, the Tyrant returns to the tomb out of longing after the lost body of the beloved; unlike these women, he is not rewarded with the miracle of his heart's desire, that of the beloved's return in living flesh. But his impossible hope (along with the soldiers' superstitious fears that the Lady will "rise" [4.3.74]) is brought closer to this scene by way of its liturgical echoes: somewhere in the back of the spectator's mind lurks the memory of a tomb evacuated for a happier reason – and the events of the subsequent tomb scene, in which the Lady herself appears before Govianus, only intensify our hope for a miracle.

And there is another potential source for miracles. This analysis, so far, has assumed that the Lady's corpse, a prominent role in the play, must be "played" by a dummy – an assumption I am not the first to make.[51] Indeed, dummies were indispensable props in a theater so often sensationally violent, and in this category we can include both early modern drama and its medieval predecessor, the passion plays and saints' lives being perhaps the worst offenders.[52] But the prompt book for Middleton's play does not call for a dummy at any point; the requirement has been extrapolated on the basis of the final scene, in which the Lady's ghost and her body are onstage simultaneously. Yet in a theater fascinated by doubling and mirroring (for instance when the twins meet in act 5 of *Twelfth Night*), there is more than one possible approach to this bifurcated role. What if the Lady's dead body is played by a living body? It makes as much sense as her live body being played by a boy. And having examined the way Webster's Duchess is forced to "play dead" while living, we are more likely to regard the living act of death as a gendered performance. Perhaps in Middleton's play, this becomes an erotic performance.

I have seen only one production of the much-neglected *Lady's Tragedy*, in Bristol in 1994, and this production cast one actress in three roles: the living Lady, her ghost, and her corpse. The latter is a role less demanding, perhaps, than that of Christ in *The Scourging* (requiring in some cases a leather leotard for protection[53]), but, nonetheless, the act of looking dead for a total of 344 lines is no inconsiderable feat. The role of Hermione in *The Winter's Tale*, who must pretend to be a statue for a mere 78 lines, looks easy in comparison.[54] And in the case of the dead Lady's role, this act entails more than lying still and not appearing to breathe; it also entails the difficult task of allowing oneself to be handled, carried (and – in the Bristol production – propped up in a contraption made of ropes), meanwhile maintaining an illusory "rigor mortis." I myself, watching this particular actress looking dead, was impressed by her performance – all the more so, I think, because I could vaguely detect her breathing.

Perhaps this scrutiny of the performance of death is, as Cartwright argues, a constitutive part of spectatorial engagement in tragedy. "Playing dead illustrates the stitching between dramatic illusion and nonillusion, drawing electricity from the ambivalence. We desire in playing dead both the triumph of realism and the certainty of just-pretending (for we always assure ourselves that the actor really breathes, lives) . . . Tragic closure depends for its full power on, unexpectedly, the audience's consciousness of theatricality."[55] But the implications of this "electricity" between audience and tragic actor may complicate the moral of the dramatic text. For the director's decision to use a live body rather than a dummy, in the Bristol production, had an apparently unintentional side-effect: it made the Tyrant's passion more comprehensible, more sane. For, however convincing this performance of deadness, the audience of course recognized it as such; the Lady's limbs were too supple, her lips too moist; she might have been, like so many bashful maidens in courtly love lyrics, merely pretending to sleep. In fact, the Tyrant's fondling of this "corpse" acquired a powerful eroticism that the use of a dummy would have prevented; even for those spectators seated too far from the stage to observe, as I did, the actress' breathing, our ontological sense of her vitality, together with the Tyrant's insistence on the same, made it too tempting to look at the actress, not the role, and to imagine how it felt to play dead and be fondled. The warm onstage body rendered virtually palpable, and hence doubly seductive, the miracle the Tyrant sought.

After all, seeing is believing.

And sure enough, after the Lady is removed from her tomb, kneeled before, kissed, and carried offstage, the miracle happens . . . or seems to. In the very next scene, she walks onstage again, interrupting her lover's lamentations. But her words forestall any hope of consummation: *"I am not here"* (4.4.40).[56] And this puzzling greeting introduces a splitting of her presence, reflected in split pronouns and a split role, which continues through the end of the play. Bergeron, addressing this "bifurcation," describes the Lady as "the 'objective correlative' for the idea of aliena-tion" (183). "Behold, I'm gone," she tells Govianus, "My body taken up"; the words echo those of the angel before Christ's empty tomb, but this lifting up is no resurrection, and the hollow space of this tomb bespeaks division, not joining, between body and soul. Govianus confirms the absence of the corpse, " 'Tis gone indeed!" (61–62), he observes, replacing her "I" with an "it," and thus pointing up the confusion of identity and presence surrounding this disembodied onstage body. When he later ponders the dead body itself, he drops the neuter pronoun but betrays no less confusion about who is there and who is not. " 'Tis strange to me / To see thee here at court, and gone from hence" (5.2.53–4).

So perhaps seeing is not believing.

The Tyrant's obsession – like Ferdinand's – is (predictably enough) presented in visual terms. Upon the Lady's entrance in act 1, the Tyrant's first words are, "Now I see my loss" (1.1.111); he then devises to lock up Govianus where "he may only have sight of her" (234); the next we see of the Tyrant, he complains, "I want her sight too long" (2.3.3), and, responding to her father's entrance, says, "Thy sight quickens me" (13). When he learns of the Lady's death, he mourns, "I've lost the comfort of her sight for ever" (4.2.30), and thus descends to the tomb, where he commands his men, "Remove the stone that I may see my mistress" (4.3.52). When finally viewing her dead body, he proclaims, "I never shall be weary to behold thee; / I could stand eternally thus and see thee" (60–61). The Lady's ghost likewise describes the Tyrant's necrophilia in terms of a lust for her image; he

> Weeps when he sees the paleness of my cheek,
> And will send privately for a hand of art
> That may dissemble life upon my face
> To please his lustful eye.   (4.4.73–76)

And these references continue. The Tyrant calls for the Lady's body: "I cannot keep from her sight so long. / I starve mine eye too much" (5.2.6–7); and beholding her, he remarks, "I can see nothing to be mended in thee" (5.2.28); noting, however, her paleness, he hires an artist, Govianus in disguise, to paint life upon her face; he instructs him to "strive / To give our eye delight" (82–83) and then dies from kissing the poisoned picture.[57] The image, in the end, kills.

The Middletonian–Calvinistic moral of this fatal, idolatrous kiss seems fairly clear, as does the point of the original staging of the finale, in which the deposed king regains his kingdom, and the spirit of the Lady returns to attend her body in its processional exit from stage. But the Bristol production complicated the flesh/spirit binary by casting one performer in the roles of body and ghost; this production consequently omitted the dual exit of the Lady's spirit and corpse, which would have required an additional body, artificial or live, for the sake of allegorical closure. Nonetheless, it is difficult to imagine an approach to staging capable of eliminating the dead Lady's troubling erotic aura – above all, though not exclusively, in a dummy-less production like the one I viewed. The Bristol production merely emphasized the tensions embedded in the text and in the theatrical medium, leaving the audience with a disturbing sense of their voyeuristic participation. After the actors filed offstage with the Lady's bier, the spotlight lingered on the empty ropes used for this crucifixion to lust. And this exit we dared not follow.

If the Lady is a female Christ, who, then, is the Tyrant? Shuger traces the influence of the Mary Magdalene legend in medieval and Renaissance devotional literature, in the process critiquing the modern critical impulse to dichotomize the erotic and spiritual in these discourses. Of particular interest to this chapter is her analysis of a Renaissance Magdalene figure, inherited from the medieval cycle plays and saints' lives, whose lamentations over the missing body of Christ strike modern readers (and some early modern readers) as flagrantly and uncomfortably sensual.[58] Standing at the mysteriously empty tomb, she pines to see and embrace the remains of her beloved. Shuger notes that, to our sensibilities, "There is something macabre in the insistent physicality of her longing for this corpse. Again, the feelings expressed are not 'religious': she has no notion of the Resurrection; what she wants is the dead body of the man she loves."[59] This is evident in the sepulcher scene in the Digby *Mary Magdalene*, where Mary laments, "I have porposyd in eche degre / To have him with me, verely" (1065–66), speaking of her missing "Lordes body" (1032) as though it were an absent, living lover. Nor do I use the latter term carelessly; Mary calls herself "his lover" (1068), much to the discomfiture of the editor, who supplies the gloss, "his devoted worshipper."

Modern confusion notwithstanding, such expressions of longing (inspired, in part, by the "Song of Songs") saturated medieval piety. Shuger explains the Aristotelian basis for this eroticism, according to which "desire and thought depend on a process of imaging." Hence, "if love requires images, then the corporeal is a sine qua non of desire. As Mary says, Christ's image has been sculpted in her soul, and she needs his body to renew the image, enabling her love to endure."[60] In just this way, Middleton's Tyrant craves the sight of his beloved, and will stop at nothing to regain it. Again, I am reminded of the witch's doll, which may be used not only to harm its referent, but alternatively to inflict love, or "to recall a truant sweetheart."[61]

However, Reformation thought, particularly that of Calvin and his followers, violently rejects this adoration of the image (or the body), giving primacy to the word and the text.[62] The editor's resistance to the term "lover" can be traced to the response of Calvin himself, according to whom Mary's longing is "folly," bespeaking "'grovelling views' and an 'earthly,' 'carnal' mind."[63] In the same fashion, Middleton's text condemns the Tyrant's grovelling before the dead Lady, and condemns the "art" with which he would preserve the image he adores. But, as we have begun to see, this is to impose a Reformist moral upon medieval materials. For medieval spirituality, as Shuger helps point out, gives priority to vision,[64] often with the effect of praising the image of Christ in terms that we would now consider profane.

To ask why these texts represent spirituality in terms of sexual desire may be a misleading question . . . One can, in fact, reverse the terms of the question, since the representation of sexual desire in the Middle Ages borrows heavily from the affective spirituality of Augustine and the twelfth-century Cistercians. That is, medieval secular eroticism (courtly love) is itself modeled on the analysis of spiritual longing, so that the latter is theoretically anterior to the former, rather than the reverse.[65]

Shuger attributes our modern bias to the "discovery of genital sexuality" which happened sometime in the middle of the seventeenth century, displacing the "ocular eroticism" prevalent from Plato through Wyatt – an eroticism which pertained to the longing for one's lady as well as the longing for God. According to the earlier model, erotic feeling moved "inward and down," from the eyes to the heart, unlike our modern, genitally based model, wherein eros moves "outward and up," from the groin to the brain, through "sublimation."[66]

And let us not forget the etymology of the word "passion": it all began with Jesus. I would like to suggest that the examples of female sacrifice we have examined in this chapter tell us something about the depiction of Christ's sacrifice that they displaced – or, put another way, these depictions tell us something about the causes of that displacement. In a culture such as our own, in which heterosexuality is normative, it is too easy to assume that the eroticization of Christ's death results from the prior feminization of his body, rather than the reverse; now, in light of Shuger's observations, we can make an alternative supposition, that Christ's passion provides the discursive materials for an eroticized female death (or a male: the "actual" gender of the victim is, in a sense, immaterial, since the act itself is heavily gendered). And perhaps it is just this mingling of the spiritual and the sensual which made the medieval view of Christ's sacrifice intolerable to Reformers like Calvin. And so Jesus was ushered offstage. In the same way that this movement rejected, abjected, the "eating" of Christ in the Eucharist; in the same way that it scorned the medieval mystics with their oozing stigmata; with this very same shudder, it chased from the stage, and from art in general, God's weeping, feminized, sacrificial body. Real presence, on stage, became real absence.

Despite its debt to medieval sources, Middleton's text is, in its conception, staunchly Calvinist. The performance, however, is another story. We have examined ways in which one particular production of *The Lady's Tragedy* complicated the moral of the dramatic text – yet in light of the nature of theater, doesn't the fact of performance itself, in a sense, undermine iconoclasm? That is why many Puritan authors avoided drama altogether, and why they strove, even in their worship, to avoid histrionics, for "the drama of salvation needed to be shifted from an outer to an inner and invisible stage."[67] Onstage, the letter *is* the spirit of the text.

By the same token, both Ferdinand and the Tyrant, with their fixations upon the image, emerge unexpectedly as figures for the male dramatist; the one artist works in wax, the other in paint. Both strive to re-present a woman they love, and both go mad when confronted with her death. During the Bristol performance of *The Lady's Tragedy*, I was struck by the puppet-like appearance of the dead Lady, once she had been strung up in the contraption intended to make her pose appear life-like. We might view this as a visual rendering of Bosola's tropic "cords of life" – severed in the Duchess by way of a rope around the neck. And although this prop was invented by a contemporary director, it seems perfectly suited to the text, especially in light of the parallels between the Lady and the imprisoned Duchess. Both heroines become well acquainted with ropes – the one strangled to death, the other driven to suicide and hung up in a mockery of life. And how fitting that the Tyrant himself has the

Lady adorned with a crucifix, even as he strives to reanimate her upon a cross-like machine. We remember that the puppeteer's magic derives from a handle whose shape mimics the cross.

The question remains, though, as to whether these women characters are killed *into* art, or killed *out of* art – especially considering the fact that (modern productions notwithstanding) there are no women on stage. And the crucifixion imagery explored in this chapter has allowed us to view misogynist violence from a different perspective, wherein transcendence, for the victim, becomes thinkable – at the very least through the admiration of the play's original, Christian audiences, for whom the language of sacrifice was likely to elicit, not just pity, but awe. The names of the Duchess and the Lady both indicate sovereignty: the latter is the female equivalent of "Lord." Does the vessel leak? Does it leak wine; does it weep blood? Sweat, milk, tears, spittle, honey, menses, oil? Luce Irigaray speaks of the "female" voice as operating according to "The 'Mechanics' of Fluids," and her contemporary, Hélène Cixous, uses the metaphor of breast-milk to describe a "woman's style in language."[68] Christ's message, by comparison, is written in blood. John Donne asks, "Who can blot out the Crosse, which th'instrument / Of God, dew'd on mee in the Sacrament?"[69] In his commendatory verses to Webster, Middleton reports that no spectator viewing the Duchess' death "could get off without a bleeding eye";[70] the image not only attests to the power of audience empathy, but also replicates the passionistic echoes of the Duchess' story. These bleeding eyes do more than weep: these are ocular stigmata.

I've heard the complaint often enough, sometimes in my own head: "All those plays where men get off on a dead woman. And all those paintings of nude women, just lying there, passive, waiting to be raped. Art is sick. Men are sick." But the same culture which eroticizes the dead female, or, at best, the nude, prone, vulnerable female, also goes to church and prays to a dead, naked, male god hung up on a wooden pole. And whether, as I theorized above, the belief in a Resurrection (a belief older than pornography as we know it[71]) made possible the eroticized portrayal of a woman's death, Jesus certainly can be credited for the transhistorical and international popularity of death – however gendered – in art. The Resurrection aestheticizes death: as George Herbert writes, Death personified "wast once an uncouth hideous thing" until Christ made him "fair and full of grace."[72] And insofar as beautification and eroticization exist on the same continuum, one could say that the Resurrection itself eroticizes death. Therefore, we can revise my theory, stated above: not only is Christ's passion a necessary precondition for the eroticization of a woman's death (or a man's) – but the erotic element itself perpetuates this theme in art. The word "martyr" is Latin for "witness": a witness of God; a death to be witnessed. Sacrifice requires an audience; thus, martyrdom is *redeemed* as a subject for art.

After all, Christ is killed into art every day.

Moreover, it is arguable that tragedy as a genre is rooted in the ethos of sacrifice. The modern understanding of Aristotelian *katharsis* as medical or moral "purgation" elides a second, equally common Greek usage, not unfamiliar to Renaissance scholars: the term also meant "sacrificial purification," that is, a ritual cleansing in blood.[73] Paster's explication of humoral physiology might complicate this notion, but need not contradict it: howsoever medical treatises tried to disparage female bleeding, none could deny the life-giving role of that uncleanly matter, the blood of menses.

This is not to say that the valorization of female self-sacrifice or victimization does not have serious implications in a society as brutal toward women as early modern England (or post-modern America, for that matter) – witness the case of Lady Arbella Stuart, one real-life version of our dead Duchess.[74] And the theoretical problem of "playing dead" should not obscure for us the fact that, in early modern England, women's lives might depend upon such an act. We recall that Desdemona, smothered in bed by hands as jealous as Ferdinand's, also revives after she is presumed dead, answering the question, "O, who has done this deed?" with a bewildering self-negation: "Nobody; I myself. Farewell" (5.2.132–33). Like the Lady's "I am not here," like the Duchess' last utterance, "Mercy," this active self-denial embodies the paradoxical nature of performing death onstage, as well as performing the living death of a circumscribed life.

Nor do I intend to rescue any of these male dramatists from their own self-contradictions, as they simultaneously wield and deny the power of the image over their female subjects. Indeed, from our critical perspective, there is something of the "poisoned kiss" effect inherent in the medium of a transvestite theater, wherein images of women made by men turn against them almost 400 years later, with the help of feminist deconstruction. A sweet, if delayed, revenge for an old prohibition. Perhaps that is why I'm not upset about the treatment of women in these plays. Are women killed into art on an all-male stage? Perhaps. But it's hard to find fingerprints, clues, when the body is missing. "There is no one inside the tomb."

And the Lady's voice within, offstage, reminds me, *I am not here.*

5   Obscene and unseen

An ordinance passed in 1606 prohibited the use of God's name on the English stage.[1] Not content to censor the image of God, the Reformists silenced his name in the mouths of the players. And there is a curious logic to this erasure, at least from the perspective of French feminist theory: Hélène Cixous writes that "Paternity is the lack of being which is called God. Men's cleverness was in passing themselves off as fathers and 'repatriating' women's fruits as their own. A naming trick. Magic of absence. God is men's secret."[2] God the Father, thus, seems an invention designed to mask the invisibility of insemination, the ambiguity of paternity. Yet insemination, we must remind ourselves, is not the only vexing ambiguity involved in that complicated physiological, psychological, and social interaction we call sexual intercourse: also indeterminate is the biological "fact" of female orgasm. Studies of pornography such as Linda Williams' *Hard Core* bring to light the futility and self-parodic potential of a male-conceived and male-marketed media obsessed with revealing and fixing the supposed secrets of female sexuality.[3] But the question remains. What does it mean that sex and God both "happen" offstage – not just in Shakespeare's theater, but in the world's theater?

It may help to ponder, a moment, that notion celebrated in the King James Bible, "carnal knowledge."[4] Iago says that the women "In Venice . . . do let God see the pranks / They dare not show their husbands" (3.3.206–7). And the puzzle of "sex" has often been phrased in terms of knowledge or ignorance. I am reminded of Chaucer's Merchant, pausing in his Tale (with, I presume, a wink at the audience) when the elderly lover beds his pretty young bride: *God knows what she thought*, he chortles (1851).[5] The Merchant implies that he does know, that his audience knows well, what May thought of old January's efforts in bed; but we can also read the sentence literally: God (only) knows what she thought. Likewise, Chaucer's Miller instructs men in his Prologue: "An housbonde shal nat ben inquisityf / of Goddes pryvetee, nor of his wyf" (3163–64).

When God's body made its exit from stage, what body replaced it? In the wake of the passion plays, the plays of the Renaissance suffered no lack of passion, as we now define it; romance and ribaldry flourished, even despite (or because of?) the material absence of women onstage. Other scholars have noted the increase in sexual language in the genre. Boose pinpoints the 1590s for the arrival of "a new and aggressively sexualized form of distinctly English literature" which quickly found its way (thanks to censorship) to the cultural niche of theater.[6] Likewise, Marliss C. Desens notes the sudden proliferation of bed-tricks in English drama at precisely the turn of the century[7] – the bed-trick being, perhaps, the most popular form of offstage sex. And if we don't want to take the critics' word for it, we can ask the playwrights themselves. The "Epistle" of *The Roaring Girl* by Middleton and Dekker – a play sharing its date, 1611, with *The Lady's Tragedy* – declares: "Now in the time of spruceness, our plays follow the niceness of our garments: single plots, quaint conceits, lecherous jests, dressed up in hanging sleeves; and those are fit for the times and the termers . . . And for venery you shall find enough, for sixpence, but well couched an you mark it" (6–15). As Middleton explains, "The fashion in play-making" (1) has turned from the Elizabethan overly "quilted" (4), to the Jacobean trim and sexy – though the "venery" may be, perforce, still "couched" in innuendo.

This is all by way of saying that what followed the Corpus Christi was equally corporeal, in its own salacious (if polysemious) way. I believe that this was no accident. At some point during the secularization process analyzed by scholars such as Shuger, *sex replaced God as the supreme signified*, particularly in theater, though arguably throughout English or even western culture. And so far, *permanently*. After all, art, like nature, abhors a vacuum, and something – or some *things* (to use that ubiquitous euphemism for the genitalia) – had to keep audiences interested, once the sacred had taken, so to speak, a back seat. A particularly crucial point of evidence is the process by which the term "profanity" – from the Latin, "before (i.e., outside) the temple" – came to be interchangeable with the term "obscenity." Medieval oaths dismembered the sacred body; modern expletives dismember the sexed body. What is the link? Profanity lost a limb; "God's blood" became, for instance, "'sblood," and "God's foot" became "'sfoot" and even then, after 1606, such terms might be censored. Thus, in early modern drama, the profanity which once invoked a particular sacred body now invokes bodies in general. And if these oaths are not explicitly sexual, they nonetheless enhance the carnal texture of a genre obsessed with bodies and littered with phallic and vaginal puns. A case in point is that of "'sfoot," which became "foot," and then was linked to the French verb *foutre*, fuck. The aforementioned oaths, those traces of an otherwise

sweeping erasure, occupy a unique position in regard to the uncensored
bodily language surrounding them, and the body of texts in which they
appear; gesturing backward toward the values of medieval Christianity
while anticipating the rise of modern obscenity, such oaths, like the genre
to which they belong, link two different realms of taboo, illustrating the
massive cultural shift best described by Foucault. "Over the centuries
[sex] has become more important than our soul, more important almost
than our life. And so it is that all the world's enigmas appear frivolous
compared to this secret . . . Sex is worth dying for."[8] With comparable
insight, Bynum critiques the modern impulse to view medieval representations of Christ's circumcision as emphasizing his sexuality, rather than
his humanity, his vulnerability; Bynum argues that the medieval mind
did not habitually associate particular body-parts (for example, a
woman's breast, medieval symbol of nurturance) with sexual acts.[9]
Simply put, we worship copulation in the way our ancestors did the
Incarnation, and the change began during the Reformation. And this
transformation has been recognized outside academia as well. D. H.
Lawrence, writing decades before Foucault, presents two male characters
discussing the sacralization of heterosexual union:

> "The old ideals are as dead as nails – nothing there. It seems to me there
> remains only this perfect union with a woman . . . and there isn't
> anything else."
> "And you mean if there isn't the woman, there's nothing?" said Gerald.
> "Pretty well that – seeing there's no God."[10]

Thanks to Cixous (who I imagine overhearing this chat), this is men's
secret no longer.

Seeing there is no God.

The profanity of the iconoclastic stage was put together, one might say,
from the relics of Christ's body. The Duchess' reference to an anchorite
kissing a skull calls to mind yet another form of medieval "idolatrie"
squelched by the Reformation – the worship of saints' remains, in whole
or in parts – and this fetishization provides an analog useful to this
chapter's study of sexual language. Relics, after all, "stand in for" a body
in the most material sense, providing a tactile as well as visual simulacrum; synecdoche *par excellence*, they operate like words, but above all
like what we now call "dirty words," defined in relation to bodies. "As
fetish, or simulacrum of a part object, the obscene word not only
represents, but replaces, its referent. It acts as a substitute for, indeed
sometimes as an improvement over its referent . . . unlike other words,
the obscene word not only represents but is, the thing itself."[11] Although
one might question whether this distinction between obscene words and

"other words" is not a matter of degree rather than kind, this notion of words as "things,"[12] in not only a material but also a sexual or genital sense, strengthens the analogy with relics, the body-parts of saints. And the early modern appetite for ribaldry seems comparable to the medieval appetite for relics – an appetite which rendered the bodies of saints virtual prey for marauding, profit-hungry relic thieves.[13] Relics, remember, work best through touch; bless, save, heal through touch. A similar, if inverted, logic inscribes the notion of "dirty words," whose utterance or reception is – as the phrase implies – conceived of in terms of soiling contact, or contact with a soiled (taboo) body-part. Also, let us not forget that the transvestite stage represented woman by way of *things* – wigs, skirts, false breasts. When do textual "things" become "the thing itself"?

The modern notion of obscenity, though, may not necessarily apply to Renaissance bawdy, that province of editors: the latter often operates by innuendo, by double-meaning. But then again, most modern obscenities, especially those which denote the genitalia, do have multiple meanings – "cock" is a bird, "pussy" a mammal – and only become "obscene" when they are used in such a way that the ornithological or feline referent is forgotten. By the same token, a bawdy "pun" only earns the label of "bawdy" – as any editor knows – when the non-sexual referent is overshadowed by the sexual. Perhaps the best litmus test for "obscene" language is the degree to which it crosses this line.

This study began with an examination of four plays with regard to the most localized – albeit offstage – erotic representations; this chapter returns to each of these plays with an eye to the overall texture of its sexual language. For bawdy also invokes offstage sex, albeit at its most general; bawdy does not show sex, but means sex, and often while pretending to mean something else. Like those offstage encounters with which this study began, bawdy is a manipulation of discursive taboos, a way of speaking the unspeakable. Moreover, by studying the ways Middleton and Shakespeare weave sexual innuendo, and, to some degree, the ways modern editors have treated this innuendo, by shifting our field of study from stage to text while adopting a wider historical lens, we can ultimately observe these texts as they work in *our* culture as well, and perhaps indulge in some hypotheses about continuities over time.

Given the constructionist view of sexuality as grounded in discourse, dictated by systems of meaning, it should come as no surprise that our search for absent bodies has led us back to those textual bodies with which we began, for one final sweep of the minutiae of sexual signification, guided by the (perhaps waning) hope of unearthing a corporeal core of language. Such a quest, of course, was doomed from the beginning, from the perspective of the theoretical discourse which provoked, merely by its certainty, my mischievous urge to try to disprove it. But the discoveries of the previous chapter, concerning the intersection of death, sex, and the sacred in theater, warrant a broader-based analysis of this semiotic conjunction. The readings of this chapter aim ultimately to anatomize language, to take it apart, to dig up its bones; returning to the sex-sounds of *Mad World* and the death-sounds of *Othello*, but this time attending to *phonics* as well as graphics,[14] we will finally glimpse in the monosyllable, and in certain monosyllabic utterances – the preposition, the oath, the ejaculation – a ghost (at least) of the body which utters. And the fact that this insight is achieved through a process of semiotic breaking-down or dismembering will provide fruitful soil for considering the nexus between texts and bodies, and the role of dissolution (or the fear of it) in our culture's erotic discourses.

For the time being, though, our main concern is the nature and use of these bawdy bones. Who is the priest of these textual relics? Not the author, who creates, but the editor, who guards and interprets – who mediates. Long before critics like myself come along with our tools for textual dissection, editors have pieced together the textual body. Editors break texts into parts before presenting them as seemingly seamless wholes, in the interests of in/corporating a multiplicity of meanings, pointing out allusion and innuendo, cataloging textual variants, censoring, or even, occasionally, un-censoring by reinserting into a text what was previously censored. Editors also, interestingly, are entrusted with *naming* the father of the textual body, even naming that body itself. Perhaps art itself is a naming trick; perhaps naming sex is the trickiest art of all.

I   Middleton: naming of parts

Middleton's sexual language tends to be more part-oriented, more genitally focused (one is tempted to say "coarser") than Shakespeare's; the latter prefers the more nuanced innuendo of an eloquent pervert such as Iago, who would rather indulge in a prolonged, allusive, and metrically sophisticated mind-fuck than blurt out a monosyllabic shocker like "prick." Valerie Traub makes an observation about Shakespeare which I find true of all early modern drama, but especially of Middleton, whose "language metaphorizes and materializes desire; . . . such terms as 'blood,' 'flesh,' 'heart,' 'appetite,' 'passion,' and 'death' locate desire in a dispersed corporeal body . . . The drama's fascination with and dependence on body parts ('mammets' and 'pricks,' as well as 'thing,' 'piece,' 'pit,' 'hell') reiterates . . . his propensity toward 'metaphorizing materialization.'"[15] Whether such terms, in early modern drama, "metaphorize" the human body is open to debate (as mentioned above, "cock" is a male bird, but how often did the audience hear the metaphor?); however, the genre's jigsaw-puzzle approach to sexuality is, as Traub indicates, a crucial factor in its overall appearance of material density. Middleton's plays also boast an array of phallic and vaginal props: the glove and the severed finger in *The Changeling*; the ring and the phallic sweets in *A Chaste Maid in Cheapside*; the Ward's "cat-stick" in *Women Beware Women*. And not unrelated to this rhetorical and symbolic dismembering is the vein of innuendo regarding the pox, which emphasizes the actual, rather than figurative dissolution which may result from sexual excess.

Our earlier analysis of *Women Beware Women* focused on the main plot, with its dark and troubled eroticism; the sub-plot, however, contains a greater quantity of explicit sexual references and presents, overall, a more boisterous, if equally cynical, view of carnal relations. Isabella's paternally enforced betrothal to the stupid and vulgar Ward provides ample opportunity for innuendo in both directions; as in any arranged match, each party is concerned with finding the prospective partner's "parts" or qualities likable. However, the only "parts" which interest the Ward are, to an absurd degree, physical, and in this respect he finds Isabella not lacking. Poor Isabella, on the other hand, is doomed to a spouse whose only "parts consist in acres" (3.2.114), whose endowments are material (and perhaps, if we buy his ribald boasting, penile) rather than spiritual or intellectual.

Of course what comes of such an unequal match is predictably tragic: Isabella goes through with the marriage only in order to facilitate a clandestine, and fatal, love-affair with her uncle. But, as in the main plot, the cuckold is hardly an object of feminist sympathy: both husbands treat their mates as objects to be appraised, purchased, and guarded. Leantio, we recall, constructs Bianca as "the best piece of theft / That ever was committed" (1.1.43–44) and thus virtually ensures that she will be "stolen" by another. Bianca becomes an object worthy of the Duke's collection, just as Isabella becomes, to the Ward, a choice collection of objects. Thus, the discourse which *takes apart* a woman constructs the threat that more than one man might *take part* in her body.

On the other hand, the language of parts and pieces is not only directed at women. The Duke first appears in his gallery as "a better piece / . . . than all these" (2.2.316–17). Similarly, Livia announces the Ward's arrival, "Here's a foul great piece of him, methinks" (1.2.86). The "piece" here indicates some oversized part of the Ward's anatomy visible onstage prior to his entrance – some editors point to his rump,[16] but given the phallic punning which follows (pointed up by the Ward's antics with his "cat-stick"), we can imagine another even bawdier alternative. Nonetheless, the reduction of the Ward to his sexual equipment seems only fair considering his attitude toward Isabella, whom he wishes to view naked before accepting her as a spouse. When Fabritio asks the Ward his opinion of Isabella's "breast" – meaning her singing voice – the Ward demonstrates his inability to see (or hear) beyond her bodily attributes: "Her breast?" he wonders, "He talks as if his daughter had given suck / Before she were married . . . / The next he praises sure will be her nipples" (3.2.156–59).

And in fact the paternal authority figures in the play are perhaps the main perpetrators of this objectifying and commodifying rhetoric. Fabritio zealously plans the display and sale of his daughter: "I will see / Her *things laid ready*, every one in order, / And have some *part* of her trick'd up tonight" (2.2.62–64; emphases added). He goes on to command, "On with her chain of pearl, her ruby bracelets, / Lay ready all her tricks and jiggambobs" (69–70). And the vaguely obscene ring of such passages deserves note. Guardino promises his nephew,

> What her good *parts* are, as far as time
> And place can modestly require a knowledge of,
> Shall be *laid open* to your understanding.   (3.2.5–7; emphases added)

This is not a promise of carnal knowledge *per se*, but the parallels are there. And such innuendo pervades the text: the word "part" or "parts" occurs thirty-eight times,[17] in contexts of varying ribaldry; the word "piece" appears seven times (aside from the recurrent homonym "peace"); in addition, "hole," "passage," "fault," "prick," "tongue," "finger," "end," "tail," "flesh," "cock," "bolt," and "thing" (this term twenty-three times in the singular, twenty-one in the plural) all play their suggestive, if not blatantly obscene, roles.

And any limb can acquire a sexual innuendo if it is treated fetishistically. Bianca jokes about taking a third "leg" – i.e. her lover's penis (4.1.48–49) – in a way that anticipates the objectifying logic with which Hippolito justifies murdering his sister's lover:

> I'll imitate the pities of old surgeons
> To this lost *limb*, who, ere they show their art,
> Cast one asleep, then cut the diseas'd *part*
> . . .
> She shall not feel him going till he's lost.   (4.1.170–74; emphases added)

Leantio here is reduced, not simply to the "third leg" of his own penis, but to a "diseas'd part" of his mistress' anatomy which must be amputated. And the amputation trope is not only troubling in itself, but also in that it implies a previous amputation. Hippolito's (and, in fact,

Bianca's) distorted view of the sexual act constructs the woman as literally "taking" the male member, and with it the entire male self (barely distinguishable, in this play, from the former), and retaining it so firmly that it cannot be removed without bloodshed. The image replaces post-coital withdrawal and/or detumescence ("she shall not feel him going") with the violence of amputation ("till he's lost") and illustrates even more vividly the confusion between parts and wholes, between organs and selves, which characterizes the play's sexual universe. The Cardinal, berating the Duke for his devotion to a "strumpet's love," looks at him and says, "The *thing* I look on seems so / To my eyes, lost for ever" (184–85; emphasis added). Clearly, when the engendering act itself is troped in terms of male dismemberment, it is only fitting that real violence follows it.

Sex therefore alters the human anatomy, and not only in terms of this, shall we call it, "dismemberment anxiety." Thus the Ward speaks of his cuckolding as if the figurative "horns" were palpable objects, a kind of cancerous growth on his brow: "I cannot wash my face but I am feeling on't" (5.1.3). And this paranoid fantasy illustrates the symbolic power of the cuckold's horns – that patriarchal nightmare of magical male disfigurement by way of female sexual agency. The imaginary horns are the inversion of the "dismemberment anxiety" mentioned above, marring the male body by manifesting a shameful, invisible "fact": that a man's wife has (in Bianca's terms) "take[n] another" – another penis to his own. Cuckolding fuses a false phallus on the male body – two, in fact – replacing the mark of legitimate, singular, male sexual power with a mocking – and mockingly doubled – surrogate.

Feminists have frequently called attention to the way poetic conventions such as the blazon dismember the female body, reducing the female subject to a collection of inanimate objects; Traub, for instance, analyzes the "male anxiety toward female erotic power" which necessitates the "metaphoric and dramatic transformation of woman into jewels, statues, and corpses" in Shakespeare.[18] But we are beginning to see that the female body is not the only victim of this metaphorical butchery, that authors may treat sexual bodies of either gender in this fashion. Could it be that dismembering is – pardon the pun – part and parcel of bawdy?

Nonetheless, there are more gentle and more comic ways of treating the parceled, commodified sexual body. Middleton's *Mad World* features a brand of bawdy that centers upon the equation of sex with money – with jewels, coins, and precious objects. The plot features a rich, old, generous, and apparently impotent lord, a trickster of an heir, a sexually under-endowed (remember our friend "Shortrod"?) and therefore jealous husband, and a wily courtesan. *Mad World* manifests the linkage of sex and dissolution in a manner more suitable to comedy; through bawdy jokes about penis size, pregnancy, pox, and impotence, the play favors the physical dissolution of age or illness – and the moral dissolution wrought by greed and material excess – over *Women Beware Women*'s disfiguring rhetoric and violence. The main plot and the sub-plot each feature a male figure of questionable potency, while the prostitute who links the two plots presents a body upon which both veins of humor converge. The courtesan makes possible much of the play's bawdy, in her play-acting of illness as a cover for adulterous doings, in the resulting speculations about her health, and in the doubt she casts upon old Sir Bounteous' sexual prowess.

Sir Bounteous, as his name suggests, is rich – that is, rich in all things save progeny – and generous toward everyone except his grandson and heir, Follywit, who for this reason schemes to rob him blind while living, rather than waiting for his death. Furthermore, Bounteous' bounty is imagined, by the envious Follywit, in orgiastic terms. Here Follywit concocts his plan:

He keeps a house like his name, bounteous, *open* for all *comers* . . . he *stands* much upon the glory of his complement, variety of *entertainment*, together with the *largeness* of his kitchen, *longitude* of his buttery, and *fecundity* of his larder, and thinks himself never happier than when some *stiff* lord or *great count*ess[19] alights to make *light* his dishes. These being well mixed together . . . make my purpose *spring forth* more fortunate. To be *short*, and *cut off* a great deal of *dirty way*, I'll *down* to my grandsire like a lord. (1.1.65–76; emphases added)

And Bounteous himself delights in this sexualization of his wealth and generosity – all of which becomes even more comical when we learn, from the courtesan's mother, of his decrepit sexual equipment (1.1.164–67). Bounteous, in fact, describes his wealth in terms of large (and primarily phallic) objects: his is "the house with the great turret o'th'top" (2.1.32), and the "fair pair of organs," and the "great gilt candlestick, and a pair of silver snuffers," and "a long dining room, a huge kitchen, large meat, and a broad dresser board" (39–46). His alternatively obsequious and bragging language brims over with phallic innuendo; he "spaciously" welcomes "Lord Owemuch" (his grandson in disguise) with apologies about his "unworthy seat" followed by boasting remarks about his "organs." Therefore it is doubly hilarious when his crafty grandson makes off with a piece of his fortunes, and then brags, "This was bounteously done of him i'faith. It *came* somewhat *hard* from him at first, for indeed nothing *comes stiff* from an old man but money, and he may well *stand* upon that, when he has nothing else to *stand* upon." (2.4.68–72; emphases added).

The ribald humor surrounding Sir Bounteous is about valuable objects which act as phallic substitutes ("Meddle not with my organs," he pleads, as Follywit gropes in his pockets for coins [2.4.62]); similarly, the humor surrounding the courtesan associates her sexual "taking" of men with the taking (even taking in) of men's money and precious objects. Her feigned sickness is not only a ploy to bring Mistress Harebrain and Penitent together; it is also a money-making scheme: she instructs Penitent, in the guise of a doctor, to "let gold, amber, and dissolved pearl be common ingredients" in her medications, so that the concerned gallants who visit her will pay abundantly to restore her health and insure their future pleasures with her (2.5.50–51). And as far as her ability to put on a good act, she assures Penitent, "Puh, all the world knows women are soon *down*. We can be sick when we have a mind to't, catch an ague with the wind of our fans, *surfeit* upon the *rump* of a lark and bestow ten pound in *physic* upon't. We're likest ourselves when we're *down*" (31–35; emphases added). The joke here is not only the courtesan's matter-of-factness about female duplicity, but the innuendo on "down" which links illness and sex, exposing the former as a cover for the latter. Also, "physic" was a euphemism for sexual intercourse, that sweet cure for the sickness of lust.

In the case of Bounteous, however, "down" has an entirely different connotation. As he enters the courtesan's sickroom, he exclaims, "Here's a sight able to make an old man *shrink*. I was *lusty* when I came in, but I am *down* now, i'faith. Mortality! Yea, this puts me in mind of a *hole* seven foot deep, my grave, my grave, my grave" (3.2.26–30; emphases added). Ascertaining that the illness is not the plague (Penitent jokes, in an aside, that the pox is the "more likely" diagnosis), Bounteous calms somewhat and then goes on to play the doctor himself.

> BOUNTEOUS. How now, my wench, how dost?
> COURTESAN [coughs]. Huh, weak, knight, huh.
> PENITENT [aside]. She says true: he's a weak knight indeed.   (36–38)

These insinuations about Bounteous' failing potency make all the more comical his self-flattering conclusion that he has impregnated the patient. Handing coins to the "doctor," he congratulates himself, "Ha, ha, I have fitted her! An old knight and a cock o'th'game still! I have not spurs for nothing, I see." The "spur" is a pun on the testicles as well as a coin called a "spur royal"; Penitent picks up on the numismatic sense in his reply, which describes the "spurs" producing not offspring but small change – an "angel," or ten shillings (3.2.87–91).

The innuendo on "spurs" thus presents us with an interesting inversion of the poetic convention analyzed by Traub, which breaks down the female body into precious objects. Bounteous' coins/testicles have, as Penitent puts it, "hatch'd" money, not children. Sexual emissions (often euphemized as "spending") become liquid gold – and in fact *aurum potabile* is one of the costly medicines the courtesan's "health" requires, along with "liquor of coral, clear amber," "unicorn's horn," pearl, and other exotic substances (61–66). Conventional romantic poetry likened the attributes of the female body to coral, pearl, gold; here the female sexual object *ingests* these materials. Thus, when another male visitor inquires of the so-called physician, "Will she take anything yet?" he answers, "Yes, yes, yes, she'll take still. Sh'as a kind of facility in taking" (110–13). Eating, invagination, and swindling are interchangeable processes in this play's physical universe.

Along these same lines, the play's numerous constipation jokes figure monetary habits in medical terms: the sickroom scene highlights, in addition to the courtesan's "facility in taking," a corresponding "looseness" of her bowels, in the same way that all of the punning on "binding" during the preceding robbery scene suggests a scatological translation of Bounteous' sexual dryness (as Follywit says, "It came hard from him"). Scatological jokes may not normally be considered "bawdy," but they warrant consideration here for the role they play in the text's commodification of the human anatomy. A body that "hatches" coins or drinks gold is equally likely to defecate jewels.

This gender equity, so to speak, in the play's objectifying language provides a different outlook upon the problem of female adornment we first looked at in chapter 3. The scene in which Follywit disguises himself in the courtesan's clothing, in order to swindle his grandfather further as well as to "put her out of favor" (3.3.77), reiterates the fetishizing logic of the play. Follywit's disguise consists of "the lower part of a gentlewoman's gown, with a mask and a chin-clout" (84–85), providing yet more punning on "a gentlewoman's lower part" (88–89). This vein of humor anticipates the following scene, in which Penitent, forswearing his adultery, asks,

> What is [woman], took asunder from her clothes?
> Being ready, she consists of a hundred pieces
> Much like your German clock.   (4.1.19–21)

The idea of taking a woman asunder reminds us powerfully of the dismemberment motif discussed above, and resonates with another later scene in which the cross-dressed Follywit discovers his grandsire's casket of jewels and calls it "a gentlewoman of very good parts: diamond, ruby, sapphire, onyx" (4.3.42–43). Yet if anyone in the play can be said to consist "of a hundred pieces," it would be no woman, but old Bounteous himself, that "knight of thousands" (1.1.64); in fact, almost all of the ornaments mentioned in the play are either male possessions or male gifts to women (we will shortly see how another time-piece resembles, not a woman, but a penis). Follywit, inspecting the treasure trove he is about to carry away, observes, "This is the fruit of old grunting venery" (43) – by "this" he refers to his own action, the theft, as the following lines make clear, but at first glance it is easy to mistake the referent as the jewels themselves. And given the previous punning on coins and testicles, we know that money is, in fact, the only "fruit" likely to result from this old man's venery. Follywit goes on, "Oh fie, in your crinkling days, grandsire, keep a courtesan to hinder your grandchild! 'Tis against nature . . . and I hope you'll be weary on't" (48–51). The phrase "crinkling days" may be read as an innocent personification of age, but it is tempting to apply the modifier to the old man's wrinkled sexual equipment, here contrasted with his collection of smooth, hard jewels. The case of jewels brings blame upon the old lecher for his unnatural actions, more than upon the whore – who, as Follywit notes with surprise, has *neglected* to steal it, though it lay well within her reach (43–45).

On the other hand, the young trickster himself does not get away scot free. Just when he thinks he's carried off one last sleight-of-hand, a watch stolen from Bounteous chimes out in Follywit's pocket; now Bounteous has the opportunity to return the favor of his earlier frisking. The old man gropes him and chortles, "*Come* with a good will or not at all! I'll give thee a better *thing*," then discovers "A *piece*, a *piece*, gentlemen!" (5.2.262–64). "Shortrod" Harebrain, ever concerned (for good reason) with size, inquires, "Great or small?" and Penitent praises the old man's "fortunate hand," which has made "all to *come* at once" (265–69). And amidst all this ribald banter, Follywit owns up to his mischief and learns, for his reward, that the "virgin" he has just married is his grandfather's whore. The play ends in a forgiving patrilinear pledge:

> SIR BOUNTEOUS. Since I drink the top, take her and hark, I spice the
> bottom with a thousand mark.
> FOLLYWIT. By my troth, she is as good a cup of nectar as any bachelor
> needs to sip at.
> Tut, give me gold, it makes amends for vice.
> Maids without coin are caudles without spice.   (312–17)

So the woman whom we once expected "to drink down a man" (3.3.102) becomes herself a drink whose "bottom" (could we miss the pun?) is spiced with gold. In the end, the "butt" of Middleton's sexual satire is neither man nor woman, but universal greed.

Before we leave the bawdy body of this text behind, some last words
are required on the doctor's behalf – on behalf of the play's quack-
medical language and its ribald effects. In an effort not to repeat myself,
I have avoided bringing up the segment of act 3 involving the offstage sex
in the sickroom. But we have yet to grasp why illness – of all the possible
ruses required by lust – was deemed necessary in this play. The climactic
moment of the scene (and arguably of the entire play) is signaled by and
signified by a series of inarticulate sounds issuing from the mouth of the
supposed patient – to repeat: "huff, huff, huff," "hey, hy, hy," and "suh,
suh" – which generations of editors have refused to gloss as what these
terms so indisputably represent: noises designed to drown out the too-
vocal lovers. The obvious explanation for this editorial reticence is plain
prudishness. But there is more to it than that. These words represent
sounds, phonemes rather than graphemes; they are monosyllabic and
devoid of the sort of etymological heritage or semantic complexity which
tends to interest editors. Moreover, how does one gloss an ejaculation?
How does one gloss an "O" or an "ah" or even an "ay me"? Henning
glosses the courtesan's "huh" as a cough, and her "huff" as a sob, but
the words "cough" and "sob" are themselves onomatopoetical, are
themselves more about sound than signification. And anyone who has
ever overheard a couple making love knows that passion can be
(mis)construed as pain.

Here it would be helpful to cite what may seem a tangential episode.
The mother of the courtesan, who is her bawd, dissembles a care for her
daughter's supposed innocence when two prospective customers solicit
her company.

> MOTHER. Upon that condition you will promise me, gentlemen, to
> avoid all profane talk . . . I am contented your suits shall be
> granted.
> POSSIBILITY. Not a bawdy syllable, I protest!
> INESSE. Syllable was well placed there, for indeed your one syllables are
> your bawdiest words. Prick that down!   (1.1.197–205)

The modern idiom for these "one syllables" is the "four-letter word";
"prick" still qualifies despite its five letters. (And how noticeable is the
non-sexual sense of Inesse's last phrase: "note that down?") There is
something about a monosyllable which lends itself to profanity: in fact,
the first letter of the oath often suffices. Later in the play, Follywit and
his companion banter about the letters "P" and "C" as initials for "two
notable fit landing places for lechers" (3.3.129), leaving the audience to
guess at the obscene referents – "prick," "cock," "cunt?" And in regard
to contemporary profanity, we all know that the self-censoring "f" can
be as effective as the whole word.

At the bawdy heart of act 3, language breaks down into "huff, huff, huff," "hey, hy, hy," and "suh, suh." And this linguistic collapse marks the nexus of illness and sex, both conceived in terms of physical collapse (Bounteous' favorite oath is "pox" – another unwholesome mono-syllable). As in any textual breakdown, however, the editors immediately arrive to put the pieces together. What happened here? Where is the body? Whodunit? What does it mean?

I have some questions of my own. Why have modern editors over-looked the medical translation and, therefore, the sexual translation of the inarticulate "huff"? I find it hard to believe that they don't know, or at least suspect, what's going on offstage. Or perhaps it is just that: one must privilege actions on stage over actions transpiring somewhere else. But isn't this, after all, what we need editors for, to point out what readers might overlook? And in any case *why* is the sex offstage? Why is it offstage even in the text, even in the gloss? And this calls to mind a related question: *Why is the sexual meaning in any "innuendo" invariably listed as secondary*? Why does the editor gloss, for instance, "stone" as "(a) gemstone, (b) testicle" – or "at a stand" as "(a) in a state of perplexity, (b) with *penis erectus*." Why is the sexual always relegated to (b)? And, excuse me, but why *penis erectus* rather than "erect penis"? Do we need the Latin?

Don't get me wrong. I like editors. One of my best friends is an editor. I, at times, have been guilty of editing.[20] But why is the sexual meaning always supplementary, always secondary, always deferred? The answer to this may, of course, ultimately have little to do with editors or even the texts that they edit. Why is sex likened to illness; why is sexual passion likened to physical pain; why is sex not fit for viewing; why is it not *normative*? What is it about sex that makes us afraid?

Perhaps it is time to turn to the man with all the answers.

II   Shakespeare: name of the father

Iago's first word in *Othello* is an oath – at least, that is what the first quarto tells us; the oath, "'Sblood," was censored out of later printings of the play, along with a good number of other profanities, among them "'swounds" (an oath originally invoking "God's wounds"), "Lord," and as many as seventeen occurrences of the name of God. On the other hand, it is not Iago's blaspheming which causes Brabanzio to ask him, "What profane wretch art thou?" (1.1.116) or Desdemona to call him "a most profane and liberal counsellor" (2.1.166–67). What bothers these characters about the way Iago speaks is the very thing that, paradoxi-cally, baffles speech in the play, driving the plot to its culmination in inarticulate, sexualized violence and a woman's literal smothering and silencing. Iago's profanity has less to do with God than with sex, although, as we shall see, it draws its force from the collision – or the confusion – of both.

There is something remarkable about the way Iago talks sex; he manages to do so with almost no direct reference to the human anatomy – two or three times he mentions fingers, palms, or lips, but in contexts only obliquely sensual; the tongue is his favorite member, but only as a metonymy for speech. Rather, Iago's most suggestive phrases feature animal bodies, and even so in a manner not very explicit:

> an old black ram
> Is tupping your white ewe. (1.1.88–89)

> your daughter covered with a Barbary horse. (113–14)

> the beast with two backs. (118–19)

> change the cod's head for the salmon's tail. (2.1.158)

> as prime as goats, as hot as monkeys,
> As salt as wolves in pride. (3.3.408–9)

One can hardly call these images graphic. Otherwise, when Iago discusses human sexuality, his terms tend toward the abstract: "gross clasps" (1.1.128); "bold and saucy wrongs" (130); "gross revolt" (136); "fresh appetite" (2.1.229); "loose affection" (241); "lust and foul thoughts" (258). The sex act is troped as "work" (2.1.118), as "sport" (228), as a man's "office" (1.3.380) or his "seat" (2.1.295). Moreover, when Iago renders his most powerful sexual impression, he does so without a ghost of indecency, in fact, more by way of silences than words; he first inspires Othello to jealousy merely by a pointed question about Cassio's familiarity with Desdemona, followed by meaningful pauses.

Nonetheless, Iago's speech is undeniably provocative, capable of endowing with sexual meaning as innocent an object as a lady's handkerchief (a far cry from the sort of phallic prop Middleton would have chosen). For Iago knows that:

> Trifles light as air
> Are to the jealous confirmations strong
> As proofs of holy writ. (3.3.326–28).

Thus Iago invokes a new scripture of jealousy and wins his first credulous convert. And the religious metaphor is worth more than a passing glance; this is the second time Iago mentions God and adultery in the same breath, each time in effect sanctifying his own lies. Yet precisely what is Iago saying about the Word of God? What seems at first another reminder that man (men) lacks divine omniscience may also serve as a reminder that nothing, not even God, can be "known." The "proof" of Desdemona's inconstancy will not be found in holy writ (nor does it matter to Iago, so long as men believe him), but this very conceit places religious faith and male sexual jealousy in disturbingly close quarters and exposes Iago at his most profane. Iago's invocation of a scriptural standard for "proof" only reiterates the problem of invisibility and drags the play deeper into its morass of skepticism and paranoia. "Her honour," he reminds Othello, "is an essence that's not seen" (4.1.16). And God is men's secret.

What holy writ "proves" is that the Word was made flesh. Iago's words enflesh a fiction of adultery, make the fantasy so vivid that Othello loses his powers of reason. And curiously enough, the words required for this magic tend to be few, and short. The discussion which opens act 4 is one example of Iago's verbal economy, and its effects.

> IAGO. Will you think so?
> OTHELLO.   Think so, Iago?
> IAGO. What, to kiss in private?
> OTHELLO.   An unauthorized kiss.
> IAGO. Or to be naked with her friend in bed
> An hour or more, not meaning any harm?   (4.1.1–4)

Of course, these words are enough of a provocation to jealousy, but what drives Othello out of his mind, what leads him to violence, is contained in one brief syllable, and not one of Middleton's prime offenders.

> OTHELLO.   What hath he said?
> IAGO. Faith, that he did – I know not what he did.
> OTHELLO. What? what?
> IAGO.   Lie –
> OTHELLO.   With her?
> IAGO.   With her, on her, what you will.

> (31–33)

The most offensive syllable here is not the word "lie." The shift from the more abstract, spatially ambiguous preposition "with" to the stunningly concrete "on" presents the imagined act between Cassio and Desdemona so palpably that Othello lapses into inarticulate rage.

Lie with her? Lie on her? We say "lie on her" when they belie her. Lie with her? 'Swounds, that's fulsome! Handkerchief – confessions – handkerchief . . . It is not words that shakes me thus. Pish! Noses, ears, and lips. Is't possible? Confess? Handkerchief? O devil!
He falls down in a trance.   (4.1.34–42)

Of course Othello deceives himself: it *is* words that shake him thus, as I am not the first reader to note.[21] His senseless raving about "noses, ears, and lips" only highlights the gap between words and bodies which he himself fails to see – perhaps because what he "sees" in his mind seems so much more real than words. Hence the "trance" which follows this outburst. Iago's prepositional lewdness, enacted in one short syllable – that smallest fragment of speech – deprives Othello of the power of speech entirely.

And prepositions tend to constitute the most material and therefore the most potentially erotic elements of English syntax – in, out, into, between.[22] Iago's use of the seemingly innocent phoneme "on" hits Othello like the proverbial ton of bricks; "on" here seems a kind of bedrock of language beyond which it cannot be broken down; it is the linguistic signifier of mass in contact with mass, body on top of body. No wonder Iago needn't dirty his hands with obscenity; he knows that the most neutral language is solid enough to make sex from. Likewise, in lieu of any material evidence for his claim, he weaves sexual fictions out of weighty, quasi-onomatopoeic verbs like "tupping," "covered," and "topped," thus setting forth not merely the concept of unchastity, but a concrete, even subliminally aural, impression of vigorous copulation.

The "on" thus implies an "in," an invagination; it gestures toward offstage sex, but more specifically toward the vaginal entrance thus analogized by Othello:

> I had rather be a toad
> And live upon the vapor of a dungeon
> Than keep a corner in the thing I love
> For others' uses.   (3.3.274–77)

Patricia Parker's analysis underscores the density, throughout the text, of this rhetoric of dilation, of holes.[23] But what strikes me about this "corner in" Desdemona (or her "thing") is the way it unfolds – in her husband's jealous fantasy – into an architectural space which engulfs him entirely. There is a lot in this "in." I am reminded of a moment in a lesser-known and contemporaneous play where the psychic space of male jealousy and the vaginal space of copulation converge in a locked offstage structure and on the preposition "in." The suspicious husband in *The Family of Love* follows his wife to a Puritan meeting-house but then botches the pass-word phrase, "Brother in the Family" (he says, "Familiar Brother"), and hence is shut out of the offstage site of cuckolding. In response to the dismissive voice *"within,"* he rages, "I made ellipsis of *in* in this place . . . the want of *in* put me clean out" (3.2.101–2).[24] Clean out of an uncleanly place, but also clean out of his wits.

This tangent into the power of prepositions may allow us to unlock the microcosmic workings of obscenity in language: it occurs to me, for instance, that some of our most potent (and popular) current-day expletives hinge upon prepositions ("up yours," "fuck off," and all of their various permutations). But the force of these expressions discloses the operation of something larger than "sex" or sexual organs. To refer again to the *Family of Love* episode, the punning on "in" has a cultural dimension not immediately available to modern readers: Puritans did in fact call themselves brothers and sisters in Christ, and the particular entrance ritual satirized here is detailed in the play's source, a pamphlet called (interestingly enough), *The Displaying of an horrible sect . . . naming themselves the Familie of Love.*[25] And there are further connections to Puritan thought. John Bunyan, writing later in the century, comments on Christ's admonition, "Strive to enter in at the strait gate" (Luke, 13.24): "Behold therefore what a great thing the Lord Jesus hath included in this little word, *in*, in this word is wrapt up an whole heaven"; he urges readers to "be heedful" so as not to "pass over . . . such a word as may have a glorious kingdom and eternal salvation in the bowels of it."[26] Prepositions, thus, can manifest or materialize – can *dilate* - the sacred as well as the sexual.

No wonder, then, Iago's potent "on" has the effect of placing Othello *"in"* a literal *"trance"* – which is, after all, a kind of inner-space, where he may "grossly gape on" things which are "impossible . . . [to] see." "Entrance," the noun, meets the verb, "en*trance*." And this spell of jealous horror is all the more significant in contrast with his first speechless moment, upon meeting Desdemona in Cyprus: "I cannot speak enough of this content. / It stops me here, it is too much of joy" (2.1.197–98). Nonetheless, in act 5 the unspeakable "too much of joy" becomes too much of shame: "Let me not name it to you, you chaste stars" (5.2.2). Likewise, Desdemona's abhorrence of a single word makes for the *non sequitur*, "I cannot say 'whore'" (4.2.165), as she also succumbs to the bewildering effects of Iago's profane suggestions.

But the name that dominates the murder scene – that crowning episode of verbal disintegration – was a name more taboo than "whore" on the early modern English stage, the very name that, even in the uncensored first quarto, Iago censored out of his own first oath: the name of God. As Desdemona is murdered, she cries, "O Lord, Lord, Lord" (5.2.93). And this prayer is nearly drowned out by similar cries, as language in the scene progressively dissolves into a battery of monosyllables. Othello's brutal "Out, strumpet!" and "Down, strumpet" (84–86) and Emilia's defiant " 'Twill out, 'twill out" (225) are prepositional bullets which transmit a world of rage. And the chaos of the page is littered with the irreducible "O" – to be exact, "O" is uttered fifty-one times in this scene,[27] sometimes in succession, in a staccato of grief.

"On," "out," "whore," "Lord," "God" . . . then the lone vowel, "O." What is the meaning of this linguistic collapse? Joel Fineman considers "the sound of *O*" repeated throughout "*Othello* to both occasion and to objectify in language Othello's hollow self" – a hollowness which he himself asserts after the murder is completed: "That's he that was Othello, here I am" (5.2.290)[28] – which is, I would add, his answer to Desdemona's "Nobody, I myself. Farewell" (5.2.133). Ejaculation ultimately equals self-negation. Having emptied his own name, his own self, finally Othello can only call upon not the name of God, but the name of the wife he has just killed, and finally, not even that: "O Desdemon! Dead Desdemon! Dead! O! O!" (288). Stanley Cavell points out "the hell and the demon staring out of the names of Othello and Desdemona,"[29] but what stares – or rather, gapes – at the very bottom of both is the anonymous, universal moan (OH-thell-OH; des-da-MOAN-ah). Othello's final strangulation of his wife's name reduces it to the bare vowel, "O," which also, oddly enough, yawns in the names "Lord," "God." The "O" at the core of God bespeaks the victim's open mouth: the inarticulate cry, the sigh, the silent prayer.[30] Both speech and its denial: voice denied a tongue.

Modern editors have quite sensibly re-inserted God's name into the text of *Othello* where it had been removed; the Riverside edition encloses these oaths in square brackets – a demure editorial sneeze. But there is something hauntingly ironic about these fingerprints of censorship, considering the subject of the play. An unspeakable act; an unspeakable name; and a woman silenced on the altar of chastity.

Juliet wonders, "What's in a name?" (2.1.85).[31] One might as easily ask, "What is in language?" According to constructionist theory, everything (and nothing). And indeed, in this chapter we have been sifting through bawdy at a frantic pace – weighing the pricks and the pieces (not to mention the suggestive pauses) – in the hopes of finding some corporeal kernel within language. And, so far, we have failed, miserably. But we cannot give up our search without at least a brief glance at the world's greatest love story. Not that I can promise to say anything new about this prodigiously analyzed and theorized play (and anyway, Zeffirelli seems to say it all in one bare shot) *but* . . .

To Juliet a name "is nor hand, nor foot, / Nor arm, nor face, *nor any other part* / Belonging to a man" (82–84; emphasis added). Romeo, however, is less certain.

> O tell me, friar, tell me,
> In what vile part of this anatomy
> Doth my name lodge? Tell me, that I may sack
> The hateful mansion.   (3.3.104–7)

From a feminist perspective, this is a pretty stupid question: we all know that Romeo's name, as the mark of patriarchal power, of course lodges in the part of him that will beget Montague heirs, as his own use of the term "vile" suggests he knows. Here Romeo threatens to wield his blade against his penis, but elsewhere in the play, as Coppélia Kahn demonstrates, the two "weapons" are equated; for in Shakespeare's Verona "it is phallic violence that ties men to their fathers."[32] Hence the machismo and ribaldry with which the play begins. As Kahn explains, "the many puns on 'stand' as standing one's ground in fighting and as erection attest that fighting in the feud demonstrates virility as well as valor."[33]

This chapter is already aswim in phallic puns, so I will not detail the handful to which Kahn refers. But more than any of the plays mentioned in this chapter, *Romeo and Juliet* presents a brand of sexual language infused with aggression and, as we shall see, a corresponding fear. Kahn argues that the text "plays out a conflict between manhood as violence on behalf of fathers and manhood as separation from the fathers and sexual union with women"[34] – but underlying both is an anxiety not particular to males or to patriarchy, an anxiety about something larger than any feud or any notion of "manhood."

This is all about bodies in contact.

The love between Romeo and Juliet is, from its inception, transcendentally dangerous. When Romeo finds his way to Juliet's balcony, they both know he is risking his life (even if his high-flung poetic raptures seem to deny it). And the feeling itself, its suddenness and power, brings its own attendant anxiety; hence they speak of vows. A vow is a way to *make words matter*, to fuse words with deeds, with the physical world. But what in the physical world, the lovers wonder, is solid enough, enduring enough to swear by? They discuss the sun, the moon. The first time I read the play, I wondered why Romeo does not simply swear to God. The name of God is conspicuously absent in this scene, although it appears elsewhere in the play, which was printed prior to the ban on profanity. Perhaps Romeo cannot swear by the name of the Father because he cannot swear by his own father's name. So Juliet finally tells him, "Do not swear at all, / Or if thou wilt, swear by thy gracious self, / Which is the god of my idolatry" (2.1.154–56). Christian doctrine distrusted earthly love for this very reason: even in wedlock, one could sin by loving one's mate for himself alone (*cupiditas*) rather than for God within him (*caritas*).[35] Juliet, however, defies the injunction to privilege

Word over flesh: she reveres what she can touch and see, and dismisses what she cannot. "What's in a name?"

Juliet dwells in the physical world, and this is not easy in a place as rugged as Verona, a city overrun by quarrelsome youths and tyrannical fathers. From early childhood, though, Juliet has proven herself capable of survival; the Nurse, calculating her age, recalls an earthquake on the day Juliet was weaned, and then reminisces about a child who

> could stand high-lone. Nay, by th' rood,
> She could have run and waddled all about,
> For even the day before, she broke her brow,
> And then my husband – God be with his soul,
> A was a merry man! – took up the child.
> "Yea," quoth he, "dost thou fall upon thy face?
> Thou wilt fall backward when thou hast more wit,
> Wilt thou not, Jule?" And, by my holidom,
> The pretty wretch left crying and said "Ay."   (1.3.38–46)

From the earthquake to the broken brow, this retelling of a bawdy joke at a child's expense tells us enough about Juliet and her world to prepare us for the play's climactic scene under the earth, in a tomb. "By th' rood" or the cross under which Jesus fell, the nurse asserts the truth of her recollection. The child breaks her brow on the hard earth as she will one day break her hymen on Romeo's "naked weapon," as she will one day break her heart upon the point of Romeo's knife. The child cries, and then stops crying; the child says, "Ay." One syllable: a homophone for "I." "Yes," an acceptance: I will fall; I will love, and die, I. "Eroticism," writes Georges Bataille, "is assenting to life up to the point of death."[36] Derrida writes of the "*yes* more ancient than knowledge" – more ancient, even, than language.[37] And for early modern women, the sex/death trope was more than a trope, considering the life-threatening nature of child-birth; bodies in contact means danger, means impact. Juliet's "Ay" is a brave syllable indeed.

Juliet also says "Ay" to the tomb, with its "loathsome smells" and horror (4.3.45). Steeling herself to swallow the Friar's potion, she briefly hesitates. What if she does not wake? Or, she wonders,

> O, if I wake, shall I not be distraught,
> Environèd with all these hideous fears,
> And madly play with my forefathers' joints,
> And pluck the mangled Tybalt from his shroud,
> And, in this rage, with some great kinsman's bone
> As with a club dash out my desp'rate brains?   (48–53)

As the plot propels the lovers away from their nuptials and toward the tomb, the language of bones takes the place of bawdy. Juliet's fantasy of madness, here, anticipates the madness of Romeo before the tomb, when he threatens Balthasar,

> If thou, jealous, dost return to pry
> In what I farther shall intend to do,
> By heaven, I will tear thee joint by joint,
> And strew this hungry churchyard with thy limbs.   (5.3.33–36)

Considering the violence of Romeo's outburst, Paris is not entirely unjustified in his fear that Romeo intends (like Middleton's Tyrant) "some villainous shame / To the dead bodies" within the tomb (52–53). The harm Romeo intends is toward himself, but this is equally "unhallowed toil" (54), the final playing out of his earlier impulse to "sack / The hateful mansion" of his body. Suicide, after all, is considered a mortal sin.

Sexual intercourse itself, in the early modern world view, was also perceived as "unhallowed toil," threatening the integrity of soul and body; each orgasm, each "expense of spirit" (in the terms of Shakespeare's Sonnet 129), shortened one's life. Thus Juliet makes her body a "sheath" for Romeo's blade, the phallic trope playing out to its inevitable conclusion: "O happy dagger, / This is thy sheath! There rust, and let me die" (168–69). In the throes of death, she imagines not only her body's dissolution, but the dissolution of the blade lodged inside her. This is the outcome of her "idolatry": flesh and metal melt and merge. Phillip Stubbes' diatribe against sumptuary excess in *The Anatomie of Abuses* includes an exhortation against the "dissolute minions" who pierce their ears, comparing them to "People in the Orientall parte of the World" who lance their skin and set "therein . . . precious Stones."[38] We recall the *aurum potabile* and the "dissolved pearl" prescribed to Middleton's whore (the diagnosis: lust); we recall the gold-spiced "cup" of her body given in wedlock. Romeo, buying the poison which enables his final union with Juliet, tells the poor apothecary, "There is thy gold – worse poison to men's souls" – even while noting that this "poison" will buy the poor man "flesh" (5.1.80–84). A final irony: to commemorate Juliet's death, Montague vows to "raise her statue in pure gold" (5.3.298).

The medieval and early modern belief systems placed bodies and things on the same continuum, the same "chain of being": the physical world and the human anatomy were composed of the same four elements.[39] From a neo-Platonic Christian perspective, the more "worldly" one's existence, the more focused on visible, palpable things, the greater the distance from heaven and the more unhallowed or thing-like one's body became. "For if ye live after the flesh," says St. Paul, "ye shall die" (Rom., 8.13).[40] In a sense, therefore, all matter was poison, and all contact deadly – body to body, body to earth.

As we observed in chapter 3, weighing Ursula's unholy bulk and pondering the Puritan's horror of puppets, the terror of *things* necessitates God, drives our belief in a "Word made flesh." Perhaps this is why *Romeo and Juliet* seems a profoundly impious text.[41] Juliet's "What's in a name?" verges on sacrilege; her injunction, "Do not swear," confirms this. On the other hand, in a world where the name of the father is the name of the feud, this repudiation seems the most (loosely speaking) Christian choice. The lovers meet in a Godless universe and build their own religion of love.

What is it about this Godless play that so moves us? Perhaps the Godlessness itself? We know all of the trite explanations: we admire the heroism and passion of the young, "star-crossed lovers"; we are moved by this "classic" story of youthful idealism versus parental corruption; et cetera, et cetera. But one thing is worth repeating: in the world's greatest love story, two people make love, and then die. And they do so unflinchingly, remorselessly, and voluptuously, and despite all the laws of their world. Juliet grabs the Friar's vial, crying, "Give me, give me! O, tell not me of fear!" (4.1.121). Romeo swallows poison and gasps over Juliet's lips, "Thus with a kiss, I die" (5.3.120). We have seen the fatal kiss before; we have seen, innumerable times, the pun on "die." One syllable. Like "God," like "yes," like Juliet's "Ay." Shave off the "D" and the vowel alone speaks, names, "I" . . . affirms, "Ay" . . .

We are back to the monosyllable, that bedrock of language upon which this chapter breaks its brow. What is the secret to these syllables; what makes them so "hard" – so persistently, so insistently palpable – and at the same time, so emotive? It seems that once we break language down to its smallest aural fragment, we get closest to the body, to the embodied "I," closest to what we describe as "real." Syllables are the bones of language. The longer words are inevitably the more abstract – not only because they are Latinate or linguistically foreign, but also because they are less onomatopoetical, less like sounds in the physical world. Long words are the most "human" sounds, the most thinking sounds, while short words, ejaculations, can resemble the cries of animals. And these cries move us. Who can forget Othello's howl, "O, O, O!?"

In life and in drama, not all sounds are intelligible, even if all sounds do inevitably come to signify. Aristotle distinguishes the human "gift of speech" from "mere voice" indicating "pleasure or pain . . . found in other animals"[42] – but, since Aristotle, western literary scholarship has had little to say about this primal "mere voice," in animals or in humans. There are some exceptions; Kristeva, for instance, outlines an entire discipline, "semanalysis," premised upon a "semiotic *chora*" driving all discursive acts; the *chora*, itself a "provisional articulation . . . analogous only to vocal or kinetic rhythm," cannot be recovered in signification, but its boundary may be observed in moments of rupture against or within the symbolic.[43] Kristeva views poetic language as recuperating or exposing these ruptures: in other words, she looks at the process in reverse. Elaine Scarry approaches the phenomenon from a different angle, through the contemplation of pain, which "does not simply resist language but actively destroys it, bringing about an immediate reversion to a state anterior to language," and producing the very "sounds and cries" made by an animal, or an infant.[44] Bearing in mind the feminist critique of evolutionary anthropology, primatology, and other origins-minded disciplines,[45] I nonetheless think it is safe to put my post-structuralist anti-positivism aside for a moment and cite a few points of what we call general scientific knowledge. Human animals, we have good reason to believe, made sounds before they made speech, and made speech more than 20,000 years before they made writing, and music may have been the earliest art form.[46] We do know that theater from its dimmest origins and throughout the Renaissance used music.[47] And music requires rhythm: percussion, repercussion.

Why are monosyllables the most thing-like, the most solid, the weightiest, the most *moving* words? Perhaps because things, when dropped, produce one syllable, one percussion. The smallest units of speech imitate the sound of matter striking matter – the thump of the apple hitting the earth, the sound of a body hitting the earth, the sound of *impact*. Speech acts themselves are described in terms of metaphorical, social "impact"; rhetoric is defined by its ability to persuade, to "move." But there are also whole classes of speech devoted to literal (bodily) impact – its sensations, its effects. We walk on two legs and so, like Juliet, we fall. That is, perhaps, the most quintessentially human action: falling. Most mammals do not have to "fall" in order to copulate; they fall when they sleep, and die. We, however, are at the mercy of gravity.[48] Hence we link sex and death. Hence we fear sexual pleasure ("What if I never awaken?"). Hence we walk in fear, and love in fear. Fear of contact; fear of impact. Ashes, ashes, we all fall down.

Sex requires impact. And in the sound of bodily impact, concussion and vocalization are often indistinguishable: the thump; the involuntary exhalation or cry. Sex is one syllable, repeated. And once it's down to "huff, huff, huff," one can scarcely – can one? – call it speech.[49] Beat a drum, toll a bell, and you send the same message: percussion, repercussion. The sexual madness of Middleton's "mad world" makes its entrance not in words but in sounds; it takes place, *pace* Derrida, *outside the text*; neither on stage nor off – in our ears, in our guts.

Ejaculations happen.

When we speak, we are doing something which is necessarily physical, although we prefer to think of it as intellectual. Speech is not only a semiotic but also a physical experience, a *felt* experience; the circling of the lips required to speak the "O" in *Othello* precedes the necessary release of air from the lungs, which precedes the vibration of the larynx, which precedes the utterance, and our hearing it. And the hearing of speech is also a physical experience; sound waves are physical phenomena; they must be registered bodily before they can be understood. Perhaps words are not (material) things, but sounds are things, produced by vibrations in the air that enter the ear canal and impact the ear drum (percussion), which then sends a message to the brain.

Perhaps our students' gut-level resistance to the post-structuralist denial of pre-discursive experience has to do with that split-second interval between our sensory perception of a word and our mental decoding of the word. This is a time-lag of which we are dimly, if at all, aware, but which haunts us; we want to say that we "just know" or we "sense" or we "feel" in an uncanny way that we do experience, or have experienced (perhaps in our infancy, or in our species' infancy) something outside any system of meaning, *something as yet unnamed*, and we want to say this because our bodies remember, even if our minds do not,[50] the priority of the *sensations of speech*.

This is all by way of saying that spoken words have impact, that they *arouse*. In most if not all cases, that arousal is mediated by discursive structures, but a shout, I believe, impacts the ear of a primate no less than my own. The audience at a production of *Othello* registers Iago's shouting at Brabanzio's window not just as meaning but as sensation, and our responses to that shout, however mediated by its signification, are partially physical – a sharp intake of breath, an increased heart-rate may result. And theater requires this response. Elin Diamond explores "the shudder of catharsis" as "a sentient convergence of body and meaning, when the material body, in all its otherness, makes itself felt to consciousness even as it enters discursive categories that make it mean."[51] The "O's" built into the murder-scene in *Othello* are designed to *excite* the listening body. Similarly, the offstage panting of Middleton's lovers (performed with gusto) could conceivably make for a real (if discursively mediated) turn-on; the very nightmare of the antitheatricalists. That is why offstage sex is almost never *heard*; obscene, and therefore unseen, God forbid it should be felt.

6   Ejaculations and conclusions: toward an erotic theoretics

> What does *the body mean to say* by trembling or crying?
> Jacques Derrida, *The Gift of Death*[1]

There's something scary in there.

I'm thinking of the conjuror's circle with which we began. I'm wondering if I made a Faustian bargain, staring into that hole in the text. Because look where it has led. After circling and circling and circling the body, tracing its traces in discourse, I am now forced to turn and look in the face the specter I have summoned. Do you see what I see?

The phenomenon I have described as early modern "boundary confusion" – the anxiety of a culture *on the brink* of new ways of seeing, knowing – is not unlike the state we're in now, post-humanism, "post-feminism," post-deconstruction, post-book. Nicholas Royle, in a paper delivered at a symposium called "Futures for Jacques Derrida," describes "all of Derrida's work," and the impact of deconstruction overall, in terms of our "trembling" before the "abyssal self-reference . . . the as yet to be named yes yes of literature."[2] The future of literary theory, and particularly of feminist theory (never mind the future of letters in general in our "virtual" culture), looks scary indeed.

But as intimidating as one might find the post-structuralist (or rather, the post-post-structuralist) textual cosmos – there is something (to me, at least) equally, if not more frightening *in there*, inside the circle this essay has drawn, inside the circles inside the texts drawn into this circling text: the ghost of a body that speaks from out of the abyss of an unspeakable past; the body which speaks in each of us, when we find ourselves speechless. And I wonder whether the post-structuralist denial of "a pre-discursive body" – a belief which arose out of a necessary move against essentialism – is not being maintained, now, past its political utility (and perhaps at a certain intellectual expense), partially out of fear – just as the dogmas of biological essentialism (and, currently, of Christian fundamentalism) were maintained, for centuries, out of fear. Fear of what's out there, but, even more so, of what's in there, in the stuff of

132

which we are composed; as all apocalyptic or existential terrors, arguably, arise from the body, from the foreknowledge of death. In this respect we seem to have made little progress in relation to the flesh/world anxieties of early modern English authors; indeed, we might have come full circle.

Let's look one last time at the conjuring circle in Renaissance drama, that hole in the world in the hole in the text, before going on to conjure a conclusion relevant to our current theoretical and political concerns. Middleton's *The Black Book* begins with a prologue delivered by Lucifer himself.

> Now is hell landed here upon the earth,
> When Lucifer, in limbs of burning gold,
> Ascends this dusty theatre of the world,
> To join his powers; and, were it numbered well,
> There are more devils on earth than are in hell.   (Moral. 1–5)

The lesson is similar to that taught Faustus by Mephostophilis, as cited in my Introduction: "Hell hath no limits"; hell has been loosed from its confines. Lucifer goes on to gloat, "That heaven is hung so high, drawn up so far, / And made so fast, nailed up with many a star" (8–9), thus building on the world/theater metaphor while also depicting heaven as both inaccessible and illusory, a matter of stagecraft: like the looking-glass heaven described by Bosola, a mere *trompe l'oeil*. But the theater trope, as we have noted before, tends to carry magic with it; with an almost mathematical regularity, depictions of the circular stage bring forth associations with necromancy, and sex. Lucifer boasts:

> to fire false embraces,
> I make the world burn now in secret places;
> I haunt invisible corners as a spy,
> And in adulterous circles there rise I;
> There am I conjured up through hot desire,
> And where hell rises, there must needs be fire.   (16–21)

Here we see the circular embrace, the circular globe, and the "secret" enclosures (in the bedroom? in the body?) where sex is staged. Yet somehow, in the midst of this spiraling imagery, Lucifer finds "invisible corners" to haunt; the spatial and geometrical oxymoron reinforces the impression of a world inside-out, epitomizing once again the boundary confusion which haunts the early modern imagination. Indeed, these impossible "corners" remind me not only of the "corner in [Desdemona's] thing," but finally, of the "round earth's imagined corners" in which Donne places the trumpeting angels of the apocalypse.[3]

Middleton depicts a world on fire. And this fire represents both illicit sex and the resulting damnation: Lucifer states that adultery is the reigning sin, "For which the world shall like a strumpet burn" (15). As I mentioned in chapter 3, in relation to Ursula's booth with its hot, smoking "pit," the vagina was often euphemized, in Renaissance literature, as hell; the conjuring circle, where Lucifer rises, is hell's microcosm. By the same token, though, the conjuring trope also equates the conjured spirit or devil with the "rising" penis. Mercutio jokes that it would "anger" Romeo "To raise a spirit in his mistress' circle / . . . letting it there stand / Till she had laid it . . . down" (2.1.24–26). *Henry V* returns, in its final scene, to the conjuring metaphor used in the Prologue, as Henry strives to "conjure up the spirit of love" in his bride, and is advised, "If you would conjure in her, you must make a circle" (5.2.286–91). The humor of the reply is that it replaces the romanticized object of conjuration, the "spirit of love," with a suggestive ambiguity (pointed up by that naughty preposition, "in"). Similarly, Robin steals one of Faustus' "conjuring books," intending to "search some circles for" himself by making "all the maidens in [his] parish dance . . . stark naked before" him (6.1–4).

But the gendered valences of circle and spirit are not always clear; a closer look at Robin's plan reveals the doubleness of the conjuring trope: he must first draw his own circle in order to get close to the vaginal "circles" he would like to "search" in the naked maidens. Here is a similar episode in Thomas Dekker's *Westward Ho!*, in which necromancy becomes a metaphor for seduction.

> EARL. Haue you pefum'd this Chamber?
> OMN.   Yes my Lord.
> EARL. The banquet?
> OMN.   It stands ready.
> EARL.   Go, let musicke
> Charme with her excellent voice and awfull scilence
> Through al this building, that her sphaery soule
> May (on the wings of Ayre) in thousand formes
> Inuisibly flie, yet be inioy'd. Away.
> 1. SERU. Does my Lorde meane to Coniure that hee drawes this
> strange Characters.
> 2. SERU. He does: but we shal see neither the Spirit that rises, nor the
> Circle it rises in.   (4.2.1–10)[4]

What strikes me about this passage is the way the Earl "sets the stage" for his erotic visitant, the way perfume, food, and music (described as "sphaery," circular) function as "Characters" a magician "drawes" in order to draw the spirit (or devil; she is called both in this scene) into his circle.

Within the magic circle, spirits could be conjured but, more importantly, contained; it functioned as both womb and stocks (to cite two
powerful symbols from *Bartholomew Fair*) for the spirits summoned
there. Analogous to the erotic matrix I call the offstage, the conjuring
circle seems a perfect symbol for the eroticism of the early modern stage
– the circle within which male dramatists (with the help of boy actors)
conjured the dangerous and desirable specter of woman. The question
remains, however, as to how well this image (and the stage which
produced it, and which it mirrored) contained the phallocentric anxieties
and fascinations it invoked. The conjuring circle is a female (womb)
symbol and a male invention; the conjuror by definition stands apart
from his art form, like the puppet-master with his invisible strings. But
the sexual puns surrounding the figure underscore the conjuror's connection to his creation: Henry cannot "conjure in" his betrothed, in the
bawdy sense, from outside the circle. Hence the slippage of the metaphor,
woman-as-spirit, woman-as-circle, man-as-magician, man-as-devil. And
anyway, the necromancer, and his devil, are both damned.

This is not to overlook the "good" magicians in Renaissance drama,
the benign Prosperos, embodying, to many critics, humanist optimism
about "man's" potential.[5] Quite the contrary: my point is that dramatists
saw their art as a kind of conjuration – involving similar glories and
similar dangers. I am struck, for instance, by the curious semantic
conjunction in Dekker's use of the word "Characters," cited above. In
the primary sense, of course, the word refers to symbols or letters drawn
in or around the magic circle, a necessary part of the conjuring exercise –
but the subtler, secondary sense points to the seducer/necromancer as an
author, as the creator of the woman he summons.[6] And there's more.
These "Characters" are, from the evidence of other sorcerous portraits,
most likely blasphemous signifiers: Faustus fills his magic circle with
"Jehovah's name, / Forward and backward anagrammatized" and
"th'abbreviated names of holy saints" (3.18–20).

On the other hand, the inscriptions of black magic do not, in
themselves, do the trick: a charm by definition is a vocalization; sound
activates the words. And having discussed the auditory backbone of at
least one erotic episode in drama, we are now in a position to appreciate
the impact of the aural. Also, it is noteworthy that Faustus conjures in
Latin. As part of a general attack on the incantatory aspects of prayer,
the Reformers objected to the ecclesiastical use of Latin, which to the
uncomprehending masses would amount to sound as divorced from
sense, and thus be no different from a charm.[7] Epitomizing the sound/
sense division, Dekker's seducer uses music to "charme" his victim, thus
supporting the antitheatricalist claim that music "stirreth up filthie lust

. . . [and] ravisheth the hart."[8] For what is to stop the music in this play from casting its sexual spell upon the audience?

The above examples invite us to view the conjuring circle as an analogy for the offstage and conjuring as a metaphor for, even as a provocation to, sexual intercourse: in one final example, the circle *is* the offstage – that is, the love-magic and the coupling it leads to are both "enacted" (in quick succession) *within*, and in such a way as to (so to speak) draw us in too. The passage, from John Marston's *Sophonisba* (printed and probably performed in that pivotal year, 1606), perfectly "rounds off" this exploration of the "hole in the text," as well as our more immediate discussion of sound and theatrical magic – for here Marston brings together music, witchcraft, and offstage sex, in a sequence designed to leave spectators breathless.

The plot of this sensational tragedy – originally titled, *The Wonder of Women; Or The Tragedy of Sophonisba* – is driven by the successive attempts of a Libyan king, Syphax, to rape the heroine, whose desperate attempts at evasion include a bed-trick using a drugged male "Negro" slave (whom Syphax immediately recognizes and kills), and a suicide threat, to which Syphax responds by threatening to rape her corpse. Finally, the would-be necrophile/rapist turns to the aid of a sorceress, Erictho, whose entrance on stage is marked by *"infernal music"* from below and a lengthy description of her grisly, sexualized uses of the dead (4.1.89–124).[9] Just before she exits to perform the promised charm, the witch explains that when he hears her "force / The air to music" – itself a kind of rape – he should "make proud [his] raised delight" (4.1.177–80) – that is, nurture the "spirit" (semen/erection) she will conjure in him. Syphax grows increasingly excited as he hears the same *"infernal music"* from below the stage, now accompanied by the voice chanting *"within"* – when *"A treble viol and a bass lute . . . within"* join in the offstage chorus, he cries "O thou power of sound, / How thou dost melt me!" (202–3).

In fact the audience is familiar with Syphax's sensitivity to sound: earlier, as he stood outside the curtained bed in which he thought Sophonisba awaited him, he sent the servants outside "ear-reach / Of the soft cries nice shrinking brides do yield" (3.1.172–73), and then called for music, complaining that "silence . . . dost swallow pleasure" (176). In the climactic later scene, however, the music eventually issues from at least two and possibly three offstage sources; at the cue, "Hark, she comes!" Marston's stage-directions call for *"A short song to soft music above"* (4.1.210.01). Syphax cries "Now hell and heaven rings" (212), mapping the cosmology of the offstage: hell below stage (under the trap-door into which Erictho will later drop), heaven *"above"* (in the upper-stage), worldly "heaven" at stage level and just out of sight. With this crescendo, the lusted-for object enters (or seems to; it's the witch herself, veiled) and quickly retires again, followed by Syphax.[10] The coupling – which is, as we soon find out, a second, successful bed-trick – occurs during the act-break, while the bass lute and treble viol continue to play, no longer "*softly.*"

It is impossible to tell, of course, just how long the act-interval would have lasted, although evidence from other sources suggests that such breaks in performance could be substantial.[11] Nor, of course, can one be sure what an interval meant to early modern audiences: there is reason to believe people talked amongst themselves, stretched, or otherwise were distracted from the play's fictional world.[12] Nonetheless, the offstage music clearly prevents a total break in the representation; the instruments, at some level, describe what we cannot see. Although music was routinely used to fill act-breaks, and though this play has been called "the most musical . . . of the era,"[13] this particular instrumentation, strongly arousing to Syphax, is unique to this scene and to this interval. Other act-breaks call for wind instruments, usually those military-sounding cornets,[14] and I suspect that here the choice of a string duet – one "voice" treble, the other bass – might have something to do with the rhythmicity, the diachrony, and the timbre of sex.

Marston elsewhere uses music to mark an offstage sexual encounter; in the even more lurid (some would say repulsive) *Insatiate Countess* (1611), "*some short song*" (not even an act-break) buys enough time for the title character to devour her third male victim and re-enter "*hanging about his neck lasciviously*" (3.4.83.01–02).[15] And if we are starting to suspect Marston of stretching credibility (never a problem with Middleton's "quickies"), it is worth pointing out that he tops it all off by having the Countess beheaded on stage. But back to *Sophonisba*. The fifth act begins with the post-coital unveiling and the triumphant cackling of the witch. And though Syphax shrieks, the audience rejoices: after the relentless, excruciating increase of tension with each thwarted rape, and after the gradual auditory intoxication of the previous scene, continuing through the teasing string-duet of the interval (I hear something building in tempo and volume, like Ravel's *Boléro*), these bullet-like ejaculations – Erictho's "Ha, ha, ha!" and Syphax's scream, "Light, light!" (5.1.1–2) – relieve us from the play's pornographical spell.

Interestingly, *Sophonisba* does not directly refer to the conjuring circle; the particular practice is only implied in her "raising" of spirits. Perhaps the female magician does not need to *draw* a circle because she *has* one: again, the entrance entrances. In lieu of the circle drawn on the ground, we find references to the womb-like subterranean space – the "labouring earth" (4.1.183) – from whence the spirits issue, and once the bed-trick is complete, and the witch gloats in the sating of her "thirsty womb" (5.1.8), it becomes hard to distinguish this organ from that larger, tropic, underground space. The "labouring" witch and the "labouring earth" are one: Faustus' conjurations, compared to these "mighty charms" (184) which "crack the trembling earth" (196), seem somewhat shallow. And if one should object that Erictho's magic is a fake, that she conjures nothing more than the satisfaction of her lust, I would answer quite simply that that is my point. Female desire is the most fearful spell.

I have chosen to end with the conjuring circle for several reasons. The symbol manifests the conjunction of scurrility and sacrilege discussed in the final chapter, hence illustrating my theory about the sexualization of profanity (and, inversely and indirectly, the sacralization of sex) during the early modern period. Moreover, the dual valence of the figure as a theatrical metaphor and a vaginal/womb image underscores and reifies the paradox which set this essay in motion: the paradox by which "woman" is both absent and omnipresent on the Renaissance stage. And finally, the conjuror's method offers insight into this problem of presence: conjuring offers a paradigm for the production, through image and sound (circle and chant), of an embodied presence which is at once seductive and threatening – but ultimately, and maddeningly, untouchable. Conjuring is an allegory for the early modern sexual imagination. And perhaps, if we listen closely, it might speak to the ear of our era as well.

I have quite deliberately shifted focus in these last pages from image to sound, from graphic to phonic, insofar as that is possible to do within the confines of a printed text. I have done so because the visual was not taking us very far (not surprisingly, since we started off in the darkness offstage) toward this book's goal of touching the body directly. Sound fills the gap between presence and absence, seen and unseen; sound *bodies forth*. That is why ritual requires music – incantation, percussion, repetition. And remember, the earliest rituals were fertility rituals, the earliest prayers for offspring, for grain, driven by fear of dearth. We unearth, alongside bone amulets, drums; tools against death, against lack, struck against stone, skin, or earth; the funeral bell and the funeral drum; wedding bells and the drum of the bacchanal: percussion, the mother of music; repetition, the mother of art.[16]

The ritualized utterance – in art or devotion – is always an attempt to speak something into being. A dream of causality; creation by fiat. A naming trick. And by the way, stringed instruments, like those which signify and sing the offstage sex in *Sophonisba*, reverb by means of *percussion* – although their sound is perhaps the most voice-like of all the instruments. Their chords approximate the sounds of our "vocal chords" – the cries, the sighs, the sobs.

In the preceding pages we examined female characterization on the all-male Renaissance stage as just such a naming trick, a conjuration through art; let us remember that the material tools for this magic – wigs, make-up, bangles, boys – only work in conjunction with the proper aural cues (in which the boy actor's *voice* is a crucial factor[17]). It is tempting to speculate whether the lush eroticism of early modern drama was a compensation (or, alternatively, a justification) for the exclusion of women performers, but contemporary theory does not encourage this approach. Judith Butler's *Bodies That Matter* theorizes the "materialization of sex" by way of the notion of "citationality," that is, "the power of discourse to produce that which it names."[18] For Butler and many feminist/gender theorists, the question of the ontological absence or presence of a female body onstage is – well, neither here nor there; the discursive construction, the naming, is all.

Whether or not the place of the stage was a site of empowerment or privilege, the effort to banish women from the stage placed them, symbolically, in the vicinity of the holy. "God knows what she thought." And the line between the unseen and the not-fit-to-be-looked-at, the unutterable and the not-to-be-uttered collapses when we look at the origins of profanity. God spelled backwards is dog (as Faustus could have read in his magic circle). Outside the walls of the medieval towns, and in the "liberties" or suburbs of the Renaissance cities, one ventured upon the playhouses, the leper colonies, the brothels, and the abbeys.[19] As anthropologists such as Mary Douglas point out, the forbidden and the sacred have always kept close company.[20]

This is why I was compelled to look at offstage sex in the first place. Cross out a word, ban a book, dig a hole, and see what happens. Someone is bound to look inside.

It was Derrida who first said – as it is most frequently translated – that there is nothing outside the text,[21] a notion which was then appropriated in the name of gender theory and has become the axiom associated with social constructionism.[22] But no sooner was the axiom born, than scholars across the United States, across disciplines, and across in Europe started scrambling to prove it wrong. Here's one of the more incisive critiques: "Though Derrida claims for discourse the glamorous infinities of modern physics, no physicist would recognize Derrida's textual universe as a convincing model of spatial reality."[23] Less sophisticated and far more impassioned (not to say hysterical) was the *Times* letter protesting Derrida's selection for an honorary degree from Cambridge, labeling the father of deconstruction a "charlatan," his work "irrational" and "nihilistic."[24] So much for dissenting voices in print. I have sat through or taught enough seminars in gender theory to know that as soon as someone denies that one can experience something "essentially female," hands shoot up, brows furrow, and the propositions begin ("What about childbirth, what about lactation, what about . . . ?").

Constructionism itself is a naming trick – at least in its purest form.[25] The assertion that "There is nothing outside of discourse," suspiciously resembles "The Word was made flesh."[26] Derrida himself pokes fun at the uses and misuses of the axiom: "If deconstruction *really* consisted in saying that everything happens in books, it wouldn't deserve *five* minutes of anybody's attention"; he then goes on to talk about why "it seemed strategically useful at a given moment to say, for example, 'a body is text, the table is text'" and so forth.[27] The question is, then, whether it might now be strategically useful to say something else. And as to the feminist application of the Derridean tenet, the very existence of Butler's 288-page follow-up to *Gender Trouble* attests to a certain ambivalence toward her work within the feminist community, an ambivalence Butler acknowledges in her Preface by citing the repeated question of certain exasperated colleagues: "What about the materiality of the body, Judy?"[28] And as much as I sympathize with Butler's own apparent exasperation (the diminutive "Judy" seems a tad patronizing), I can also sympathize with her critics; theirs is an impatience I too have felt, confronting Butler's (and her imitators') excessively Latinate, technical, and curiously *dis-embodied* prose. In the battery of -ation -ation -ation and -ivity -ivity -ivity, prefix upon prefix and suffix upon suffix, I do not hear a body speaking. If someone were talking that way in person, I'd be tempted to step on her toe.

It is the effort to attend to the body which leads to the perhaps misguided attempt of feminists like myself to think a way out of discourse. This may be why Butler herself concedes that "There is an 'outside' to what is constructed by discourse, but this is not an absolute 'outside' . . . ; as a constitutive 'outside,' it is that which can only be thought – when it can – in relation to that discourse."[29] In the end, constructionism can always fall back upon one irrefutable point: "The body posited as prior to the sign, is always *posited* or *signified* as *prior*."[30] In other words, we cannot speculate about the "outside" of discourse without, in the process, bringing that "outside" into our discursive field – it is like looking at the horizon: however much it beckons, it will always be "over there." On the other hand, anthropologist Eric Gans, defending his own theory on the origins of language, responds curtly to this theoretical "Gordian knot": "The objections of philosophical nihilism cannot be answered on their own terms."[31]

Perhaps they can, though. Elizabeth Grosz twists the constructionist Gordian knot in a very useful way. Grosz presents as a model for understanding sexual difference the Möbius loop or double-sided figure-eight, which demonstrates "that there can be a relation between two 'things' – mind and body – which presumes neither their identity nor their radical disjunction."[32] A brilliant resolution to the conundrum of the inside/outside binary in all its theoretical manifestations, the model allows "subjectivity to be understood as fully material and for materiality . . . to include . . . the operations of language, desire, and significance."[33]

This is why I find the conjuror's circle a compelling paradigm: opening from within onto a vast "beyond," it represents the untapped plenitude of both body and imagination, and the resistance of both to stasis and closure. Elizabeth Meese upholds as a model for feminist theory "an infinite progression that refuses to identify a center because it is always decentered, self-displacing and self-contradictory."[34] In just this spirit I have set down this essay, with its vertiginous, inside-out path, its collapsing of entrances and exits, its backward (in places) chronology, its naive determination to escape its own discursivity. In just this spirit I have questioned the body of theory which I inhabit. And in just this spirit I urge you to question me too.

This exploration began with a self-consciously essentialist question regarding the early modern stage: where does sex "really" happen? And that led me to search the stage for wombs, wineskins, and wigs, wondering whether or in what sense these things could build women; to play with dolls and puppets and crosses, wondering what part death played in it all; it finally drove me to tear four texts to pieces in an effort to get between the lines. But perhaps the real question is not where does sex happen but why does sex happen – or better yet, why does it matter? *Why must we make it mean something?* I'll grant this to constructionism. We are essentially, if we are essentially anything, creatures who make meaning.

The abundance of erotic texts, and the abundance of texts about these texts, and the abundance of theories, laws, letters, treatises, confessions about "sexuality" lumped all together – this "proliferation of discourse," to borrow Foucault's terminology – attests to the fact that we want to make sex mean. We want to *make sense* of our bodies. Why do we speak about whether or not a sexual encounter "means anything?" "He was drunk; he was using me; it didn't mean anything to him. The bastard." But why *should* sex mean anything? We do not expect this of a cheese sandwich. Perhaps we want sex to make sense because we are no longer concerned about whether it makes babies.

As Derrida explains, writing (language) is about desire, about reaching out across the gap between self and world, self and other: "For to write is to draw back . . . Language is the *rupture* with totality itself."[35] Jacques Lacan argues that the entry into consciousness comes with the recognition of the "I," with the realization of the split between self and world, self and other.[36] Thus, language both constitutes and is premised upon our separateness, our vulnerability.

I have a new story for the old story, if you care to listen.

Constructionism argues that there is no unmediated bodily experience, but we want to touch ourselves directly, so we wrestle with the seeming abstraction, the seeming impalpability of the "discursive body." But instead of trying to situate a body inside or outside discourse, why not ground discourse, first and foremost, inside the body? We might consider an alternative to Lacan's "mirror stage" in the slap applied to the baby's behind which evokes at once its first breath and its first cry (the "sign" of life, in response to which the mother's breasts involuntarily lactate). From this perspective, language arises in the realization of embodiedness – which is to say, of bodily separation – but also in the concurrent attempt to heal this separation, to heal through touch. Sex is worth dying for (as Juliet well knows) because without communion, we die.

I would like to try reversing the terms of the constructionist equation, as reversal brings fresh insight (god/dog). Instead of saying that language constitutes "sex," let us ask whether sexual contact itself constitutes a language; or, even more daringly, let us ask whether bodily discourse constitutes an *essential* discourse, an originary discourse. Was the word made flesh, or was flesh the first word? Intercourse: discourse of hands. Does not touch communicate? Commune, communion, communication. Some anthropologists have hypothesized a gestural language which preceded speech.[37] We know that gestures speak: why not touch? We know that pictures speak: why not touch? We know sound speaks: why not touch?

For before we made books, we made pictures, and before we made pictures, we made speech, and before we made pictures or speech, we made love. Before we made God, we made love.

Appendix 1

Note: my own emendations of Harbage are enclosed in square brackets.

Erotic activity	No erotic activity
1595	
Singing Simpkin (William Kempe?)	*Richard II* (Shakespeare)
Sir Thomas More (Munday *et al.*)	*Edmond Ironside, or War Hath*
Love's Labour's Lost (Shakespeare)	*Made All Friends* (Anon.)
A Midsummer-Night's Dream	
(Shakespeare)	
Romeo and Juliet (Shakespeare)	
total: 5	total: 2
1596	
The Blind Beggar of Alexandria	
(George Chapman)	
A Tale of a Tub (Jonson)	
King John (Shakespeare)	
The Merchant of Venice	
(Shakespeare)	
Captain Thomas Stukeley (Anon.)	
total: 5	
1597	
An Humorous Day's Mirth	
(Chapman)	
The Case Is Altered (Jonson)	
I Henry IV (Shakespeare)	
II Henry IV (Shakespeare)	
total: 4	

1598

The Death of Robert, Earl of
  Huntingdon (H. Chettle,
  A. Munday)
The Downfall of Robert . . .
  (Chettle, Munday)
Englishmen for My Money (William
  Haughton)
Every Man in His Humour (Jonson)
Much Ado About Nothing
  (Shakespeare)
The Wooing of Nan (Anon.)
    total: 6

1599

Old Fortunatus (Dekker)   *Histriomastix, or the Player*
The Shoemakers' Holiday (Dekker)   *Whipped* (Marston)
I Sir John Oldcastle (Drayton *et al.*)
I & II Edward IV (T. Heywood?)
Every Man out of His Humour
  (Jonson)
Antonio and Mellida (Marston)
As You Like It (Shakespeare)
Henry V (Shakespeare)
Julius Caesar (Shakespeare)
A Larum for London (Anon.)
Look about You (Anon.)
The Thracian Wonder (Anon.)
A Warning for Fair Women (Anon.)
The Wisdom of Doctor Dodypoll
  (Anon.)
    total: 14:   total: 1

1600

I *The Blind Beggar of Bednal Green* (Chettle *et al.*)	*Thomas Lord Cromwell* (Anon.)
Patient Grissil (Chettle *et al.*)	
Lust's Dominion, or The Lascivious Queen (Anon.)	
The Devil and His Dame (Haughton)	
The Four Prentices of London (Heywood)	
Antonio's Revenge (Marston)	
Jack Drum's Entertainment (Marston)	
The Merry Wives of Windsor (Shakespeare)	
Twelfth Night, or What You Will (Shakespeare)	
Charlemagne, or The Distracted Emperor (Anon.)	
The Maid's Metamorphosis (Anon.)	
The Weakest Goeth to the Wall (Anon.)	
total: 12	total: 1

1601

Satiromastix, or the Untrussing . . . (Dekker, Marston ?)	*The Contention between Liberality and Prodigality* (Anon.)
Cynthia's Revels, or The Fountain of Self-Love (Jonson)	
Poetaster, or the Arraignment (Jonson)	
What You Will (Marston)	
Hamlet (Shakespeare)	
Blurt, Master Constable ([Dekker])	
The Trial of Chivalry (Anon.)	
total: 7	total: 1

1602
The Gentleman Usher (Chapman)
May-Day (Chapman)
Sir Giles Goosecap (Chapman)
Hoffman, or a Revenge for a Father
    (Chettle)
How a Man May Choose a Good
    Wife from a Bad (Heywood)
The Royal King and the Loyal
    Subject (Heywood *et al.*)
The Family of Love ([Lording
    Barry])
All's Well That Ends Well
    (Shakespeare)
Troilus and Cressida (Shakespeare)
The Fair Maid of the Exchange
    (Anon.)
The Merry Devil of Edmonton
    (Anon.)
Wily Beguiled (Anon.)
        total: 12

1603
A Woman Killed with Kindness
    (Heywood)
Sejanus His Fall (Jonson)
        total: 2

1604

All Fools (Chapman)
Bussy D'Ambois (Chapman)
Monsieur D'Olive (Chapman)
Philotas (Samuel Daniel)
*Law Tricks, or Who Would Have
  Thought It* (J. Day, G. Wilkins?)
*I The Honest Whore (I The
  Converted Courtesan)* (Dekker,
  Middleton)
Westward Ho (Dekker)
The Wise Woman of Hogsdon
  (Heywood)
*The Dutch Courtesan (Cockle de
  Moye)* (Marston)
The Malcontent (Marston, Webster)
The Phoenix (Middleton)
When You See Me You Know Me
  (Rowley)
Measure for Measure (Shakespeare)
Othello (Shakespeare)
The Fair Maid of Bristow (Anon.)
*I Jeronimo, with the Wars of
  Portugal* (Anon.)
The London Prodigal (Anon.)
       total: 17

Sir Thomas Wyatt (Dekker,
  Webster)
*I If You Know Not Me You Know
  Nobody . . .* (Heywood)

                                            total: 2

1605
The Widow's Tears (Chapman)
Eastward Ho (Chapman *et al.*)
II The Honest Whore (*II The
   Converted Courtesan*) (Dekker)
Northward Ho (Dekker *et al.*)
*I If You Know Not Me You Know
   Nobody* . . . (Heywood)
Parasitaster, or The Fawn (Marston)
*The Wonder of Women; Or The
   Tragedy of Sophonisba* (Marston)
A Trick to Catch the Old One
   (Middleton)
Your Five Gallants (Middleton)
King Lear (Shakespeare)
Nobody and Somebody (Anon.)
   total: 11

1606
The Woman Hater (*The Hungry   *The Whore of Babylon* (Dekker)
   Courtier*) (Beaumont, Fletcher)
The Isle of Gulls (Day)
Volpone, or The Fox (Jonson)
A Mad World, My Masters
   (Middleton)
Michaelmas Term (Middleton)
Macbeth (Shakespeare)
The Miseries of Enforced Marriage
   (George Wilkins)
*The Puritan, or The Widow of
   Watling Street* ([Middleton])
The Revenger's Tragedy
   ([Middleton])
A Yorkshire Tragedy ([Middleton])
   total: 10   total: 1

1607

The Devil's Charter (Barnabe
   Barnes)
The Knight of the Burning Pestle
   (Beaumont, Fletcher?)
*The Travels of the Three English
   Brothers* (Day *et al.*)
The Rape of Lucrece (Heywood)
Every Woman in Her Humour
   (Machin?)
The Turk (J. Mason)
Antony and Cleopatra (Shakespeare)
Timon of Athens (Shakespeare,
   Middleton)
Cupid's Whirligig (Edward
   Sharpham)
      total: 9

1608	
The Two Maids of More-Clacke (R. Armin)	*Coriolanus* (Shakespeare)
Ram Ally, or Merry Tricks (Barry)	
The Conspiracy . . . of Charles Duke *of Byron* (Chapman)	
Humour out of Breath (Day)	
The Roaring Girl, or Moll Cutpurse (Dekker, Middleton)	
The Faithful Shepherdess (Fletcher)	
Cupid's Revenge (Fletcher, Beaumont)	
The Dumb Knight (G. Markham *et* *al.*)	
A Shoemaker a Gentleman (Rowley)	
The Birth of Merlin . . . (Rowley)	
Pericles (Shakespeare, [Wilkins])	
total: 11	total: 1

1609

Philaster, or Love Lies a-Bleeding
  (Beaumont, Fletcher)
The Coxcomb (Fletcher, Beaumont)
Wit at Several Weapons (Fletcher *et
  al.*)
A Woman Is a Weathercock
  (Nathan Field)
Fortune by Land and Sea (Heywood,
  Rowley)
Epicoene, or The Silent Woman
  (Jonson)
Cymbeline (Shakespeare)
*The Atheist's Tragedy, or The
  Honest Man's Revenge* (Cyril
  Tourneur)
        total: 8

1610

The Maid's Tragedy (Beaumont,
  Fletcher)
The Revenge of Bussy D'Ambois
  (Chapman)
A Christian Turned Turk (Robert
  Daborne)
*I The Fair Maid of the West, or A
  Girl Worth Gold* (Heywood)
*The Golden Age, or The Lives of
  Jupiter and Saturn* (Heywood)
The Alchemist (Jonson)
The Insatiate Countess (Marston,
  Barkstead)
The Winter's Tale (Shakespeare)
        total: 8

1611
A King and No King (Beaumont,
    Fletcher)
*Greene's Tu Quoque, or The City
    Gallant* (John Cooke)
Match Me in London (Dekker)
If It Be Not Good, the Devil Is in It
    (Dekker, Daborne?)
Amends for Ladies (Field)
*The Night Walker, or The Little
    Thief* (Fletcher)
*The Woman's Prize; or, The Tamer
    Tamed* (Fletcher)
The Brazen Age (Heywood)
The Silver Age (Heywood)
Catiline His Conspiracy (Jonson)
A Chaste Maid in Cheapside
    (Middleton)
The Tempest (Shakespeare)
The Second Maiden's Tragedy [*The
    Lady's Tragedy*] ([Middleton])
        total: 13

1612
The Valiant Welschman ("R. A.")
The Captain (Fletcher, Beaumont?)
*Four Plays, or Moral
    Representations, in One* (Fletcher
    et al.)
I The Iron Age (Heywood)
II The Iron Age (Heywood)
The White Devil (Webster)
        total: 6

1613
Bonduca (Fletcher)
The Scornful Lady (Fletcher,
  Beaumont)
The Honest Man's Fortune (Fletcher
  et al.)
No Wit, No Help Like a Woman's
  (Middleton)
Henry VIII (Shakespeare, Fletcher)
The Two Noble Kinsmen
  (Shakespeare, Fletcher)
The Hog Hath Lost His Pearl
  (Robert Tailor)
     total: 7

1614
Valentinian (Fletcher)
Wit Without Money (Fletcher)
Bartholomew Fair (Jonson)
The Hector of Germany . . .
  (W. Smith)
The Duchess of Malfi (Webster)
The Faithful Friends (Anon.)
     total: 6

1615
Aemilia (T. Cecil)
More Dissemblers Besides Women
  (Middleton)
The Witch (Middleton)
The Honest Lawyer ("S. S.")
     total: 4

1616
Love's Pilgrimage (Fletcher,
  Beaumont?)
*The Nice Valour, or The Passionate
  Madman* ([Middleton])
The Devil Is an Ass (Jonson)
The Widow (Middleton)
     total: 4

1617
The Poor Man's Comfort (Daborne)
The Mad Lover (Fletcher)
The Queen of Corinth (Fletcher *et al.*)
Thierry and Theodoret (Fletcher *et al.*)
A Fair Quarrel (Middleton, Rowley)
The Devil's Law Case (*When Women Go to Law the Devil is Full of Business*) (Webster)
    total: 6

1618
The Loyal Subject (Fletcher)
The Knight of Malta (Fletcher *et al.*)
Hengist, King of Kent (Middleton, Rowley?)
The Old Law . . . (Middleton *et al.*)
The Martyred Soldier (H. Shirley, Heywood?)
Swetnam the Woman-Hater Arraigned by Women (Anon.)
    total: 6

1619
The Two Merry Milkmaids . . . ("I. C.")
The Fatal Dowry (Field, Massinger)
The Humorous Lieutenant (Fletcher)
The Bloody Brother (Fletcher *et al.*)
The Little French Lawyer (Fletcher, Massinger)
The Laws of Candy (Fletcher)
All's Lost by Lust (Rowley)
    total: 7

Sir John van Olden Barnavelt (Fletcher; Massinger)

    total: 1

1620

The Virgin Martyr (Dekker,
    Massinger)
Women Pleased (Fletcher)
The Custom of the Country
    (Fletcher, Massinger)
The Double Marriage (Fletcher,
    Massinger)
The False One (Fletcher, Massinger)
The Heir (Thomas May)
The Costly Whore (Anon.)
        total: 7

1621

The Witch of Edmonton (Dekker *et
    al.*)
The Island Princess (Fletcher)
The Pilgrim (Fletcher)
The Wild Goose Chase (Fletcher)
The Duke of Milan (Massinger)
The Maid of Honour (Massinger)
A New Way to Pay Old Debts
    (Massinger)
Anything for a Quiet Life
    (Middleton, Webster)
Women Beware Women (Middleton)
        total: 9

Grand total: 216 works   10 works
95.6% of total   4.4% of total

Appendix 2

Note: my emendations of Harbage are enclosed in square brackets. Titles may not correspond to those in Appendix I, as the list below includes titles of lost plays.

love, -er(s), lust:
 1 *Disguises, or Love in Disguise, a Petticoat Voyage* (Dekker?, 1595)
 2 *Love's Labour's Lost* (Shakespeare, 1595)
 3 *Romeo and Juliet* (Shakespeare, 1595)
 4 *Love Prevented* (H. Porter, 1598)
 5 *Love's Labour's Won* (Shakespeare, 1598)
 6 *Dido and Aeneas* (Anon., 1598)
 7 *Troilus and Cressida* (H. Chettle, Dekker, 1599)
 8 *Leander* (W. Hawkesworth, 1599)
 9 *War without Blowes and Love without Suit* (Heywood, 1599)
10 *Antonio and Mellida* (Marston, 1599)
11 *The Love of a Grecian Lady* (Anon., 1599)
12 *Lust's Dominion, or The Lascivious Queen* (Anon., 1600)
13 *Antony and Cleopatra* (F. Greville, 1601)
14 *Cynthia's Revels, or The Fountain of Self-Love* (Jonson, 1601)
15 *Love Parts Friendship* (Chettle *et al.*, 1602)
16 *The Family of Love* ([Barry] 1602)
17 *Troilus and Cressida* (Shakespeare, 1602)
18 *Antony and Cleopatra* (Shakespeare, 1607)
19 *Aeneas and Dido* (Anon., 1607)
20 *Philaster, or Love Lies a-Bleeding* (Beaumont, Fletcher, 1609)
21 *Four Plays . . . (. . .* [including] *The Triumph of Love)* (Fletcher *et al.*, 1612)
22 *Ulysses and Circe* (W. Browne, 1615)
23 *Romeus et Julietta* (Anon., 1615)
24 *Love's Pilgrimage* (Fletcher, Beaumont?, 1616)
25 *The Lovesick King* (A. Brewer, 1617)
26 *The Mad Lover* (Fletcher, 1617)

27 *Pathomachia, or The Battle of Affections (Love's Loadstone)* (Anon., 1617)
28 *All's Lost by Lust* (W. Rowley, 1619)

woman, -en

1 *The Kitchen Stuff Woman* (W. Kempe?, 1595)
2 *The Wonder of a Woman* (Anon., 1595)
3 *A Woman Hard to Please* (Anon., 1597)
4 *The Fount(ain) of New Fashions (The Ill [Jill?] of a Woman)* (G. Chapman, 1598)
5 *The Woman's Tragedy* (Chettle, 1598)
6 *Englishmen for My Money, or A Woman Will Have Her Will* (W. Haughton, 1598)
7 *II The Two Angry Women of Abingdon* (Porter, 1599)
8 *Two Merry Women of Abingdon* (Porter [same as above?], 1599)
9 *A Warning for Fair Women* (Anon., 1599)
10 *Friar Rush and the Proud Woman of Antwerp* (Day, Haughton, 1601)
11 *Arabia Sitiens . . . (. . . or, The Weather-Woman)* (W. Percy, 1601)
12 *A Woman Killed with Kindness* (Heywood, 1603)
13 *How to Learn of a Woman to Woo* (Heywood, 1604)
14 *The Wise Woman of Hogsdon* (Heywood, 1604 [same as above?])
15 *The Wit of a Woman* (Anon., 1604)
16 *The Wonder of Women; Or The Tragedy of Sophonisba* (Marston, 1605)
17 *The Woman-Hater (The Hungry Courtier)* (Beaumont, Fletcher, 1606)
18 *Every Woman in Her Humour* (L. Machin?, 1607)
19 *A Woman Is a Weathercock* (N. Field, 1609)
20 *Epicoene, or The Silent Woman* (Jonson, 1609)
21 *The Woman's Prize; or, The Tamer Tamed* (Fletcher, 1611)
22 *A Yorkshire Gentlewoman and Her Son* (Chapman?, 1613)
23 *No Wit, No Help Like a Woman's* (Middleton, 1613)
24 *A Right Woman* ("Beaumont, Fletcher," 1615)
25 *More Dissemblers Besides Women* (Middleton, 1615)
26 *The Devil's Law Case (When Women Go to Law the Devil is Full of Business)* (Webster, 1617)
27 *Swetnam the Woman-Hater Arraigned by Women* (Anon., 1618)
28 *The Woman's Mistaken* (R. Davenport et al., 1620)
29 *Women Pleased* (Fletcher, 1620)
30 *The Woman's Plot* (Massinger, 1621)
31 *Women Beware Women* (Middleton, 1621)
32 *The Woman Is Too Hard for Him* (Anon. [same as *Woman's Prize?*], 1621)

maids, ladies, etc.

1 *A Toy to Please Chaste Ladies* (Anon., 1595)
2 *Mother Redcap* (M. Drayton, A. Munday, 1598)
3 *The Fair Maid of London* (Anon., 1598)
4 *Arcadian Virgin* (Chettle, Haughton, 1599)
5 *Joan as Good as My Lady* (Heywood, 1599)
6 *The Fair Maid of Italy* (Anon., 1599)
7 *The Devil and His Dame* (Haughton, 1600)
8 *The Merry Wives of Windsor* (Shakespeare, 1600)
9 *The Maid's Metamorphosis* (Anon., 1600)
10 *I Lady Jane (The Overthrow of Rebels)* (Chettle *et al*, 1602)
11 *A Medicine for a Curst Wife* (Dekker, 1602)
12 *II Lady Jane* (Dekker, 1602)
13 *How a Man May Choose a Good Wife from a Bad* (Heywood, 1602)
14 *The Widow's Charm* ("Antony the Poet," 1602)
15 *The Fair Maid of the Exchange* (Anon., 1602)
16 *A Royal Widow of England* (Anon., 1602)
17 *The Fair Maid of Bristow* (Anon., 1604)
18 *Lady Amity* (Anon., 1604)
19 *The Widow's Tears* (Chapman, 1605)
20 *The Puritan, or The Widow of Watling Street* ([Middleton], 1606)
21 *The Faithful Shepherdess* (Fletcher, 1608)
22 *The Two Maids of More-Clacke* (Armin, 1608)
23 *The Roaring Girl, or Moll Cutpurse* (Dekker, Middleton, 1608)
24 *I The Fair Maid of the West, or A Girl Worth Gold* (Heywood, 1610)
25 *The Maid's Tragedy* (Beaumont, Fletcher, 1610)
26 *Amends for Ladies* (Field, 1611)
27 *A Chaste Maid in Cheapside* (Middleton, 1611)
28 *The Second Maiden's Tragedy* [*The Lady's Tragedy*] ([Middleton], 1611)
29 *The Proud Maid's Tragedy* (Anon., 1612)
30 *The Scornful Lady* (Fletcher, Beaumont, 1613)
31 *The Widow* (Middleton, 1616)
32 *The Two Merry Milkmaids . . .* ("I. C.," 1619)
33 *The Careless Shepherdess* (Goffe?, 1619)
34 *Look to the Lady* (Anon., 1619)
35 *The Virgin Martyr* (Dekker, Massinger, 1620)
36 *The Maid of Honour* (Massinger, 1621)

whores, cuckolds, etc.

1 *The Triangle* [or *Triplicity*] *of Cuckolds* (Dekker, 1598)
2 *The Witch of Islington* (Anon., 1599)

3 *The Cuckqueans and Cuckolds Errants . . .* (Percy, 1601)
4 *I The Honest Whore (I The Converted Courtesan)* (Dekker, Middleton, 1604)
5 *The Dutch Courtesan (Cockle de Moye)* (Marston, 1604)
6 *II The Honest Whore (II The Converted Courtesan)* (Dekker, 1605)
7 *The Viper and Her Brood* (Middleton, 1606)
8 *The Whore of Babylon* (Dekker, 1606)
9 *The Witch* (Middleton, 1615)
10 *The Costly Whore* (Anon., 1620)
11 *The Witch of Edmonton* (Dekker *et al.*, 1621)

wooing/wedding

1 *The Wooing of Nan* (Anon., 1598)
2 *The Wooing of Death* (Chettle, 1600)
3 *The Miseries of Enforced Marriage* (Wilkins, 1606)
4 *Iphis and Iantha, or A Marriage without a Man* ("Shakespeare," 1613)
5 *Technogamia, or The Marriage of the Arts* (Barten Holiday, 1618)
6 *The Fatal Dowry* (Field, Massinger, 1619)
7 *The Bridegr[oom]* (Anon., 1619)
8 *The Double Marriage* (Fletcher, Massinger, 1620)

Cupid and/or Hymen

1 *Cupid and Psyche (The Golden Ass)* (Chettle *et al.*, 1600)
2 *A Country Tragedy in Vacunium, or Cupid's Sacrifice* (Percy, 1602)
3 *Cupid's Whirligig* (Edward Sharpham, 1607)
4 *Cupid's Revenge* (Fletcher, Beaumont, 1608)
5 *Hymen's Holiday, or Cupid's Vagaries* (Rowley, 1612)
6 *Cupid's Festival* (Anon., 1614)

Others

1 *Lucretia* (Anon., 1605)
2 *The Rape of Lucrece* (Heywood, 1607)
3 *The Insatiate Countess* (Marston, Barkstead, 1610)

Notes

I   ENTRANCES: SEX, WOMEN, GOD

1 Marie-Louise von Franz, *Creation Myths* (Boston: Shambhala, 1995).

2 I have found only one in-depth discussion of offstage action in Renaissance drama, Anthony Brennan's *Onstage and Offstage Worlds in Shakespeare's Plays* (Routledge, 1989). Brennan's perspective, however, is foremost that of a director, not a literary theorist; his tabulations of performance time and dramatic structure are meticulous and sweeping, but do not particularly explore the sexual "action" which concerns me here, nor bring the question of stage absence to bear on post-structuralist literary theory.

3 Michel Foucault's *The History of Sexuality, Vol. I*, trans. Robert Hurley (New York: Random House, 1990) critiques the widely held view of western society as historically sexually repressed, making the case for a massive and widespread "incitement to discourse" about sexuality, often driven by the notion of repression itself. Although I do find aspects of this argument quite compelling, I have from time to time been frustrated by its application, which tends to produce – ironically enough – its own brand of *repression* in scholarly writing. Note, for instance, the sequence of admonishments comprising Foucault's "Methods" chapter, a veritable Ten Commandments of scholarly discourse, beginning, "Hence the objective is to analyze a certain form of knowledge . . . *not* in terms of repression or law, but in terms of power" (92); then follows five statements defining what "Power is *not*" (94–95), followed by four "cautionary prescriptions": "One must *not* suppose" and "We must *not* look for" and "What is said about sex must *not*" and so on (98–102; emphases added).

4 In dating *Romeo and Juliet* at 1595, I am following Gary Taylor, "The Canon and Chronology of Shakespeare's Plays," in *William Shakespeare: A Textual Companion*, ed. Stanley Wells and Gary Taylor (Oxford University Press, 1987), 89–109, as well as Alfred Harbage, *Annals of English Drama*, rev. by S. Schoenbaum (Cambridge, MA: Harvard University Press, 1964). Because in this case and others the newer edition of Harbage is of debatable authority, I have used the 1964 edition consistently.

5 For a detailed tabulation, see Appendix I. My sincere thanks to my research assistant, Tim VandeBrake, for his tireless and painstaking efforts for this project.

6 Included in this survey are all works, extant or lost, performed or intended for performance by all-male companies or (in rare cases) guilds; that is, I have not

counted masques, royal entertainments, civic pageants, closet dramas, or any other work which might have been performed by women. In the case of court masques this is, I believe, a rather fine distinction, for in this period female roles in court theatricals were invariably *silent*. For feminist readings of the masque form, both as a method of containment and a potential site of subversion, see Suzanne Gossett, "'Man-maid, Begone!': Women in Masques," *English Literary Renaissance* 18 (1988), 96–113, and Marion Wynne-Davies, "The Queen's Masque: Renaissance Women and the Seventeenth-Century Court Masque," *Gloriana's Face: Women, Public and Private, in the English Renaissance*, ed. S. P. Cerasano and Marion Wynne-Davies (New York: Harvester, 1992), 79–104.

7 Under "lovers," I include generic references (e.g., *The Mad Lover*), as well as particular references to famous lovers (*Leander*) or pairs of lovers (*Romeo and Juliet*). For the entire list, see Appendix II.

8 Omitting, once again, masques and the like, the *Annals* lists 668 titles for the 26-year period, or an average of 25.69 per year.

9 For accounts of performances which were censored for representing the Queen, see Susan Frye, *Elizabeth I: The Competition for Representation* (Oxford University Press, 1993), 70–71, and E. K. Chambers, *The Elizabethan Stage, Vol. III* (Oxford University Press, 1951), 361–62.

10 See Frye, *Elizabeth I*, for a thorough and engaging discussion of the way the Queen constructed her image throughout her reign.

11 Antitheatrical polemicists objected fiercely to the transvestite boy actor but found the thought of women acting even more repellent – an affront to female modesty. See J. W. Binns, "Women or Transvestites on the Elizabethan Stage?: An Oxford Controversy," *Sixteenth-Century Journal* 5.2 (1974), 95–120.

12 Frye, *Elizabeth I*, 11.

13 V. A. Kolve, *The Play Called Corpus Christi* (Stanford University Press, 1966), 30–31.

14 Sarah Beckwith, *Christ's Body: Identity, Culture and Society in Late Medieval Writings* (London: Routledge, 1993), 22.

15 A word or two about methodologies may be in order here. Like many or most English scholars today, I have been deeply influenced by the historicisms developed since the 1980s; however, I am not embarrassed to admit my privileging of literary texts over other discourses, my focus on theater above other cultural practices, throughout the ensuing chapters. After all, the evidence from the *Annals* strongly suggests that the theater was the dominant site for the production of erotic discourses in early modern England.

16 See Jonathan Sawday, *The Body Emblazoned: Dissection and the Human Body in Renaissance Culture* (London: Routledge, 1995), 70. On the impact of Copernican theories, see Hans Blumenberg, *The Genesis of the Copernican World*, trans. Robert M. Wallace (Cambridge, MA: The MIT Press, 1987). Blumenberg's explanation of "the enlargement of space that emerged as a consequence of Copernicanism" (130) is relevant to the spatial confusion I am discussing.

17 Sawday elaborates on the parallel between Renaissance anatomy and

cartography: "Like the Columbian explorers, these early discoverers" of the internal organs "dotted their names, like place-names on a map, over the terrain which they encountered. In their voyages, they expressed the intersection of the body and the world at every point, claiming for the body an affinity with the complex design of the universe" (*The Body Emblazoned*, 23–24).

18 See Norman Sanders, Richard Southern, T. W. Craik, and Lois Potter, eds., *The Revels History of Drama in English, Vol. II* (London: Methuen, 1980), 24–30; see also Gary Taylor, *Cultural Selection* (New York: Basic Books, 1996), 47–62.

19 A complementary viewpoint on space and Renaissance English drama is offered by Steven Mullaney, who emphasizes the significance of the commercial theaters' location in the "Liberties," a liminal and symbolically charged space. See *The Place of the Stage: License, Play, and Power in Renaissance England* (University of Chicago Press, 1988), 1–25.

20 Christopher Marlowe, *Doctor Faustus*, ed. John D. Jump, Revels Plays (Manchester University Press, 1962).

21 All quotations are from John Webster, *The Duchess of Malfi*, ed. Elizabeth M. Brennan, New Mermaids (London: A. & C. Black, 1993).

22 David L. Hodges, *Renaissance Fictions of Anatomy* (Amherst: University of Massachusetts Press, 1985), 18; and Sawday, *The Body Emblazoned*, 88.

23 All Shakespeare quotations are from William Shakespeare, *The Complete Works*, gen. eds. Stanley Wells and Gary Taylor (Oxford University Press, 1988).

24 Sawday, *The Body Emblazoned*, 92.

25 Hodges, *Renaissance Fictions of Anatomy*, 68–69 and 82.

26 Julia Kristeva, *Powers of Horror: An Essay on Abjection*, trans. Leon S. Roudiez (New York: Columbia University Press, 1982), 1. Along similar lines, Valerie Traub argues that the production of gender in early modern anatomy is "a defense against the body's abjection." See "Gendering Mortality in Early Modern Anatomies," in *Feminist Readings of Early Modern Culture: Emerging Subjects*, ed. Valerie Traub, M. Lindsay Kaplan, and Dympna Callaghan (Cambridge University Press, 1996), 44–92.

27 Mark Breitenberg, *Anxious Masculinity in Early Modern Culture* (Cambridge University Press, 1996), 183.

28 Sawday, *The Body Emblazoned*, 76. See also Luke Wilson, "William Harvey's *Prelections*: The Performance of the Body in the Renaissance Theater of Anatomy," *Representations* 17 (1987), 62–95. On the specific question of anatomy and gender, see Traub, "Gendering Mortality"; Thomas Laqueur, *Making Sex: Body and Gender from the Greeks to Freud* (Cambridge, MA: Harvard University Press, 1990); Karen Newman, *Fashioning Femininity and English Renaissance Drama* (University of Chicago Press, 1991), 3–12; and Howard Marchitello, "Vesalius' *Fabrica* and Shakespeare's *Othello*: Anatomy, Gender and the Narrative Production of Meaning," *Criticism* 35.4 (Fall 1993), 529–58.

29 Sawday, *The Body Emblazoned*, 222. Traub goes as far as to say that "anatomy, as an emerging 'scientia sexualis,' would appropriate for its own use images from the . . . *ars erotica*," thereby offering the male viewer "the

psychic safety provided by pornographic conventions" ("Gendering Mortality," 82).

30 Another early modern phenomenon to be considered is the male encroachment into the field of midwifery, both aided and signaled by the publication of midwifery manuals in the vernacular. See Elizabeth D. Harvey, *Ventriloquized Voices: Feminist Theory and English Renaissance Texts* (London: Routledge, 1992), 76–115.

31 John Gillies, *Shakespeare and the Geography of Difference* (Cambridge University Press, 1994), 37.

32 Gillies, *Geography of Difference*, 1–98, and Shakespeare, *As You Like It* (2.7.139).

33 Gillies, *Geography of Difference*, 13.

34 See Michael Camille, *Image on the Edge: The Margins of Medieval Art* (Harvard University Press, 1992). Of the "Psalter Map," Camille observes, "the further one moves away from the centre-point of Jerusalem, the more deformed and alien things become"; he also states that "illuminators were often not inventing monsters but depicting creatures they might well have assumed existed at the limits of God's creation" (14). See also Evelyn B. Tribble, *Margins and Marginality: The Printed Page in Early Modern England* (Charlottesville: University Press of Virginia, 1993).

35 Gillies, *Geography of Difference*, 188.

36 William E. Engel, noting the same cartographical paradox, views the exuberant monsters of the Iceland map (Figure 4) as demonstrating "a will to represent what exceeded . . . the powers of mortal vision." See *Mapping Mortality: The Persistence of Memory and Melancholy in Early Modern England* (Amherst: University of Massachusetts Press, 1995), 139.

37 Shakespeare, *The Complete Works*, 1167.

38 Anthony Grafton, *New Worlds, Ancient Texts: The Power of Tradition and the Shock of Discovery* (Cambridge, MA: Belknap Press of Harvard University Press, 1992), 5.

39 Kathleen M. Kirby, *Indifferent Boundaries: Spatial Concepts of Human Subjectivity* (New York: Guilford Press, 1996), 37–67 and *passim*.

40 Catherine Belsey, *The Subject of Tragedy: Identity and Difference in Renaissance Drama* (London: Methuen, 1985), 13–54; 43. See also Robin F. Jones, "A Medieval Prescription for Performance," in *Performing Texts*, ed. Michael Issacharoff and Robin F. Jones (Philadelphia: University of Pennsylvania Press, 1988), 101–15.

41 Gary Taylor argues for the inextricable, though generally invisible, connection between the roles of authors and editors, makers and transmitters. See *Cultural Selection* (New York: Basic Books, 1996), 121–42.

42 The play is also known by an alternative title: *The Woman's Prize; or, the Tamer Tamed*.

43 Kirby, *Indifferent Boundaries*, 6.

44 Foucault, *The Order of Things: An Archaeology of the Human Sciences* (New York: Vintage, 1973), 17–45.

45 Stephen Gosson, *The School of Abuse* (London, 1579), sig. B6–B7.

46 Jacques Derrida, *Writing and Difference*, trans. Alan Bass (University of Chicago Press, 1978), 295.

2   OFFSTAGE SEX AND FEMALE DESIRE

1 See Susan Estrich, *Real Rape* (Cambridge, MA: Harvard University Press, 1987), 8–26. Contemporary US definitions of rape vary from state to state, of course, but a glance at current Kentucky legislation provides an example of a system which has, very recently, been re-shaped in response to critiques like Estrich's. "Forcible compulsion," the key term in determining first-degree rape, is defined as "physical force *or the threat* of physical force, *express or implied*, which places a person in fear of immediate death, physical injury to self or another person, fear of the immediate kidnap of self or another person . . . *Physical resistance shall not be necessary to meet this definition*" (Ky. Rev. Stat. Ann. Section 510.010 [Michie 1996]; emphases added). For this reference, I am indebted to Karen Quinn, Legal Counsel, Office of Child Abuse and Domestic Violence Services, Office of the Governor of Kentucky.

2 See Breitenberg's chapter on *Othello*, in which he links "sexual jealousy and the anxiety of interpretation," arguing that "sexual jealousy is both constitutive and symptomatic of the normative operations of early modern patriarchy" (*Anxious Masculinity*, 175–201).

3 See Laura Mulvey, "Visual Pleasure and Narrative Cinema," *Screen* 16 (1975), 6–18; Teresa de Lauretis, *Alice Doesn't: Feminism, Semiotics, Cinema* (Bloomington: Indiana University Press, 1984), esp. 12–69; and Jill Dolan, *The Feminist Spectator as Critic* (Ann Arbor: UMI Research Press, 1988).

4 Gillian Rose, *Feminism and Geography: The Limits of Geographical Knowledge* (Minneapolis: University of Minnesota Press, 1993), 153–60.

5 Determining the authority of stage directions in even the earliest surviving copy of a play can be tricky business; J. R. Mulryne points out that the stage directions in the 1657 edition of *Women Beware Women* may have derived from marks made by a theater functionary upon an earlier stage-manuscript, now lost. See the introduction to Mulryne's Revels Plays edition (London: Methuen, 1975), xxiii–xxv. For a more wide-ranging discussion of the problem of stage directions, see William B. Long, "Stage-Directions: A Misinterpreted Factor in Determining Textual Provenance," *Text* 2 (1985), 121–37.

6 On performance as text, or "a language of sound, light, and movement, to be interpreted by the audience," see Michael Issacharoff and Robin F. Jones, eds., *Performing Texts* (Philadelphia: University of Pennsylvania Press, 1988), 1. For an extended discussion of *mise-en-scène*, defined as "the bringing together . . . in a given space and time, of different signifying systems, for an audience" (86), see Patrice Pavis' essay, "From Text to Performance," in the same volume (86–100). In discussing possible performative approaches to dramatic texts – some of which lack a substantial stage history – I will have to generalize, in the ensuing chapter, about the responses of a hypothetical audience. Of course audiences are not homogeneous entities: the sex scene one spectator finds titillating might cause the person sitting next to him discomfiture or boredom. Nonetheless, theater is by definition a collective experience, and countless instances of "mob" or collective action prove that responses can be shared by a group. In theater, Pavis states, "the dramatic text no

longer has an individual reader, but a *possible collective* reading" (91; emphasis in original); it is this possibility which I will address.

7 I have borrowed the term "proximity" from one of the few contemporary editors to engage with Derridean theory: Gary Taylor. See "The Renaissance and the End of Editing," in *Palimpsest: Editorial Theory in the Humanities*, ed. George Bornstein and Ralph G. Williams (Ann Arbor: University of Michigan Press, 1993), 121–49. Taylor's work will be more fully addressed below.

8 Suzanne Gossett, " 'Best Men are Molded out of Faults': Marrying the Rapist in Jacobean Drama," *English Literary Renaissance* 14.3 (1984), 305–27. Gossett discusses the play in light of the custom – no longer legal, but practically in effect, in early modern England – whereby the victim could opt to marry her rapist, who otherwise would be executed. Historical records indicate that charges of rape against aristocratic males were infrequent and could prove disastrous for the plaintiff, therefore "a girl might consider herself lucky to marry her rapist, especially if she was pregnant" (312).

9 Engaging in sexual intercourse with anyone under sixteen is punishable as third-degree rape in the state of Kentucky (Ky. Rev. Stat. Ann. Section 510.060). The evidence for Bianca's age comes from the Duke's messenger, who says she is "about sixteen" (3.1.180).

10 All quotations from the work of Middleton are from *The Collected Works of Thomas Middleton*, gen. ed. Gary Taylor (Oxford University Press, forthcoming).

11 The offstage rape in Thomas Heywood's *The Rape of Lucrece* is only slightly shorter, transpiring in the space of twenty-three lines.

12 Andrew Gurr, *The Shakespearean Stage 1574–1642* (Cambridge University Press, 1970), 161.

13 Galenic anatomy, which was still the model in early modern medicine, upheld female orgasm as necessary for conception and thus instructed men to solicit their partners' pleasure during intercourse. See Laqueur, *Making Sex*, 43–52.

14 Just before the incident on the upper stage, Livia declares, "Here's a duke / Will strike a sure stroke for the game anon; / Your pawn cannot come back to relieve itself" (2.2.302–4). Livia points out that the pawn is the only piece that cannot move backwards and hence retreat from danger.

Oddly enough, a number of modern editors have noted this *double entendre* and the way it casts Bianca as a defenseless victim; yet these same editors consistently describe the incident as a "seduction." J. R. Mulryne, for instance, devotes seven full pages to the critical conundrum of Bianca's sudden "change of heart," without pausing to consider the simple explanation provided within the play itself. This speech of Isabella's may be the most apt description of Hostage Syndrome outside contemporary studies on domestic violence:

> When women have their choices, commonly
> They do but buy their thraldoms and bring great portions
> To men to keep 'em in subjection:
> As if a fearful prisoner should bribe
> The keeper to be good to him, yet lies in still,
> And glad of a good usage, a good look

> Sometimes, by'r Lady; no misery surmounts a woman's.
> Men buy their slaves but women buy their masters.   (1.2.168–75)

The Duke himself echoes this language, as he assaults Bianca: "Why art so fearful?" (325); "So is captivity pleasant" (335).

15 For the 1969 Royal Shakespeare Company production, director Terry Hands conceived of a set which would highlight the chess/art tropes for sex by way of a chess-board stage and an enormous statue of Venus.

16 Stalemate was not possible according to Renaissance rules. See David Hooper and Kenneth Whyld, *The Oxford Companion to Chess* (Oxford University Press, 1992), 388.

17 A. H. Bullen, Introduction to Thomas Middleton, *The Works of Thomas Middleton, Vol. I*, ed. A. H. Bullen (Boston: Houghton, Mifflin, 1886), lxxiv. The only previous edition, by Alexander Dyce in 1840, has nothing to say about Bianca in particular, but his attitude can be extrapolated on the basis of his comment about the entire "dramatis personae," whom he describes as "almost all repulsive from their extreme depravity" (qtd. in Sara Jayne Steen, *Ambrosia in an Earthen Vessel: Three Centuries of Audience and Reader Response to the Works of Thomas Middleton* [New York: AMS Press, 1992], 101). The ensuing critique of Middleton editions does not pertain to the forthcoming Oxford *Collected Works*, which explicitly aims for a more inclusive perspective. The Oxford Middleton is, in fact, the first project of its kind to involve a significant proportion of female and feminist editors, of whom I am one.

18 J. R. Mulryne, Introduction to Thomas Middleton, *Women Beware Women*, ed. J. R. Mulryne, Revels Plays (London: Methuen, 1975), lxix; emphasis added.

19 Thomas Middleton, *The Selected Plays of Thomas Middleton*, ed. David L. Frost (Cambridge University Press, 1978).

20 R. V. Holdsworth, "*Women Beware Women* and *The Changeling* on the Stage," in *Three Jacobean Revenge Tragedies*, ed. R. V. Holdsworth, Casebook Series (London: Macmillan, 1990), 259.

21 Michael Issacharoff, "Space and Reference in Drama," *Poetics Today* 2.3 (1981), 211–24.

22 Derrida, *Writing and Difference*, 8.

23 Roland Barthes, *The Pleasure of the Text*, trans. Richard Miller (New York: Hill and Wang, 1975), 9–10.

24 Roland Barthes, *Camera Lucida*, trans. Richard Howard (New York: Hill and Wang, 1981), 59.

25 Jacques Derrida, *Of Grammatology*, trans. Gayatri Chakravorty Spivak (Baltimore: Johns Hopkins University Press, 1974), 152.

26 Barthes, *The Pleasure of the Text*, 10.

27 Derrida, *Of Grammatology*, 154.

28 See Edward Engelberg, "Tragic Blindness in *The Changeling* and *Women Beware Women*," *Modern Language Quarterly* 23 (1962), 20–28.

29 Lynn Lawner, Introduction to Giulio Romano, Marcantonio Raimondi, Pietro Aretino, and Count Jean-Frederic-Maximilien de Waldeck, *"I modi": The Sixteen Pleasures, An Erotic Album of the Italian Renaissance*, trans. and ed. Lynn Lawner (Evanston: Northwestern University Press, 1988), 4. See

also Walter Kendrick, *The Secret Museum: Pornography in Modern Culture* (New York: Viking, 1987), 58–62. The other reference to "Aretine's pictures" is in Middleton's *A Game At Chess* (2.2.257–61).

30 *Of Grammatology*, 155.

31 Rescuing editorial theory for post-modern chic, Taylor astutely points out that "The absence of the author – a discovery so revolutionary for post-modernist literary theory – is, and has always been, the foundation of editing" ("End of Editing," 125). Taylor is alluding to Barthes' famous essay, "The Death of the Author," in *Image Music Text*, trans. Stephen Heath (New York: Hill and Wang, 1977). See also Taylor's "The Rhetoric of Textual Criticism," *Text* 4 (1988), 39–57.

32 See Peter Saccio's critical introduction in the forthcoming Oxford *Collected Works*. I take this opportunity to single out this particular Middleton editor for perceiving, despite the oversights of all available editions, the erotic/comic potential of the scene about to be discussed. My working with Saccio on the commentary for *Mad World* has enormously benefited this chapter.

33 This innuendo has been studiously ignored by critical commentaries, though there is ample evidence that the sexual usage of "come" was current in Middleton's time. See Eric Partridge, *Shakespeare's Bawdy* (New York: E. P. Dutton, 1948), 89. Partridge does not include, however, the most decisive example, from Middleton and Dekker's *Honest Whore*: "A wench that will come with a wet finger" (1.2.4). My thanks to Peter Saccio for bringing this to my attention.

34 Curiously enough, Henning does gloss the earlier "huh" as a cough, though why the Courtesan should leave off the sick-noises as she supposedly "draws nigh her end" (175), he seems not to have considered.

35 In the recent Oxford World's Classic edition (1995), Michael Taylor does catch the innuendo here, glossing it as, "jealousy is alert to the sounds of copulation." Nonetheless, the commentary fails to apply this lesson to the ensuing scene – or, if it does so, it does so confusingly, and obliquely. Taylor makes the unprecedented admission that "Penitent Brothel and Mistress Harebrain are copulating off-stage," but then adds in the same note, "We are to imagine Mistress Harebrain's voice to be too soft to be heard by her husband." The stage directions are no help either, remaining faithful to Henning's interpretation.

36 Philippe Ariès and Georges Duby, *A History of the Private Life, Vol. 3: Passions of the Renaissance* (Cambridge, MA: Harvard University Press, 1989), 1–11. See also Lawrence Stone, *The Family, Sex, and Marriage in England 1500–1800*, abr. edn. (New York: Harper & Row, 1979), 384.

37 Michael Neill, "Unproper Beds: Race, Adultery, and the Hideous in *Othello*," *Shakespeare Quarterly* 40.4 (1989), 406.

38 Katharine Eisaman Maus, "Horns of Dilemma: Jealousy, Gender, and Spectatorship in English Renaissance Drama," *English Literary History* 54 (1987), 561–83.

39 Taylor, "Farrago," *Textual Practice* 8.1 (1994), 40.

40 All quotations from the work of Shakespeare are from Shakespeare, *The Complete Works*.

41 Neill points out that "The power of the offstage scene over the audience's

prying imagination is immediately suggested by the irritable speculation" of the critics themselves, from the earliest onward ("Unproper Beds," 395).

42 *Ibid.*

43 See Patricia Parker, "Fantasies of 'Race' and 'Gender': Africa, *Othello* and Bringing to Light," in *Women, "Race," and Writing in the Early Modern Period*, ed. Margo Hendricks and Patricia Parker (London: Routledge, 1994), 84–100.

44 *Ibid.* 91.

45 For a detailed account of the compression of time in *Othello*, see A. C. Bradley, *Shakespearean Tragedy* (New York: Meridean Books, 1955), 338–44.

46 Partridge, *Shakespeare's Bawdy*, 64.

47 Maus' reflections on the issue of "ocular proof" at times parallel my own. "One of the many ironies of 'ocular proof' is that it does not exist and could never exist in a theater in which the representation of sexual intercourse is taboo." She goes on to argue that "Shakespeare sometimes arranges for his audience's surmises about the offstage world of the characters to overlap . . . with the surmises of the jealous male who plays the spectator onstage" ("Horns of Dilemma," 575).

48 This is all the more necessary since Kenneth Branagh does not, I feel, make a believable Iago. Villainy just does not suit this adorably comic/romantic actor. The credits could read: "Winnie-the-Pooh as Iago."

49 Maus, *Inwardness in English Renaissance Drama* (University of Chicago Press, 1995), 120.

50 For a more thorough treatment of this preoccupation, see Patricia Parker's "*Othello* and *Hamlet*: Dilation, Spying, and the 'Secret Place' of Woman," *Representations* 44 (Fall 1993), 60–95.

51 Taylor, "A World Elsewhere" (presented at the Shakespeare Centre in Stratford-upon-Avon, 1994), 25.

52 Stephen Greenblatt, *Shakespearean Negotiations: The Circulation of Social Energy in Renaissance England* (Berkeley: University of California Press, 1988), 89.

53 Neill, "Unproper Beds," 385.

54 *Ibid.* 384. The tally of twenty-five references to Desdemona's bed is from Lynda E. Boose, "Othello's Handkerchief: 'The Recognizance and Pledge of Love,'" *English Literary Renaissance* 5 (1975), 370.

55 Jill Colaco, "The Window Scenes in *Romeo and Juliet* and Folk Songs of the Night Visit," *Studies in Philology* 83.2 (1986), 141.

56 Harley Granville-Barker, *Prefaces to Shakespeare, Vol. 4* (London: B. T. Batsford, 1963), 16–17.

57 Peter S. Donaldson, *Shakespearean Films / Shakespearean Directors* (Boston: Unwin Hyman, 1990), 167–70.

58 *Ibid.* 146–47.

59 Donaldson also details the undercurrent of "loss" in this scene, yet he emphasizes the interrupted homosexual bond between Romeo and Mercutio – rather than Romeo's exile – as the film's primary locus of loss (*ibid.* 170–71).

60 Maus, *Inwardness*, 104–81.

61 *Ibid.* 128–81.

62 Laqueur, *Making Sex*, 1–113.
63 Sue-Ellen Case, *Feminism and Theatre* (New York: Methuen, 1988), 22–23.
64 See Alan Bray, *Homosexuality in Renaissance England* (London: Gay Men's Press, 1982); Gregory W. Bredbeck, *Sodomy and Interpretation* (Ithaca: Cornell University Press, 1991); Jonathan Goldberg, *Sodometries: Renaissance Texts, Modern Sexualities* (Stanford University Press, 1992); and Bruce R. Smith, *Homosexual Desire in Shakespeare's England: A Cultural Poetics* (University of Chicago Press), 1991.
65 Orgel reconsiders the evidence for the claim that no women performed, citing visits by European companies, which always included actresses, in addition to cases which have been treated as exceptional, such as the famous appearance of Moll Frith. In calling attention to the way in which critical history has, in a sense, colluded in the taboo against female performance by overstating the "all male" qualification, Orgel's caveat must be heard. For the purposes of my argument, however, the prohibition itself, as a cultural gesture, is significant enough to assume its efficacy, at least on the public stage during the years 1595–1621. See *Impersonations: The Performance of Gender in Shakespeare's England* (Cambridge University Press, 1996), 1–9.
66 *Ibid.* 18.
67 Richmond Barbour, " 'When I Acted Young Antinous': Boy Actors and the Erotics of the Jonsonian Theater," *PMLA* 110.5 (1995), 1010.
68 Derrida, *Spurs: Nietzsche's Styles / Eperons: Les styles de Nietzsche*, trans. Barbara Harlow (University of Chicago, 1978), 71.
69 Orgel, *Impersonations*, 10–11.
70 Barbour, "Boy Actors," 1017.
71 Linda Woodbridge, *Women and the English Renaissance: Literature and the Nature of Womankind 1540–1620* (University of Illinois Press, 1984), 250–52; 258.
72 T. S. Eliot, *Selected Essays* (London: Faber and Faber, 1951), 166.
73 Linda Williams, *Hard Core: Power, Pleasure, and the "Frenzy of the Visible"* (Berkeley: University of California Press, 1989), 1–9.

3   BODY BENEATH / BODY BEYOND

1 See also Mario Perniola's fascinating essay, "Between Clothing and Nudity," trans. Roger Friedman, in *Fragments for a History of the Human Body, Part Two*, ed. Michel Feher, with Ramona Naddaff and Nadia Tazi (New York: Zone, 1989), 237–65. Perniola argues, "In the figurative arts, eroticism appears as a relationship between clothing and nudity . . . [and] is conditional on the possibility of movement – transit – from one state to another" (237).
2 The debate on the cultural significance and visibility of the boy actor is more wide-ranging than a footnote could ever do justice to. The previous chapter mentioned two critics, Case and Orgel, who treat the transvestite stage as, at least in part, an institution fueled by masculinist anxieties. Similarly, Greenblatt argues, "The open secret of identity – that within differentiated individuals is a single structure, identifiably male – is presented literally in the all-male cast" (*Shakespearean Negotiations*, 93), and Lisa Jardine, in *Still Harping on Daughters: Women and Drama in the Age of Shakespeare*

(Totowa, NJ: Barnes and Noble, 1983), underscores the male homoerotic response of the audience to this cast (9–36). Other critics such as Kathleen McLuskie emphasize the role of theatrical convention in obscuring the material fact of the boy actor. McLuskie argues that "the question of theatrical representation of femininity cannot be restricted to the physical: gender has never been coterminous with sex" ("The Act, the Role, and the Actor: Boy Actresses on the Elizabethan Stage," *New Theatre Quarterly* 3.10 [1987], 125). In a more recent article, Michael Shapiro looks at some previously unnoticed evidence from the period and finally opts for a more middle-of-the-road approach, stating that consciousness of the art-form need not preclude engagement in the fiction ("Lady Mary Wroth Describes a 'Boy Actress,'" *Medieval and Renaissance Drama in England* 4 [1989], 187–94). I take this opportunity to face up to the political awkwardness of my position with regard to the historical boy actors; because my analysis traverses their material presence, I might be perceived as dismissing the value of their experiences. But there is already an outpouring of excellent scholarship attending to these boy bodies. Suffice it to say that, historically speaking, the boy actors were there, and they *mattered*.

3 Peter Stallybrass, "Transvestism and the 'Body Beneath': Speculating on the Boy Actor," *Erotic Politics: Desire on the Renaissance Stage*, ed. Susan Zimmerman (London: Routledge, 1992).

4 Woodbridge, *Women and the English Renaissance*, 184–223.

5 All quotations are from John Fletcher, *The Tamer Tamed*, ed. Gary Taylor and Celia R. Daileader, Revels Plays (Manchester University Press, forthcoming).

6 See McKluskie, *Renaissance Dramatists*, Feminist Readings (Atlantic Highlands, NJ: Humanities International, 1989), 215–16.

7 See Sara Jayne Steen, Introduction to *The Letters of Lady Arbella Stuart*, (Oxford University Press, 1994), 1–111.

8 Mikhail Bakhtin, *Rabelais and His World*, trans. Helene Iswolsky (Bloomington: Indiana University Press, 1984), 282–83.

9 Molly Easo Smith, "John Fletcher's Response to the Gender Debate: *The Woman's Prize* and *The Taming of the Shrew*," *Papers in Language and Literature* 31 (1995), 38–60.

10 Stallybrass, "'Body Beneath,'" 73.

11 Stallybrass, "Worn Worlds: Clothes and Identity on the Renaissance Stage," in *Subject and Object in Renaissance Culture*, ed. Margreta de Grazia, Maureen Quilligan, and Peter Stallybrass (Cambridge University Press, 1996), 313. See also Newman, *Fashioning Femininity*, 111–27.

12 Masculine attire for women was as fashionable as it was controversial during the early seventeenth century; Orgel makes the point that, despite objections such as the *Hic mulier* pamphlet, the very existence of these fashions indicates their appreciation by at least *some* men (*Impersonations*, 118–19).

13 The association dates at least as far back as Augustine, who wrote of Christ's Incarnation as a process by which he was "clothed with a body of earthly mortality, that He might clothe it with heavenly immortality" (*The City of God*, ed. and trans. Marcus Dods, 2 vols. [New York: Hafner, 1948], vol. I, bk. XIII, ch. 23, 550). As in any trope for the flesh, Christian iconography

was quite capable of positively portraying the body/robe – for example, in images of the pregnant Virgin Mary knitting a child's garment representing the Incarnation. See Gail McMurray Gibson, *The Theater of Devotion: East Anglican Drama and Society in the Late Middle Ages* (University of Chicago Press, 1989), 155–66. Another late medieval source is Julian of Norwich (1342–1416), who says "our filthy, dying flesh which the Son of God took upon himself, like Adam's old coat, tight, threadbare, and too short, the Saviour transformed into something beautiful, fresh, bright and splendid" (*Revelations of Divine Love*, trans. Clifton Wolters [New York: Penguin, 1966], 150).

14 *Certaine Sermons or Homilies Appointed To Be Read in Churches in the Time of Queen Elizabeth I, Vol. II* (London, 1623), 105. Regarding the argument of this chapter, it is noteworthy that the "Homilie," placed back-to-back with the "Homilie Against Gluttony and Drunkennesse," makes little distinction between sumptuary, sexual, and alimentary appetite, often collapsing all three under the category of "wanton lustes." Here is one characteristic passage: "For the proude and haughtie stomacks of the daughters of England, are so maintained with divers disguised sortes of costly apparell, that . . . there is left no difference . . . between an honest matrone and a common strumpet" (105).

15 Maus' *Inwardness* compellingly reconsiders recent critiques of Hamlet's claim to interiority, exposing the post-modern critical biases which have influenced such objections. The list of scholars engaged is impressive. See Anne Ferry, *The "Inward" Language: Sonnets of Wyatt, Shakespeare, Donne* (University of Chicago Press, 1983), 1–30; Francis Barker, *The Tremulous Private Body* (New York: Methuen, 1984), 31, 58; Catherine Belsey, *The Subject of Tragedy: Identity and Difference in Renaissance Drama* (New York: Methuen, 1985), 48; Jean E. Howard, "The New Historicism in Renaissance Studies," *English Literary Renaissance* 16 (1986), 15. These critics claim that belief in psychic inwardness was nonexistent or at most nascent at the time that Shakespeare penned Hamlet's speech, and warn readers against such anachronistic projections of modern "bourgeois subjectivity." A second group of critics taken on by Maus concedes "that the rhetoric of inwardness is highly developed in the English Renaissance, but maintain that these terms inevitably refer to outward, public, and political factors" (Maus, *Inwardness*, 2). Sources in this second category include: Jonathan Goldberg, *James I and the Politics of Literature* (Baltimore: Johns Hopkins University Press, 1983), 86; Ann Rosalind Jones and Peter Stallybrass, "The Politics of *Astrophil and Stella*," *Studies in English Literature* 24 (1984), 54; Kay Stockholder, "'Yet Can He Write': Reading the Silences in *The Spanish Tragedy*," *American Imago* 47 (1990), 3–124; and Patricia Fumerton, *Cultural Aesthetics: Renaissance Literature and the Practice of Social Ornament* (University of Chicago Press, 1991).

16 Stallybrass, "'Body Beneath,'" 66.

17 For a very different analysis of this broadside, see Taylor, "Thomas Middleton: Lives and Afterlives," in the *Collected Works.*

18 Stallybrass, "'Body Beneath,'" 66–70.

19 *Ibid.* 76; emphasis added.

20 Perniola, "Between Clothing and Nudity," 258–59. Perniola compares these

lovingly detailed images of dissection to the sartorial excess of Bernini's *Saint Theresa*, wherein the robe takes on a life of its own.

21 In my gendering of the (literal or figurative) skeleton as male, I am diverging from Traub's reading of early modern anatomy practice, wherein "the body slips progressively into a representational realm where gender difference holds no meaning" ("Gendering Mortality," 55). Although I do agree that dissection of the male cadaver runs the risk of disclosing a messy, and therefore effeminizing, physical interior, I do feel that the final product (whether or not it is achieved) of a clean skeleton is always unambiguously male (even, arguably, if it once belonged to a woman). After all, Gloriana's skull must be "dressed up" to act the woman's part in the fatal bed-trick.

22 Laurie A. Finke, "Painting Women: Images of Femininity in Jacobean Tragedy," *Theatre Journal* 35.3 (1984), 357–70.

23 Augustine, *The City of God*, bk. XIII, ch. 13, p. 534.

24 Laura Levine, *Men in Women's Clothing: Anti-theatricality and Effeminization 1579–1642* (Cambridge University Press, 1994), 14 and *passim*.

25 Leonard Tennenhouse analyzes Shakespearean drama in light of "a poetics of surface" which inscribed the Elizabethan social body – above all, through the markings of apparel. Players often received as donations the rich attire which servants inherited from their masters but were forbidden by law to wear, and the players, an otherwise marginalized group, could then strut with impunity in rags worth a fortune ("Simulating History: A Cockfight for Our Times," *Drama Review* 34.4 [1990], 140–42). Stallybrass goes so far as to argue, and convincingly, that "the commercial theater is directly *derived* from the market in clothes" ("Worn Worlds," 294).

26 Patricia Parker discusses the "feminine" gendering of this literary fleshiness or *copia*, in contradistinction to a more "masculine" style marked by simplicity and "rigor," in her essay "Virile Style," in *Premodern Sexualities*, ed. Louise Fradenburg and Carla Freccero (London: Routledge, 1996), 201–22.

27 Hyphenated terms such as "Toast-and-Butter" have only been counted once.

28 Gordon McMullen, *The Politics of Unease in the Plays of John Fletcher* (Amherst, MA: University of Massachusetts Press, 1994), 125.

29 Gail Kern Paster, *The Body Embarrassed: Drama and the Disciplines of Shame in Early Modern England* (Ithaca: Cornell University Press, 1993), 45–46. See also an important precursor to Paster's argument: Peter Stallybrass, "Patriarchal Territories: The Body Enclosed," *Rewriting the Renaissance: The Discourses of Sexual Difference in Early Modern Europe*, ed. Margaret W. Ferguson, Maureen Quilligan, and Nancy J. Vickers (University of Chicago Press, 1986), 123–42. Both Stallybrass and Paster elaborate on the Bakhtinian paradigm which pits the "grotesque" body against its "classical" antithesis, but apply these terms to gender as well as class conflict.

30 All quotations are from Ben Jonson, *Bartholomew Fair, Three Comedies*, ed. Michael Jamieson (London: Penguin, 1966).

31 Paster, *The Body Embarrassed*, 46.

32 Frances Teague, *The Curious History of* Bartholomew Fair (Lewisburg, PA: Bucknell University Press, 1985), 17.

33 *Ibid.* 37.

34 My own blocking of the scene strongly qualifies Jamieson's interpolated stage

direction at the opening of act 4, scene 4, whereby Knockem, Mistress Overdo, and the others are "*discovered drinking in Ursula's booth*"; later in the same scene, Ursula enters from somewhere else, and answers Mistress Overdo's request for her "pot" by saying it is "employed . . . within" (202–4). So, if the "vapours" game is played inside the now partially opened booth, there must be an additional enclosure "within" – perhaps the same space from which Ursula enters.

35 Maus, *Inwardness*, 182–209.

36 Derrida uses the notion of a structural "abyss" to illustrate his axiom that "there is nothing outside the text": "the concept of the supplement and the theory of writing designate textuality itself . . . in an indefinitely multiplied structure – *en abyme* . . . Representation *in the abyss* of presence is not an accident of presence; the desire of presence is, on the contrary, born from the abyss (the indefinite multiplication) of representation" (*Of Grammatology*, 163).

37 Kristeva, *Powers of Horror*, 54.

38 The *Oxford English Dictionary* (*OED* hereafter) confirms that the use of the word "pig" to mean "the animal or its flesh as an article of food" is generally for humor.

39 See Jamieson's note to 3.1.72.

40 The use of the word "belly" to mean "stomach" or "bowels" predates its usage for "womb" by almost a century, according to the *OED*. Interestingly, though, the Old English "womb" appeared to mean "uterus" and "stomach" interchangeably, as did the Latin *uterum*. Laqueur explains this early anatomical confusion with the supposition "that ancient medicine is less interested in specific organic causes than in corporeal metaphors that correlate with symptoms." Early modern medicine, however, recognized two discrete organs (*Making Sex*, 251 nn.3, 4).

41 On Ursula as earth mother, see C. G. Thayer, *Ben Jonson: Studies in the Plays* (Norman: University of Oklahoma Press, 1963), 132–33. See also Jonathan Haynes' Bakhtinian analysis, "Festivity and the Dramatic Economy of Jonson's *Bartholomew Fair*," *English Literary History* 51 (1984), 647.

42 Luce Irigaray, *This Sex Which Is Not One*, trans. Catherine Porter (Ithaca: Cornell University Press, 1985), 111.

43 Paster, *The Body Embarrassed*, 38–39.

44 On vagina as hell, see Gordon Williams, *A Dictionary of Sexual Language and Imagery in Shakespearean and Stuart Literature*, 3 vols. (London: Athlone Press, 1994), 660.

45 Stallybrass, "'Body Beneath,'" 66.

46 Levine, *Men in Women's Clothing*, 101.

47 *Ibid.* 105. Another argument against the "sterile" reading of Ursula's body can be made on strictly biochemical grounds: anyone familiar with the effects of anorexia nervosa knows that a woman's "fat" is essential to her fertility – the more, the better. This is not to say that Ursula's sexuality is not treated with some ambivalence. I should emphasize here that my strongest objection to Levine concerns the attribute of sterility, rather than that of anti-eroticism (eroticism being, after all, in the eye of the beholder). Still, we should be cautious in dismissing Ursula's erotic potential to an early modern audience.

The same is true of the "tired prostitutes" whose attraction Levine also dismisses in the passage cited above. In our age of relative sexual freedom, it is too easy to overlook the *frisson* a sexually available "whore" might provoke in a different culture.

48 Grace Tiffany, *Erotic Beasts and Social Monsters: Shakespeare, Jonson, and Comic Androgyny* (Newark: University of Delaware Press, 1995), 157. Parker also refers to Jonson's corpulence in order to point up a contradiction in his work; the author himself perpetuated the gendered binary of lean versus fleshly or effeminate styles, despite his contributions to the latter category, specifically in *Bartholomew Fair* ("Virile Style," 208).

49 The phrase is John Dryden's; see *Preface to the Fables*, in *Essays of John Dryden, Vol. II*, ed. W. P. Ker (New York: Russell & Russell, 1961), 262.

50 Geoffrey Chaucer, *Prologue to Sir Thopas, The Canterbury Tales, The Riverside Chaucer*, ed. Larry D. Benson (Boston: Houghton Mifflin, 1987), vol. VII, 701. (All subsequent quotes of Chaucer are from this edition.) The *OED* cites this Chaucerian passage under the definition of "popet" as "small or dainty person," but the term also applied to any miniature human figure or doll, including those used in witchcraft; although the *OED* dates the secondary meaning ("puppet") at 1586, I believe Chaucer's "popet" subtly anticipates this usage: the referent is, after all, the author's fictional representative, whose motions are dictated, so to speak, from above.

51 Scott Cutler Shershow, " 'The Mouth of 'hem All': Ben Jonson, Authorship, and the Performing Object," *Theatre Journal* 46 (1994), 189.

52 Teague, *Curious History*, 19.

53 Levine, *Men in Women's Clothing*, 101.

54 Maus, *Inwardness*, 267. Another recent analysis of the womb metaphor in male-authored texts of the period appears in Elizabeth D. Harvey's *Ventriloquized Voices: Feminist Theory and English Renaissance Texts* (London: Routledge, 1992), 76–115. Harvey, interestingly, links the popularity of the trope with the encroachment of the male medico-scientific establishment into the field of midwifery.

55 Maus, *Inwardness*, 274.

56 Stallybrass, "Worn Worlds," 314.

57 Tennenhouse, "Simulating History," 139.

58 Sawday, *The Body Emblazoned*, 85.

59 Paster, *The Body Embarrassed*, 38.

60 Judith Butler, *Gender Trouble: Feminism and the Subversion of Identity* (London: Routledge, 1990), 33; emphasis added.

4 (OFF)STAGING THE SACRED

1 See Stanley Wells, *Re-Editing Shakespeare for the Modern Reader* (Oxford: Clarendon, 1984), 91–92, 103–5; 109.

2 See George B. Ferguson, Introduction to John Fletcher, *The Woman's Prize; or, the Tamer Tamed: A Critical Edition*, ed. George B. Ferguson, Studies in English Literature (The Hague: Mouton, 1966), vol. XVII, 33.

3 See Stanley Wells and Gary Taylor, *A Textual Companion to the Works of William Shakespeare* (Oxford University Press, 1987), 476–91.

4 For a detailed chronology of this suppression, see *The Revels History of English Drama, Vol. II*, gen. ed. T. W. Craik (London: Methuen, 1980), 7–11. For an account which traces the opposition to and censorship of religious drama into the twentieth century, see John R. Elliott, Jr., *Playing God: Medieval Mysteries on the Modern Stage* (University of Toronto Press, 1989), 3–24. Astonishingly enough, the ban on theatrical representation of the deity was not legally overturned in England until 1968 – that is, until my own lifetime (24).

5 Christopher Hill, *The English Bible and the Seventeenth-Century Revolution* (London: Penguin, 1993), 20.

6 Debora Kuller Shuger, *The Renaissance Bible: Scholarship, Sacrifice, and Subjectivity* (Berkeley: University of California Press, 1994), 5.

7 Shuger, *The Renaissance Bible*, 192–96.

8 Caroline Walker Bynum, *Holy Feast and Holy Fast: The Religious Significance of Food to Medieval Women* (Berkeley: University of California Press, 1987), *passim*. See also Barbara Newman, *From Virile Woman to WomanChrist: Studies in Medieval Religion and Literature* (Philadelphia: University of Pennsylvania Press, 1995). Of particular relevance to this chapter is Newman's discussion of a female godhead in the writings of female mystics such as Hadewijch, Mechthild of Magdeburg, and Marguerite Porete; see 153–58. Though qualifiable as "esoteric" and removed by far from our period of focus, these thirteenth-century authors became part of a movement Newman terms "the feminization of Christianity" (244) which flourished in late medieval mariolatry and culminated in Cornelius Agrippa's radical treatise in defense of women, *De nobilitate et praecellentia foeminei sexus*, published in 1529 and reprinted well into the next century (224–48).

For an account of a sixteenth-century woman who proclaimed herself Christ, see Auke Jelsma, "A 'Messiah for Women': Religious Commotion in the North-East of Switzerland, 1525–1526," in *Women in the Church*, ed. W. J. Sheils and Diana Wood, Studies in Church History 27 (Oxford: Blackwell, 1990), 295–306.

9 Closer scrutiny of the two works mitigates the apparent contradiction. The latter piece is a critique of Leo Steinberg's thesis about images of Christ which call attention to his penis and thereby his (male) "sexuality." Bynum counters this claim with evidence of Christ's feminization; she also makes the more general point that medieval people did not necessarily "read" the body and its various organs the way we do. As to whether medieval mystics experienced sexual arousal in their communion with Christ, Bynum essentially declares the matter beside the point, since what worried medieval theologians was not the physical nature of these sensations, but rather the uncertainty about who was causing them, Christ or the devil. See *Fragmentation and Redemption: Essays on Gender and the Human Body in Medieval Religion* (New York: Zone Books, 1991), 79–117. Similarly, in *Holy Feast and Holy Fast*, Bynum argues against modern treatment of mystical writings as "sublimated sexual desire," stating that "In the eucharist and in ecstasy, a male Christ was handled and loved; sexual feelings were . . . not so much translated into another medium as simply set free" (248). A footnote provides a more thorough defense of this

affective spirituality against our post-Freudian assumptions about sex and eros (403 n.21).

10 Shuger, *The Renaissance Bible*, 176–91.

11 This classical critical tenet is from chapter 14 of Samuel Taylor Coleridge's *Biographia literaria*, in *The Norton Anthology of English Literature*, gen. ed. M. H. Abrams, 5th edn. (New York: Norton, 1982), vol. XI, 397.

12 William E. Engel elaborates on the Renaissance interest in cartographical/ spatial metaphors for the *terra incognita* of death; see *Mapping Mortality*, 129–94. For a rather bleaker view of attitudes toward this "ultimate departure," see Robert N. Watson, *The Rest Is Silence: Death as Annihilation in the English Renaissance* (Berkeley: University of California Press, 1994). Watson argues that "Despite its ferocious displays of Christian conviction, Jacobean culture struggled with the suspicion that death was a complete and permanent annihilation of the self" (3). On the rhetorical treatment of death in drama specifically, see Michael Cameron Andrews, *This Action of Our Death: The Performance of Death in English Renaissance Drama* (Newark: University of Delaware Press, 1989).

13 Sara Jayne Steen argues for a measure of popular sympathy for the character of the Duchess of Malfi, contrary to a number of critics who uphold the view that early modern audiences, indoctrinated by antifeminism, condemned her. Steen bases her argument on popular reactions to a close contemporary parallel, the case of Lady Arbella Stuart, imprisoned by male relatives for marrying against their wishes. Stuart also died in prison, through self-starvation. See Steen's essay, "The Crime of Marriage: Arbella Stuart and *The Duchess of Malfi*," *Sixteenth Century Journal* 22.1 (1991), 61–76, as well as her Introduction to *The Letters of Lady Arbella Stuart*.

Other contemporary feminists view Webster as subverting the misogyny of his culture; see, for instance, Woodbridge, *Women and the English Renaissance*, 259–61, and McLuskie, "Drama and Sexual Politics: The Case of Webster's Duchess," in *Drama, Sex, and Politics* (Cambridge University Press, 1985). For a reading of the play which focuses specifically on the problem of female political power, see Theodora Jankowski, "Defining/ Confining the Duchess: Negotiating the Female Body in John Webster's *The Duchess of Malfi*," *Studies in Philology* 87.2 (1990), 221–45.

14 All quotes are from John Webster, *The Duchess of Malfi*, ed. Elizabeth Brennan, New Mermaids Series (London: A. & C. Black, 1993).

15 Finke borrows the phrase from Sandra Gilbert and Susan Gubar's exegesis of a comment made by Virginia Woolf, declaring that a woman writer must "kill" the "angel in the house" (qtd. in Gilbert and Gubar, cited below); "in other words," they write, "women must kill the aesthetic ideal through which they themselves have been 'killed' into art" (*The Madwoman in the Attic: The Woman Writer and the Nineteenth-Century Literary Imagination* [New Haven: Yale University Press, 1979], 17); see also Finke, "Painting Women," 360–64.

16 Finke, "Painting Women," 360–61.

17 Mary Beth Rose, *The Expense of Spirit: Love and Sexuality in English Renaissance Drama* (Ithaca: Cornell University Press, 1988), 161.

18 Finke, "Painting Women," 369.

19 Stone, *The Family, Sex, and Marriage*, 64.

20 On the political meaning of the Duchess' blood, see Jankowski, "Defining/ Confining," and also Tennenhouse, *Power on Display: The Politics of Shakespeare's Genres* (New York: Methuen, 1986), 118–22.

21 Frank Whigham argues that "the point of Ferdinand's incestuous rage is not the achievement of sexual relations, but the denial of institutional slippage *via* contaminating relation" (*Seizures of the Will in Early Modern English Drama* [Cambridge University Press, 1996], 188–224; 196) – and whereas I find Whigham's reading of Ferdinand as a "threatened aristocrat" compelling, I also feel strongly that the invasive speech-acts the Duke directs at his sister provide an outlet for his incestuous desires; in other words, they are a consummation in themselves.

22 Paster, *The Body Embarrassed*, 64–112.

23 Paster draws these examples from Shakespeare's *Julius Caesar*, where Antony describes Caesar's wounds as "poor, poor, dumb mouths" (3.2.225), in contrast to Portia's "voluntary wound" (2.1.300), offered as proof of a continence transcending her sex (*The Body Embarrassed*, 106, 111–12).

24 Laqueur, *Making Sex*, 35–36.

25 Bynum, *Holy Feast and Holy Fast*, 260–76.

26 Shuger, *The Renaissance Bible*, 96.

27 See Dale B. J. Randall, "The Rank and Earthy Background of Certain Physical Symbols in *The Duchess of Malfi*," *Renaissance Drama* 18 (1987), 171–203.

28 See R. F. Whitman, "Webster's *Duchess of Malfi*," *Notes and Queries* 6 (1959), 174, and M. C. Bradbook, *Themes and Conventions*, 2nd edn. (Cambridge University Press, 1980), 82–84.

29 Richard Allen Cave, *Text and Performance*: The White Devil *and* The Duchess of Malfi, Text and Performance Series, gen. ed. Michael Scott (London: MacMillan, 1998), 66.

30 David M. Bergeron, "The Wax Figures in *The Duchess of Malfi*," *Studies in English Literature* 18 (1978), 331.

31 A 1989 RSC performance in Stratford used this method (Brennan edn., 85; 4.1.55n). As the text of the play post-dates its performance, and "was published with the reader rather than the actor in mind" (Brennan edn. Introduction, xl), it is quite possible that Webster's elaborate stage direction, "*Here is discover'd behind a traverse, the artificial figures of* Antonio *and his child; appearing as if they were dead*" (4.1.55.01–02), addresses the fiction rather than the material conditions of performance.

32 Kent Cartwright, *Shakespearean Tragedy and Its Double: The Rhythms of Audience Response* (University Park: Pennsylvania State University Press, 1991), 5–7.

33 Andrews, *This Action of Our Death*, 66.

34 John Wesley Harris, *Medieval Theater in Context: An Introduction* (London: Routledge, 1992), 140.

35 Passion Play II (N Town), in *Medieval Drama*, ed. David Bevington (Boston: Houghton Mifflin, 1975), line 448. All subsequent quotations of medieval plays are from this edition.

36 Cartwright, *Shakespearean Tragedy and Its Double*, 3.

37 For a defense of the title used here, see the forthcoming Oxford edition.

38 According to the *OED*, the religious sense of the word predates all others by at least two centuries. The earliest reference to the passion of Christ appears in 1175; the first use of the word to mean "painful affliction" arises in 1382; not until the 1590s (and thanks, in part, to Shakespeare) do we find the word used in its modern sexual sense.

39 Anne Lancashire, Introduction to Thomas Middleton, *The Second Maiden's Tragedy*, ed. Anne Lancashire, Revels Plays (Baltimore: Johns Hopkins University Press, 1978), 27–28.

40 *Ibid.* 26.

41 Contrast his attitude to that of Tarquin toward Lucrece, whose construction as "Lucrece the Chaste" compels him to rape her. See Sara E. Quay, "'Lucrece the Chaste': The Construction of Rape in Shakespeare's *The Rape of Lucrece*," *Modern Language Studies* 25 (1995), 1–15.

42 Lancashire, Introduction, 55.

43 Elisabeth Bronfen, *Over Her Dead Body: Death, Femininity, and the Aesthetic* (London: Routledge, 1992), xii.

44 Bevington, Introduction, *Medieval Drama*, 32.

45 Bergeron, "Art Within *The Second Maiden's Tragedy*," *Medieval and Renaissance Drama in England* 1 (1984), 173–86.

46 Bynum, *Holy Feast and Holy Fast*, 113–86.

47 The process of extricating the Pharaoh from his funerary encasements took Carter well over a year. The outermost of these gilded enclosures measured 17 by 11 feet and stood 9 feet high – leaving only a 2-foot crawl-space for the archaeologist to work in. The outer shrine housed 3 interior shrines and 3 coffins, the innermost solid gold; once Carter had penetrated this far, he could remove Tut's gold mask and begin the painstaking task of cutting through the 13 layers of linen wrappings, uncovering, one by one, 143 pieces of jewelry, down to the very last: a gold sheath over the penis. See Howard Carter, *The Tomb of Tutankhamen* (London: Dutton, 1972), esp. 103–33.

   The cultural phenomenon of Tut-mania is material for another book in itself. Its pertinence to this chapter lies in its illustration of a collective love-affair with, not just a dead person, but a dead *body*. The appellation of "boy king" is telling in itself: modern culture insisted on reminding itself of the youth of a 3,300-year-old mummy, the nickname appearing in newspaper captions under his ossified profile. The eternizing conceit lives on.

48 Lancashire, Introduction, 43.

49 "*Here they pulle of[f] Jhesus clothis and betyn him with whippys*" (Passion Play II, 440 stage direction).

50 [The Service] For Representing the Scene at the Lord's Sepulchre, lines 25–27.

51 Bergeron speculates "that the 'effigy' necessary in the production to represent this dead Lady could have been used for one of the 'wax' figures in Webster's play, both plays written for production by the King's men" ("Webster's Allusion to *The Second Maiden's Tragedy*," *English Language Notes* 17 [1980], 255).

52 "The medieval audience loved its tortures. Saints were continually being decapitated, roasted on gridirons, burnt in ovens, torn limb from limb, or otherwise carved up. St Denis . . . was progressively whipped, racked, tormented on a red-hot grill, savaged by wild animals, steeped in a furnace,

crucified, beheaded and disemboweled . . . St Barbara, in another play, was stripped naked, bound to a stake, beaten and burnt, had her breasts cut off, was rolled in a nail-studded barrel and dragged over a mountain by her hair, before being executed. Presumably in these cases dummies were substituted at some point for the actors" (Harris, *Medieval Theater in Context*, 145).

53 *Ibid.* 144.

54 Bergeron points out the relationship between this Shakespearean scene and that in which the Duchess views the wax figures of her husband and children. "Leontes and the others who gaze on this figure assume that this is the life-like representation of Hermione, dead for some sixteen years . . . Paulina pulls the curtain in order to reveal Hermione just as Bosola 'discovers' the figures behind a 'traverse.' The Duchess believes, in contrast to Leontes, that what she sees are dead persons. Not only is Hermione alive, but this is no statue, as we discover. The transformation of Hermione leads to transcendent joy and reconciliation, while the wax figures belie the truth to the Duchess and encourage her longing for death" ("The Wax Figures," 333).

55 Cartwright, *Shakespearean Tragedy and Its Double*, 6.

56 The line actually precedes her entrance, and is attributed in the MS to an anonymous voice "*Within*" or offstage. There is no question that the line must be spoken by the person playing the Lady, but the offstage placement of the speaker, as well as the convention which situates the offstage *within*, strengthens the parallel between the absent body of woman and the absent body of Christ.

57 This deadly kiss of a poisoned/painted female corpse resembles the lethal kiss of Gloriana's skull in *The Revenger's Tragedy*. An interesting analysis of this moment is provided by Stallybrass in his essay, "Reading the Body: *The Revenger's Tragedy*," *Renaissance Drama* 18 (1987), 121–48. Stallybrass reads the fatal kiss in light of "the centrality of the mouth and the tongue in the topography of the staged body" (122). Finke's compelling feminist reading of the female *memento mori* also points out that the notion of "paint" or cosmetics as poison had a practical basis, for the make-up available in early modern England was often mercury-based and led to "gradual decomposition" ("Painting Women," 363).

Along different lines, this kiss reminds me of the medieval Christian adoration of relics, a practice I will foreground in the next chapter. Medieval worshippers believed that the body of a dead martyr or a member taken from that body held both the power to heal the faithful and the power to harm an infidel; a profane touch to the relic would cause the limb or hand of the offender to shrivel or lose its function. See Ann Eljenhom Nichols' essay, "The Hierosphthitic Topos, or the Fate of Fergus: Notes on the N-Town Assumption," in *Iconographic and Comparative Studies in Medieval Drama*, ed. Clifford Davidson and John H. Stoupe (Kalamazoo: Medieval Institute, 1991), 29–41.

58 Shuger, *The Renaissance Bible*, 167–91.

59 *Ibid.* 170.

60 *Ibid.* 173–74.

61 George Lyman Kitteredge, *Witchcraft in Old and New England* (Cambridge, MA: Harvard University Press, 1929), 73–103.

62 Martin Luther adopted a somewhat more moderate approach to the problem of images, even combating the radical iconoclasm of his contemporary, Andreas Bodenstein von Karlstadt: the rioters who, inspired by Karlstadt, stormed churches and tore down altars were themselves making an idol of iconoclasm, Luther said. As material objects were in themselves neutral, idolatry was in the mind. Furthermore, Luther argued against body/soul dualism, insisting that God could only be reached through Christ's humanity, and hence, in part, through the material world. Calvin, by contrast, issued stern warnings against the dangers of images in worship. See Carlos M. N. Eire, *War Against the Idols: The Reformation of Worship from Erasmus to Calvin* (Cambridge University Press, 1986), 65–73, 195–233.

63 Qtd. in Shuger, *The Renaissance Bible*, 175.

64 Clifford Davidson argues that medieval drama cannot be fully understood without taking into account the relation of the stage to iconography, cult images, relics, "and various additional representations that illustrate aspects of religious devotion in an age when *seeing* was more important than hearing" ("Positional Symbolism and English Medieval Drama," *Iconographic and Comparative Studies*, 66).

65 Shuger, *The Renaissance Bible*, 176.

66 *Ibid.* 178.

67 Jonas Barish, *The Antitheatrical Prejudice* (Berkeley: University of California Press, 1981), 159.

68 See Irigaray, *This Sex Which Is Not One*, 106–18, and Hélène Cixous and Catherine Clément, *The Newly Born Woman*, trans. Betsy Wing, Theory and History of Literature 24 (Minneapolis: University of Minnesota Press, 1986), 93.

69 John Donne, "The Crosse," in *The Complete English Poems of John Donne*, ed. C. A. Patrides (London: J. M. Dent, 1985), 443–50; lines 15–16.

70 See Brennan's New Mermaids edition, 6.

71 Although sexually explicit representations date at least as far back as Pompeii, "pornography" as a term and a category seems to have been invented in the nineteenth century. See Walter Kendrick, *The Secret Museum: Pornography in Modern Culture* (New York: Viking, 1987), 1–32. See also *The Invention of Pornography: Obscenity and the Origins of Modernity, 1500–1800*, ed. Lynn Hunt (New York: Zone, 1993). Building on Kendrick, Hunt argues that pornography as a discursive category arose in response to the spread of literacy – that is, pornography was defined as such in order to regulate its consumption (9–18).

72 George Herbert, "Death," in *The English Poems of George Herbert*, ed. C. A. Patrides (London: J. M. Dent & Sons, 1974), 189; lines 1, 15.

73 Shuger, *The Renaissance Bible*, 128–30. Although this may not be the sense in which Aristotle's *Poetics* employs the term, the dual meanings, Shuger argues, "would have been obvious to any Renaissance Graecist." Moreover, the association between tragedy and sacrifice might even have been grasped by readers unschooled in Greek: sixteenth-century translations of Greek tragedy into Latin or the vernacular overwhelmingly focus on human and "*especially female* sacrifice" (129; my emphasis).

74 Steen, "Crime of Marriage," 61–76.

5 OBSCENE AND UNSEEN

1 "For the preventing and avoyding of the great Abuse of the Holy Name of God in Stageplayes Interludes Maygames Shewes and such like; Be it enacted by our Soveraign Lorde the Kinges Majesty, and by the Lordes Spirituall and Temporall, and Comons in this present Parliament assembled . . . That if at any tyme or tymes . . . any p[er]son or p[er]sons doe or shall in any Stage play Interlude Shewe Maygame or Pageant jestingly or p[ro]phanely speake or use the holy Name of God or of Christ Jesus, or of the Holy Ghoste or of the Trinitie, which are not to be spoken but with feare and reverence, shall forfeite for everie such Offence by hym or them comitted Tenne Pound" (qtd. in Gary Taylor and John Jowett, *Shakespeare Reshaped 1606–1623* [Oxford University Press, 1993], 51).

2 Cixous and Clément, *The Newly Born Woman*, 101.

3 See Williams, *Hard Core, passim*. See also Celia R. Daileader, "The Uses of Ambivalence: Pornography and Female Heterosexual Identity," *Women's Studies* 26.1 (1997), 73–88. For an entertaining overview of the widely diverging feminist responses to and uses of pornography, see M. G. Lord, "Pornutopia: How Feminist Scholars Learned to Love Dirty Pictures," *Linguafranca* 7.4 (1997), 40–48.

4 Maus quite pointedly remarks of this phrasing, "Men 'know' their wives but the expression is not reciprocal" (*Inwardness*, 193).

5 The Merchant's wisecrack refers to the old bridegroom's post-nuptial dawn song, but also, indirectly, to his previous "labors" of love. I include a sizable passage, lest there be any doubt as to the speaker's (and perhaps even Chaucer's) own sympathies:

> Thus laboureth he til that the day gan dawe;
> And thanne he taketh a sop in fyn clarree,
> And kiste his wyf, and made wantown cheere.
> And upright in his bed thanne sitteth he,
> And after that he sang ful loude and cleere.
> He was al coltissh, ful of ragerye,
> And ful of jargon as a flekked pye.
> The slakke skyn aboute his nekke shaketh
> Whil that he sang, so chaunteth he and craketh.
> But God woot what that May thoughte in hir herte,
> Whan she hym saugh up sittyng in his sherte,
> In his nyght-cappe, and with his nekke lene;
> She preyseth nat his pleyyng worth a bene.   (1842–54)

6 Much of this new literature was, as Boose points out, satirical, and therefore its content was objected to on political more than on moral grounds, but the 1599 ban which targeted many such works constitutes a turning point in the history of English censorship and letters. The ban drove authors such as Middleton and Marston to the theater, where they sought "sanctuary" from censorship – a move which resulted in the "sexualized, politicized, spectacularized," and "radicalized" Jacobean stage (197–98). See "The 1599 Bishops' Ban and the Sexualization of the Jacobean Stage," in *Enclosure Acts: Sexuality, Property, and Culture in Early Modern England*, ed. Richard Burt

and John Michael Archer (Ithaca: Cornell University Press, 1994), 185–200. Note that my use of the term "cultural niche" puts into practice the theory of cultural evolution elaborated in Taylor's *Cultural Selection.*

7 I applaud Desens for correcting, in her survey of the bed-trick in Renaissance English drama, centuries of critical neglect surrounding the convention and its cultural significance. Critics have tended to dismiss the convention as either overworn or inherently "theatrical" (and therefore, socially and theoretically neutral), ignoring the complete absence of the device (itself as old as the Bible) in plays of the 1500s. Desens accounts for the bed-trick's sudden popularity by pointing out that it "is best suited to exploring issues of gender and sexuality in a less idealized context than that of the romantic comedies of the 1580s and 1590s" (Marliss C. Desens, *The Bed-Trick in English Renaissance Drama: Explorations in Gender, Sexuality, and Power* [Newark: University of Delaware Press, 1994], 35). The author in part supports her point by quoting R. A. Foakes, who observed that "satire brought into drama what romantic comedy had kept out: sexuality"; and that tragicomedy arises when "the world of romantic comedy is invaded by the forces of sexuality" (qtd. in Desens, 52). Desens does not comment on the invasion metaphor, peculiarly appropriate to the matter at hand.

I would only make the further point that the genre issue cited by Foakes, as well as Boose (see note 6, above), may or may not be pertinent here. Despite the reverence with which modern intellectuals talk sex, satire and eroticism are far from mutually exclusive categories: in fact, Hunt argues that modern pornography originated in satire (*Invention of Pornography*, 9–45). There is also the problem of defining satire – which is, to a large degree, in the eye of the beholder. In fact, Foakes' own language suggests the very sort of notions about "sexuality" which precondition its satirical treatment and/or reception in literature. What results is a kind of feedback loop: "sexuality" consists of invasive, primal "forces" which ought to be "kept out"; therefore, when "sex" sneaks into plays it must be read as satire; it must be meant to ridicule something (the subject, the object, the body, mankind?). Satire is, in fact, a classic form of abjection.

8 Foucault, *The History of Sexuality, Vol. I*, 156.

9 Bynum, *Fragmentation and Redemption*, 87.

10 D. H. Lawrence, *Women in Love* (New York: Bantam Books, 1969), 52.

11 Lucienne Frappier-Mazur, "Truth and the Obscene Word in Eighteenth-Century French Pornography," Hunt, *Invention of Pornography*, 221.

12 Lacan has a different, but logically compatible, approach to the words/things relationship: "the symbol manifests itself first of all as the murder of the thing" – in other words, the signifier displaces the (material) signified (Jacques Lacan, *Ecrits*, trans. Alan Sheridan [London: Tavistock, 1979], 104). Which is to say, there are no "things," only words; which is to say, words are everything, all things; which is as good as saying every word is a thing. In other words, sexual signification, once again, simply crystallizes or manifests in microcosm larger signifying processes. Obscenity is beginning to look like a hyper-discourse. Of course, whether we want to follow Lacan's theory – or any of its post-structuralist counterparts – to its seemingly Cartesian conclusion is another matter entirely – more on that below.

13 Patrick Geary, in his analysis of this peculiar medieval trade, argues that "a real conviction that the relic was the saint, that the relic was a *person and not a thing*, undoubtedly helped mitigate the more blatantly immoral aspects of stealing. Paralleling the custom of ritual 'kidnappings' of brides by their prospective husbands, the theft of relics was at once a kidnapping and a seduction" (*Furta Sacra: Thefts of Relics in the Central Middle Ages* [Princeton University Press, 1978], 162; emphasis added).

14 This turn toward the phonic may be the most counter-Derridean move that I dare. The critique of structuralist "phonocentrism" – that is, the prioritizing, temporally and logically, of the spoken word over its written representation – was *Of Grammatology*'s most radical and liberating intellectual contribution (see esp. 3–73). But in the decades between the book's publication and my entry into the profession, the proverbial pendulum may have swung farther than Derrida himself imagined (see his comments in "Deconstruction in America," quoted in the Conclusion): the danger of "graphocentrism" is especially evident to a student of theater, and may be accountable for some of the mis-editing of plays diagnosed in chapter 1. These are all strategic matters: the ontological question of temporality and human development, of the origins of discourse, will be dealt with later – as such questions will continue to vex me, despite my best post-structuralist intents.

15 Valerie Traub, *Desire and Anxiety: Circulations of Sexuality in Shakespearean Drama* (London: Routledge, 1992), 12–13.

16 This is Frost's term for it; Loughrey and Taylor use "arse." The Revels edition stays mum. To my knowledge, no edition considers the Ward's perhaps oversized cod-piece, or else the cat-stick itself, clearly a kind of quasi-dildo. Livia's very next line supports the phallic hypothesis: "What will he be, when he comes altogether?" (1.2.87).

17 In all such calculations in this chapter, I have made use of a draft concordance compiled by John Lavagnino, based on texts in the forthcoming Oxford *Collected Works*.

18 Traub, *Desire and Anxiety*, 25–49. See also Nancy Vickers, "Diana Described: Scattered Woman and Scattered Rhyme," *Critical Inquiry* 8 (1981), and Patricia Parker, *Literary Fat Ladies: Rhetoric, Gender, Property* (London: Methuen, 1987), 126–54.

19 Pronounced "cunt-ess."

20 I have resisted harping on the overwhelming male-dominance of the profession of editing, not only because I have edited, but also because women are equally capable of editorial prudery, as we are pointedly reminded by the namesake of bowdlerization, Henrietta Maria Bowdler, editor of *The Family Shakespeare*. Nonetheless, gender imbalance, or rather gender bias, is a problem, and I can even cite a male editor here (Gary Taylor, "Textual and Sexual Criticism: A Crux in *The Comedy of Errors*," *Renaissance Drama* 19 [1988], 195–225).

21 Stallybrass observes, "If it is 'not words,' it is the body ('Noses, ears, and lips') that shakes him. But . . . there can be no simple opposition between language and body because the body maps out the cultural terrain and is in turn mapped out by it. The connection between the handkerchief and 'Noses, ears, and lips' is not only metonymic; it is also metaphoric, since those parts

of the body are all related to the thresholds of the enclosed body, mediating, like the handkerchief, between inner and outer, public and private" ("Patriarchal Territories," 138). Peter Cummings also observes the irony of the statement, "It is not words"; noting the play's anticipation of modern "male pornography," he asserts that Iago's revenge is a kind of rape of Othello: he "fucks" him, in the negative sense of the word (79). See "The Making of Meaning: Sex Words and Sex Acts in Shakespeare's *Othello*," *Gettysburg Review* 3.1 (1990), 75–80. I quite agree that the trance episode manifests Iago's violation of Othello, but I would use a different expression: this is a literal "mind-fuck."

22 This was certainly clear to John Donne, whose speaker in "Elegie [XIX]. To his Mistress Going to Bed" wants his lover to "Licence [his] roving hands, and let them go, / Before, behind, between, above, below" (*The Complete English Poems of John Donne*, 183–85; lines 25–26).

23 See Parker, "Dilation," 60–72.

24 The play has usually been attributed to Middleton, but the Oxford editors now attribute it to Lording Barry. I am quoting from Simon Shepherd's edition (Nottingham Drama Texts, 1979).

25 J. Rogers, *The Displaying of an horrible sect . . . naming themselves the Familie of Love* (London, 1579).

26 John Bunyan, *The Strait Gate, The Miscellaneous Works of John Bunyan, Vol. V*, ed. Graham Midgley (Oxford: Clarendon Press, 1986), 73–74.

27 For this calculation, I consulted Martin Spevack's *Harvard Concordance to Shakespeare* (Cambridge, MA: Harvard University Press, 1969).

28 Joel Fineman, *The Subjectivity Effect in Western Literary Tradition: Essays Toward the Release of Shakespeare's Will* (Cambridge, MA: MIT Press, 1991), 151.

29 Stanley Cavell, "Epistemology and Tragedy: A Reading of *Othello* (Together with a Cover Letter)," *Daedalus* 108.3 (1979), 42.

30 Parker notes of Desdemona's death: "the closing or stifling of her mouth, an act that makes explicit the links between the two orifices [mouth and vagina] throughout, [is] a symbolic 'close' both to her speech and to the assumed crime of sexual openness enacted on her wedding sheets" ("Dilation," 71).

31 It hardly seems necessary to point out the enthusiasm with which deconstruction takes up the question of names, signatures, and their referents. Derrida writes, "The critic and the philologist . . . may wonder whether a certain piece of writing is indeed assignable to a certain author, but as regards the event of the signature, the abyssal machinery of this operation, the commerce between the said author and his proper name, . . . whether his proper name is truly his name and truly proper, before or after the signature . . . no question is ever posed by any of the regional disciplines which are, as such, concerned with texts known as literary" (*Signsponge*, trans. Richard Rand [New York: Columbia University Press, 1984], 24–26). Concerning this particular Shakespearean quote, Derrida writes, "A proper name does not name anything which is human, anything which belongs to a human body, a human spirit, an essence of man. And yet this relation to the inhuman only befalls man . . . in the name of man" ("Aphorism Countertime," trans. Nicholas Royle, in *Acts of Literature*, ed. Derek Attridge [London: Routledge, 1992], 427). See also

Royle's engaging discussion of these remarks (and Juliet's) in *After Derrida* (Manchester University Press, 1995), 85–123.

32 Coppélia Kahn, *Man's Estate: Masculine Identity in Shakespeare* (Berkeley: University of California Press, 1981), 83.

33 *Ibid.* 88.

34 *Ibid.* 83.

35 The distinction originates with Augustine: "I call 'charity' the motion of the soul toward the enjoyment of God for His own sake, and the enjoyment of one's self and of one's neighbor for the sake of God; but 'cupidity' is a motion of the soul toward the enjoyment of one's self, one's neighbor, or any corporal thing for the sake of something other than God" (*On Christian Doctrine*, trans. D. W. Robertson, Jr. [New York: Liberal Arts Press, 1958], III, X, 16; p. 88).

36 Georges Bataille, *Eroticism: Death and Sensuality*, trans. Mary Dalwood (San Francisco: City Lights Books, 1986), 11.

37 This arises in a discussion of the famous, erotic "yes" spoken by Molly Bloom at the end of James Joyce's *Ulysses*, in particular with regard to the question of whether the "signature" of the text here belongs to the heroine or the author: Derrida states that "there is no signature without a *yes*," because the "yes" is presupposed by all language. See *Acts of Literature*, 253–309.

38 Phillip Stubbes, *The Anatomie of Abuses* (London, 1583), sig. F4.

39 The idea of the "chain of being" is a critical tenet which has, I believe, stood the test of time; the phrase was coined by E. M. W. Tillyard in *The Elizabethan World Picture* (New York: Vintage, 1946), 25–36 and *passim*.

40 The popularity in Renaissance piety of Pauline body/soul dualism is evident in the widely circulated and royally authorized *Certaine Sermons*, first published in 1547 (book 1) and 1563 (book 2), and regularly reprinted throughout the next century (the authorized Folio edition combining both books shares its birthday with that of Shakespeare's First Folio). Paul is heavily quoted in thunderous denunciations of carnality such as the *Homilie Against excesse of Apparell*, where the faithful are urged to avoid luxury "least desiring to bee enriched with aboundance, wee fall into temptations, snares, and many noysome lustes, which drowne men in perdition and destruction" (*Certaine Sermons*, 104).

41 Dympna C. Callaghan views the play as manifesting the "new orthodoxy" of romantic love over and against the waning medieval ethic of "spiritual self-transcendence": the co-existence of the two ideologies engenders the tension between "transgressive" and idealistic readings of the lovers, and renders the play a kind of emblem of "the historical moment when the ideologies and institutions of desire . . . were being negotiated" ("The Ideology of Romantic Love: The Case of *Romeo and Juliet*," in *The Weyward Sisters: Shakespeare and Feminist Politics*, ed. Dympna C. Callaghan, Lorraine Helms, and Jyotsna Singh [Oxford: Blackwell Press, 1994], 59–101; 59–60). Although I do not share Callaghan's Marxist theoretical concerns or her emphasis on the "oppressive effects" of the ideology (this is not to say I could dispute them), and though I balk (on a far too personal level) at her characterization of romantic love as "false consciousness," nonetheless her somewhat sharper-toned Marxist feminist analysis

wonderfully complements my thesis on the play's pivotal role in the
sacralization of heterosexual eroticism.

42 Aristotle, *Politics*, in *The Complete Works of Aristotle, Vol. II*, ed. Jonathan
Barnes, 2 vols. (Princeton University Press, 1984–88), book I, chapter 2 (II,
1988).

43 Julia Kristeva, *Revolution in Poetic Language*, trans. Margaret Waller (New
York: Columbia University Press, 1984), 25–26, 43–44, and *passim*. Another
French theorist who ponders the prediscursive articulation is Michel de
Certau, who describes the cry as "a revolt or flight of that which, within the
body, escapes the law of the named" (*The Practice of Everyday Life*, trans.
Steven Rendall [Berkeley: University of California Press, 1988], 131–64;149):
he locates the imprint of the "voices of the body" in "contextless voice-gaps,
these 'obscene' citations of bodies, these sounds waiting for a language"
which "seem to certify . . . that there is something else" (163).

44 Elaine Scarry, *The Body in Pain: The Making and Unmaking of the World*
(Oxford University Press, 1985), 4.

45 See Micaela di Leonardo, ed. *Gender at the Crossroads of Knowledge: Feminist
Anthropology in the Postmodern Era* (Berkeley: University of California Press,
1991), 1–48, for an overview of the field as it has been reshaped by the various
feminisms since the 1970s. Initially a political project, "to alter the male-
biased presumptions of scholarly and popular culture" (2), 1970s feminism
exposed the gender stereotypes and gender-based oversights which saturated
primatology and physical anthropology, calling for alternative models and
methodologies, even for "an anthropology of women." Later, the influence of
social constructionism brought forth more sophisticated, less totalizing
approaches to the objects of study. However, Di Leonardo clearly distinguishes between this theoretical stance and the post-structuralism of Foucault
(and implicitly, of Derrida): "Although social constructionism can shade into
poststructuralism, it cannot, when it is located inside historical and social
scientific analysis, degenerate into a nihilist stance holding either that there is
no truth or that . . . we are all trapped in the prisonhouse of language" (30).
See also Alison M. Jaggar and Susan R. Bordo, eds., *Gender/Body/Knowledge:
Feminist Reconstructions of Being and Knowing* (New Brunswick, NJ: Rutgers
University Press, 1989), esp. 207–92.

For an anthropologist's rebuttal of the post-structuralist attack on originary research, see Eric Gans, *Originary Thinking: Elements of Generative
Anthropology* (Stanford University Press, 1993), 1–28.

46 See David Crystal, ed., *The Cambridge Encyclopedia of Language* (Cambridge
University Press, 1987), 291; Denis Arnold, ed., *The New Oxford Companion
to Music* (Oxford University Press, 1983), 73–74 and 859; and Taylor,
Cultural Selection, 201, 213.

47 Oscar G. Brockett, *History of the Theatre*, 4th edn. (Boston: Allyn and Bacon,
1982), 4–6.

48 For a fascinating exploration of the dream of bodily ascension in art, see
Clive Hart and Kay Gilliland Stevenson, *Heaven and the Flesh: Imagery of
Desire from the Renaissance to the Rococo* (Cambridge University Press,
1995). Hart and Stevenson observe that "Contrasts of vertical and horizontal
are frequently embedded in the ordinary language and imagery of sexuality."

Linking arousal to verticality and consummation with horizontality, the authors argue that "The difficulty of reconciling vertical and horizontal modes and phases of eroticism, central to the tension of the Petrarchan tradition, lies at the heart of the debates of love throughout the later Middle Ages and the Renaissance" (3).

49 The phenomenon of Tourette's Syndrome provides a case-study for the kind of linguistic archaeology I attempt here. The illness manifests itself in uncontrollable bursts of obscene speech, generally in the form of monosyllabic repetitions (e.g., fuck fuck fuck). Even more pertinent to the close of this chapter is the case of small children with Tourette's Syndrome, who, having not yet learned the obscenities, make "peculiar coughing and grunting noises." See Daniel Rancour-Laferriere, *Signs of the Flesh: An Essay on the Evolution of Hominid Sexuality* (Berlin: Mouton de Gruyter, 1985), 222–27; 226–27.

50 In addition to cognitive memory, there is an entire class of memory which scientists term "somatic memory" or "body memory." See, for instance, Judith Lewis Herman, *Trauma and Recovery* (New York: Basic Books, 1992), 37–39. Paul Connerton critiques the "cognitive imperialism" of social constructionism in neglecting the study of non-cognitive memory, which he calls "habit-memory." Connerton argues, "Habit is a knowledge and a remembering in the hands and in the body; and in the cultivation of habit it is our body which 'understands'" (*How Societies Remember* [Cambridge University Press, 1989], 94–95).

51 Elin Diamond, "The Shudder of Catharsis in Twentieth-Century Performance," *Performativity and Performance*, ed. Andrew Parker and Eve Kosofsky Sedgwick (New York: Routledge, 1995), 154.

6   EJACULATIONS AND CONCLUSIONS

1 Jacques Derrida, *The Gift of Death*, trans. David Wills (University of Chicago Press, 1995).

2 Nicholas Royle, "Ouijamiflip," presented at the University of Alabama, 1996.

3 Holy Sonnet VII, *The Complete English Poems*, 438; line 1.

4 Thomas Dekker, *Westward Ho! The Dramatic Works of Thomas Dekker*, ed. Fredson Bowers (Cambridge University Press, 1964).

5 John S. Mebane relates the figure of the magician to the humanist "conviction that humankind should act out its potential in free exercise of its powers on the social and natural environment." See *Renaissance Magic and the Return of the Golden Age: The Occult Tradition and Marlowe, Jonson, and Shakespeare* (Lincoln: University of Nebraska Press, 1989), 3. Barbara Howard Traister views the same figure as registering a profound ambivalence about the question of knowledge; the magician manifests both human "potential and limitation"; see *Heavenly Necromancers: The Magician in English Renaissance Drama* (Columbia: University of Missouri Press, 1984), 2.

For a discussion of magical beliefs in the general population of sixteenth and seventeenth-century England, see Keith Thomas, *Religion and the Decline of Magic* (New York: Macmillan, 1971). Thomas argues persuasively for the interdependence between religious and magical faith in the common people; this viewpoint presents as deeply problematic the Reformist attack upon "magical" elements of Catholic ritual, which had offered people a comforting sense of control over their environments (51–57).

6 The *OED* demonstrates the co-existence of both the literal and the literary sense during the seventeenth century.

7 On the Protestant attack upon the incantatory aspects of prayer, see Thomas, *Religion and the Decline of Magic*, 61–62.

8 Stubbes, *Anatomie of Abuses*, sig. O4V.

9 I will be quoting from John Marston, *Sophonisba*, in *The Selected Plays of John Marston*, ed. Macdonald P. Jackson and Michael Neill, Plays by Renaissance and Restoration Dramatists (Cambridge University Press, 1986).

10 There is some confusion about where the actors disappear to, and how this corresponds to the precise location of the viol and lute. There may in fact be a curtained bed on stage – the same used in the bed-trick, and in various other episodes of deferred coitus – from which the actors would emerge in the next scene. Or, the bed-curtains mentioned could mark off a "discovery space" in the tiring-house wall, the same *"within"* from whence the chant issued, and possibly the string duet as well. Here are Marston's stage directions:

> *A treble viol and a bass lute play softly within the canopy.*   (4.1.200sd)

> *A short song to soft music above.*   (210sd)

> *Cantant.*   (212sd)

> *Enter* ERICTHO *in the shape of* SOPHONISBA, *her face veiled, and hasteth in the bed of* SYPHAX.   (213sd)

> SYPHAX *hasteneth within the canopy, as to* SOPHONISBA's *bed.*
> *A bass lute and a treble viol play for the Act.*   (218sd)

> SYPHAX *draws the curtains and discovers* ERICTHO *lying with him.*   (5.1.0sd)

> *They leap out of the bed*   (5.1.3sd)

The confusion arises from the occurrence of the phrase *"within the canopy"* in reference to both the (onstage?) bed and the offstage music. Richard Hosley resolves the problem by positing more than one canopy, one closing off a music station in the upper-stage, and one veiling the onstage bed. He thus extrapolates, from the line *"short song to soft music above,"* that the *"soft music"* is the same string duet mentioned earlier (J. Leeds Barrol, Alexander Leggatt, Richard Hosley, and Alvin Kethan, eds., Revels *History of Drama, Vol. III*, 220–24). But it is equally possible, as Jackson and Neill surmise (see their note to 200sd), that music issues from the tiring-house as well; this would make for a stereophonics as masterful as the magic. The second mention of *"soft music"* need not be redundant, or the *"above"* could modify *"short song"* alone, so that the heavenly voices are responding to the earthier strains of the viol and bass (which themselves have responded to *"infernal music"* from below). This would mean that the string duet would occupy the same offstage stratum as the sex, either embracing the curtained bed, or – if the formulation "*as to . . . bed*" means the bed is a tiring-house fiction – issuing from the very place where we imagine two bodies lust-locked. On "*as*" as an index of stage economy, and the particular formulation of *as from bed*, see Alan C. Dessen, *Recovering Shakespeare's Theatrical Vocabulary* (Cambridge University Press, 1995), 127–49; 136. My thanks to Leslie Thompson for her input on this problem.

11 The convention of musical act-breaks, as opposed to the single, long intermission of modern performance, seems to have been a requirement by 1616; in the children's companies, for whom Marston wrote, the practice began much earlier, and was the rule by 1599. See Taylor, "The Structure of Performance," in Taylor and Jowett, *Shakespeare Reshaped 1606–1623*, 3–50. Taylor notes one case in which the interval has to allow for an elaborate costume change, something which elsewhere requires at least 15–20 lines of dialogue (7–8); in some cases, the text itself would mark the break as "*long*" (5).

12 Taylor cites instances of playwrights complaining about, or even mimicking, audience chit-chat, within the plays themselves (24–25).

13 Linda Phyllis Austern, *Music in English Children's Drama of the Later Renaissance* (Philadelphia: Gordon and Breach, 1992), 42. Austern also reads the inter-act music as continuing the sexual fiction, relating it to the pantomime which fills the break between acts 1 and 2 (91).

14 One exception is the interval after act 3, which calls for "*organs, viols and voices*"– clearly, though, this would make for an entirely different sound than the duet after act 4.

15 Authorship of *The Insatiate Countess* has been a bit of a problem for editors: it is generally believed that Marston penned much of the original draft, but there are signs of revision by William Barksted. Act 3, scene 4, in particular is considered more Marstonian than others. See Giorgio Melchiori, Introduction to John Marston, *The Insatiate Countess*, ed. Giorgio Melchiori, Revels Plays (Manchester University Press, 1984), 9–17. I believe the "*short song*" in this scene strengthens the attribution to Marston, who is known for his innovative use of stage music, as well as for his relatively elaborate stage directions. See, in addition to Jackson and Neill's Introduction to the play (*Selected Plays*, 397–400), Austern, *Music in English Children's Drama*, 44, 91, 186.

16 "Tambourines, cymbals, and castanets infiltrated from orgiastic cults (e.g. of Dionysus and Cybele) into the realm of light entertainment" in ancient Greece. And long before this, in ancient Sumer, percussion instruments such as drums and clappers accompanied oracular and ritual utterance (Arnold, *Oxford Companion to Music*, 73–74). On the ritualistic precedents for theater, see Brockett, *History of the Theatre*, 1–6.

17 See Dympna Callaghan, "The Castrator's Song: Female Impersonation on the Early Modern Stage," *Journal of Medieval and Early Modern Studies* 26.2 (1996), 321–53.

18 Judith Butler, *Bodies That Matter: On the Discursive Limits of "Sex"* (London: Routledge, 1993) 1–23, 225.

19 Steven Mullaney, *The Place of the Stage: License, Play, and Power in Renaissance England* (University of Chicago Press, 1988), 22.

20 Mary Douglas, *Purity and Danger: An Analysis of Concepts of Pollution and Taboo* (New York: Routledge, 1966), 8.

21 "[Reading] cannot legitimately transgress the text toward something other than it, toward a referent . . . or toward a signified outside the text . . . *There is nothing outside of the text* [there is no outside-text; *il n'y a pas de hors-texte*] . . . In what one calls the real life of these existences 'of flesh and bone,' . . . there has never been anything but writing; there have never been anything but supplements, substitutive significations which could only come forth in a chain of differential references" (*Of Grammatology*, 158–59). See also *Writing and Difference*, 278–93.

22 Note that I am not treating the categories of gender theory, feminist theory, and social constructionism as interchangeable, although the three do often overlap. Here for the sake of argument it might be best to distinguish feminism, the political position, along with its outgrowth in feminist literary criticism/theory, from gender theory of the social constructionist bent, which can subsume the former, but doesn't have to. Note also that the relationship of feminism and feminist theory to specifically Derridean theory is not always comfortable; even feminists who espouse or are influenced by Derridean notions of the discursive constitution of subjectivity may express ambivalence, frustration, or hostility when discussing the political implications of Derrida's work. See Elizabeth Grosz's defense in *Space, Time, and Perversion: Essays on the Politics of Bodies* (New York: Routledge, 1995), 59–101.

23 Taylor, "End of Editing," 127.

24 I am quoting the letter as quoted at the opening of Royle's delightful homage to/elaboration of Derrida's work, *After Derrida*. In answer to the charge of nihilism, Royle, like Grosz, cites Derrida's own insistence that his work is a form of *affirmation* – Royle goes so far as to speak of Derridean thought as heralding a "new enlightenment" (1–2). And I can't resist quoting another of Royle's (un)quotes of something Derrida said (Royle makes a point of removing the quotation marks, true to his own principle of "excitation," that is, ex-citation): "Deconstruction is love" (140). On deconstruction as affirmation, see Derrida, "The Principle of Reason: The University in the Eyes of Its Pupils," trans. Catherine Porter and Edward P. Morris, *Diacritics* 13.3 (1983), 15. On the theory and practice of "excitation" see Royle, *After Derrida*, 168–71.

25 Diana Fuss offers a compelling re-thinking of the constructionist/essentialist division. She points out, for instance, that "Constructionism is fundamentally dependent upon essentialism in order to do its work" (xiii), and that "There is a sense in which social constructionism can be unveiled as merely a form of sociological essentialism, a position predicated upon the assumption that the subject is, in essence, a social construction" (*Essentially Speaking: Feminism, Nature, and Difference* [London: Routledge, 1989], 6). This last point is well illustrated by Butler herself, positing not so much a sociological as a *linguistic* essentialism: " . . . This linguistic bearing might well qualify as something *essential* to who these subjects are, something without which they could not be said to exist" (*Excitable Speech: A Politics of the Performative* [London: Routledge, 1997], 30; emphasis added). Grosz sounds a similar warning against over-strident attacks on "essentialism" – a move which, considering

her defense of its seeming antithesis, deconstruction, demonstrates more than simply her open-mindedness, but, more importantly, the fact that feminism need not or should not freeze itself in a single statement of repudiation. See *Space, Time, and Perversion*, 45–57.

26 On the theological resonances and implications of Derridean theory, see Graham Ward, *Theology and Contemporary Critical Theory* (New York: St. Martin's Press, 1996), 24–29, 39–42. Ward's lucid and thoughtful analysis helps explain Derrida's delicately poised resistance to the standpoint from which his textual aporiae suggest a "negative theology" – that is, a placing of God in the ellipses.

27 James Creech, Peggy Kamuf, and Jane Todd, "Deconstruction in America: An Interview with Jacques Derrida," *Critical Exchange* 17 (1985), 15.

28 Butler, *Bodies That Matter*, ix. For a critique of Butler's views by a theorist within the social constructionist "camp," see Allison Weir, *Sacrificial Logics: Feminist Theory and the Critique of Identity* (London: Routledge, 1996), 90–134.

29 Butler, *Bodies That Matter*, 8.

30 *Ibid.* 30.

31 Gans, *Originary Thinking*, 4.

32 Grosz, *Volatile Bodies: Toward a Corporeal Feminism* (Indianapolis: Indiana University Press, 1994), 209.

33 *Ibid.* 210.

34 Elizabeth Meese, *Crossing the Double-Cross: The Practice of Feminist Literary Criticism* (Chapel Hill: University of North Carolina Press, 1986), 150.

35 Derrida, *Writing and Difference*, 70–71.

36 See, for example, Jacques Lacan, "The Signification of the Phallus," in *Ecrits*, trans. Alan Sheridan (London: Tavistock, 1977), 281–91. See also Freud's discussion of the "*fort/da*," here/there, game, signaling an infant's realization of the mother's separate existence, in Sigmund Freud, *Beyond the Pleasure Principle, On Metapsychology: The Theory of Psychoanalysis*, ed. Angela Richards, Penguin Freud Library, Vol. II (London: Penguin, 1984), 269–338.

37 Evidence for highly developed community life precedes the evidence for speech capacities in pre-hominids, suggesting some pre-verbal form of communication (Crystal, *Cambridge Encyclopedia of Language*, 291).

Index

Cambridge Studies in Renaissance Literature and Culture

General editor
STEPHEN ORGEL
Jackson Eli Reynolds Professor of Humanities, Stanford University